BRAD PITT

THE RISE TO STARDOM

BRAD PITT
THE RISE TO STARDOM

BRIAN J. ROBB

Plexus, London

Copyright © 1995, 1998 by Brian J. Robb;
copyright © 2002 by Plexus Publishing Limited
Published by Plexus Publishing Limited
55a Clapham Common Southside
London SW4 9BX
www.plexusbooks.com

British Library Cataloguing in Publication Data
Robb, Brian J.
Brad Pitt: the rise to stardom. - Rev. & updated ed.
1.Pitt, Brad, 1963- 2. Motion picture actors and actresses -
United States - Biography
I.Title
791.4'3'028'092

ISBN 0 85965 288 2

Printed in Spain by Bookprint, S.L., Barcelona
Designed by Phil Smee
Cover design by Bradley Davis at White Light

Acknowledgements

My love and thanks to my wife Brigid and son Cameron for
their patience with my working hours and constant
support.

Special thanks are due to the dynamic duo George and
Fergus and John Lavaille; John Ridley at BFI Information
and Library Services and Mike Wingate at C&A video.

Organisations and individuals whose assistance was
invaluable include The Directors Guild of America and The
American Film Institute. Also gratitude to everyone at
Plexus and The Central Times, as well as everyone at the
various film production, distribution and publicists offices.

I'd like to thank the following magazines, newspapers,
TV Shows and websites for the coverage of Brad Pitt over
the years: *TV Hits*/Liz Simon; *Film Review*; *Sky
Magazine*; *Entertainment Weekly*; *People Weekly*;
Company; *Live & Kicking*; *Nineteen*; *Options*; *Big*; *Mizz*;
My Guy; *New Musical Express*; *New Woman*; *OK!*; *Prima*;
Smash Hits; *Cinescape*; *Bliss*; *Gay Times*; *Screen
International*; *Vanity Fair*; *National Enquirer*; *Select*;
Maxim; *Cosmopolitan*; *The List*; *Sci-Fi Entertainment*;
Time Out; *The Face*; *Rolling Stone*; *Monthly Film
Bulletin*; *Time*; *Variety*; *New Yorker*; *New Statesman &
Society*; *Film Monthly*; *The Guardian*; *Daily Record*; *Mail
on Sunday*; *Daily Mail*; *Sunday Telegraph*; *The
Independent*; *The Evening Standard*; *Daily Telegraph*;
Edinburgh Evening News; *Sunday Express*; *Spectator*;
Today; *The Hampstead and Highgate Express*; *The New
York Times*; *The Observer*; *The Irish Times*; *The Belfast
Telegraph*; *The Financial Times*; *The Morning Star*; *The
Sunday Post*; *The People*; *The Daily Express*; *The Los
Angeles Times*; *The Times*; *Premiere*; *USA Today*;
Washington Post; *Newsweek*; *Chicago Sun-Times*; *The
International Herald Tribune*; *Village Voice*; *Austin
Chronicle*; *Heat*; *Elle*; *TV Guide*; *Empire*; *Sight and Sound*;
Now; *San Francisco Examiner*; *Esquire*; *Seattle Post-
Intelligencer*; *Details*; *Jay Leno Show*; *Entertainment
Tonight*; *Spin*.

Also thanks are due to the staff of BFI Stills, Posters
and Designs and the following libraries and film companies
for supplying photographs: Jon Ragel/Onyx/Retna; All
Action; Michael Putland/Retna; La Moine/Katz; John
Paschal/Celebrity Photo; C. Delmas/Sygma; Ian
McKell/Retna/Levi's; Mark Anderson/Retna; George
Holz/Retna; Steve Granitz/Retna; MGM; The Ronald Grant
Archive; The British Film Institute; Richard Corman/Onyx/
Retna; Morgan Creek International; Jean Cummings/All
Action; Tri-Star Pictures; Rob Brown/Retna; Geffen
Pictures; People in Pictures; Warner Brothers;
Entertainment; Doug Peters/All Action; New Line
Productions Inc/New Line Cinema/Peter Sorel; PolyGram
Filmed Entertainment; Richard Hogan/All Action; Sam
Levi/Retna; Mojgan B. Azimi/Retna; Brad
Fierce/Snap/Katz; Michael Benabib/Retna; Laura
Luongo/People in Pictures; Fred Prouser/Popperfoto/
Reuters; Ian Waldie/Popperfoto/Reuters; Rose Prouser/Pop
perfoto/Reuters.

Film Stills courtesey of: Guild Film; Columbia TriStar;
PolyGram Filmed Entertainment; Rank Film Distributors
Limited; Paramount Pictures; Entertainment; New Line
Productions Inc/New Line Cinema; Warner Brothers
Entertainment; MGM; Pathe Entertainment/United
International Pictures; Morgan Creek International; Geffen
Pictures; Nelson Entertainment; Shuler-Donner
Productions; Miramax; Vega Film Productions; Allied
Filmmakers; Viacom Pictures; Propoganda Films;TriStar
Pictures/Entertainment Film Distributors; Universal
Pictures; Fox 2000; Ska Productions/Columbia Pictures;
Dreamworks.

Contents

1 The Missouri Kid

IN THE HOLLYWOOD of the 1990s Brad Pitt is one of the biggest stars, and he seems to have reached this enviable position with almost next to no effort. His rise has been unstoppable, from his first 15 minutes of fame as a sensual robber in 1991's controversial hit movie *Thelma and Louise*. In 1995 he won great acclaim for his role as a cop on the trail of a satanic serial killer in the surprise box office smash *Seven*. An Oscar nomination followed for his supporting role in the sci-fi thriller *Twelve Monkeys*. From the boy in a Levi jeans TV advert to a pay packet of $10 million a movie in the space of just under a decade is no mean feat for any aspiring actor.

Brad Pitt, however, is not just any actor. He's been blessed with the kind of good looks and easy charm that guarantee a huge fan following, regardless of true acting talent. The advantage that Pitt has over most other TV-to-movies teen idols is that he can actually turn in a more than worthy performance, as his dramatic turns in Robert Redford's *A River Runs Through It* and his challenging work alongside Bruce Willis in Terry Gilliam's *Twelve Monkeys* and Robert DeNiro in *Sleepers* show.

Bill and Jane Pitt's first born son, William Bradley Pitt, came into the world in the small town of Shawnee, Oklahoma on 18th December 1963. For his mother Jane, working as a school counsellor, the health and well-being of her new son was uppermost in her mind. For his father, William Senior, known as Bill, the arrival of his son was a welcome break from the routine of his life as a trucker. However, he knew that his work meant that he wouldn't be seeing as much of 'little Brad', as the new child was known to distinguish him from his father, as he might like to.

One of Pitt's college friends felt he could see Pitt's parents in his own make-up. 'Brad looks like his father and has the personality of his mother,' Chris Schudy told *Rolling Stone* in a 1994 profile. 'His mother is so down to earth, just a super woman. His dad is a great guy, but more reserved. *A River Runs Through It* is almost a mirror of Brad's family. When I saw the movie, I called him and said "You're not even acting, it's just your home unit."'

The home unit was on the move soon after Brad's birth. Bill Pitt was offered a better-paid trucking job based in Springfield, a larger metropolis than the small town of Shawnee. Pitt's new home town was located in the shadow of the Ozark Mountains, which cross the borders of Missouri and Arkansas.

Relocating to Springfield was the first and last move for the new family. Pitt's parents and his brother Douglas, born when Brad was three years old, and sister Julie, born two years after Douglas, still live happily in the town while the elder Pitt pursues his career in Hollywood.

The young Pitt doesn't seem to have suffered from his father's absence for long periods of time due to work. Bill Pitt made sure he spent plenty of time with his children when he was at home, and whenever possible he'd try and take the kids on the road with him. These journeys were the nearest thing to real holidays that the family enjoyed.

Sister Julie describes the family as happy and close-knit: 'I always looked up to both of my brothers. I just thought they were the greatest. Doug and Brad really played off each other. We just had such a close family, and I think that gave us confidence. I think that's what allowed Brad to become an actor. Sometimes I can't believe that this guy from Springfield made it, but Brad has always succeeded in what he's done, and he's always had a way with people.' Now with a young family of her own, Julie maintains those close ties with her parents and brothers.

Brother Doug, who now runs his own computer company in Springfield, reinforces the impression of a well-balanced, loving family. 'He's a regular Joe,' he says of his $10 million per picture superstar brother. It's Brad Pitt's stubborn streak, his willingness to work against the flow that Doug reckons has allowed him to succeed in the shark-infested waters of modern Hollywood. 'If the rush was for everyone to go out and buy Harleys, Brad wouldn't buy one.'

'Brad has always done things his own way or not at all. When he was told to walk on the right, he would walk on the left. But he's so good at things and so charming he has always got away with it. Whenever I tried to imitate him, I always got into trouble.'

Pitt would later call his parents 'the biggest guides in my life,' laying any blame or credit for his acting success on his mother. It was Jane who encouraged her son to express himself and who began to suspect he might have some acting talent. 'She just thought it from day one,' said Pitt.

It wasn't only family members who recognised the talents brewing in Brad. As a six-year-old choir boy, Pitt came to the attention of piano accompanist Connie Bilyeu at South Haven Baptist Church. 'You couldn't keep from watching Brad because his face was so expressive,' she told *People* magazine. She was so impressed with Pitt's scene stealing at the choir that she later became his high school drama coach. 'He would move his little mouth so big with all the words that he would attract everyone's attention.'

Family life for the Pitts seems to have been quite idyllic. The family weren't well off, but neither were they particularly poor. Springfield, Missouri was a typical middle-income, mid-Western town. There was no trauma from a parents divorce to fuel Brad Pitt's acting ambitions. There was no peripatetic childhood, with the family crossing the States in search of happiness. There was no childhood insecurity or parental abuse to be poured out later into press interviews. In fact, although they enjoyed only a modest standard of living there was no real lack whatsoever in Brad Pitt's early life. His parents worked hard to provide for the family. 'I understand that people work – my father spent 36 years, six days a week on the job,' Pitt later told *Vanity Fair*.

His parents, for all their Baptist-inspired discipline and strictness, provided Brad with an emotional stability and moral guidance that allowed him to grow up in a safe, secure and carefree environment. Although tough on him about following their religion and about attending church, Bill and Jane were not typically restrictive Baptist parents in most other ways.

According to Pitt, one incident with his father during his early teen years illustrates his parents' enlightened approach to discipline and child-rearing. Losing his juvenile temper during a heated game of tennis, Pitt ended up screaming and shouting and throwing his racket to the ground in an out-of-control tantrum. Approaching his son between games, Bill Pitt asked him a simple question. 'He just said "Are you having fun?" I got all huffy and said "no". He looked at me and said, "Then don't do it," and then walked away. Boy, that put me in my place. I should have gotten my ass kicked, but he was so above that.'

Although young Pitt saw benefits in his parents' Baptist religion and its effects on him - 'it kept my mind on bigger things' - he was like any other child who had to sit through church services: easily bored and in search of a distraction. His rebellion took the childish form of wanting to disrupt the service by making a loud noise and drawing attention to himself – always good skills for any would-be actor to develop at an early age. 'I wanted to stand up and yell.'

Kickapoo High School was another source of stability in Pitt's early life, along with his family and their religion. The school allowed him to discover the academic subjects, including writing and sciences, that interested him and at which he excelled. He also took the opportunity to get involved in non-academic activities, from student government to madrigal singing, an interest developed from his choir days. But even in his school days, Pitt seems to have been unusually aware of his physical attractiveness, and he won an entry in his yearbook, *The Kickapoo Gold*, as 'Best Dressed Student'.

It wasn't all sweetness and light, though, at school, when a scuffle with another pupil turned into a physical fight with one of his teachers. 'The teacher got involved,' Pitt told *Movieline* magazine, 'and she got her dress ripped. It was over something stupid - I can't even remember. I'm the one who hit the teacher. I know I didn't win, but I didn't get my ass kicked.'

Brad in his freshman year at college. The future still looks unexceptional.

School friend Greg Pontious witnessed the incident: 'He wouldn't back down once he confronted a situation. One day in class somebody spouted off at him and he went after the guy. A teacher got in the middle of the fight and was punched in the face. It was a bloody fight that shocked everyone. No one thought he had it in him to hurt someone badly. It nearly got him thrown out of school.'

Pam Senter, another friend who'd known Pitt since they were both aged five, remembered a different side to Pitt's school days. 'Brad and I went on church trips together and he was always fun to be with – constantly entertaining. He and his friends sang at assembly. They called themselves The Brief Boys. It was ridiculous. They wore their underwear and sang Beach Boys songs with made up lyrics. I think it was Brad's idea – he showed off his body anytime he could. He never talked about wanting to be an actor but now I look back on it, he was an entertainer all along.' It was another example of the young Pitt being conscious of his looks and using them to his advantage.

Like the well rounded, all-American student he was, Pitt was inevitably involved in baseball. Although he didn't excel at the sport, his experiences on the field of play did scar him for life – literally. 'This one is from baseball,' Pitt told *Rolling Stone* writer Chris Mundy, pointing to a cheekbone scar, 'a pop fly that I lost in the sun. I still threw the guy out on the second after it dropped on my face.'

School plays were his real passion, although at this early stage in his acting career he hardly swept audiences off their feet, gaining only supporting parts. It seems that he never pushed himself forward for the leading parts in the school productions, as if he didn't yet have the confidence to emerge from the wings to claim the spotlight for himself. But they did give him the chance to turn his hand to drama and comedy, and even musicals.

Movies were a constant in Pitt's teenage years, and he can remember to this day the films of the late 1970s that made an impact on him. He enjoyed *Saturday Night Fever* on its first release in 1977. It wasn't the obvious attraction, though,

that made Pitt remember the movie. 'Not because of the dancing, but because they got the street life. It was a whole 'nother world than I'd been living in, but I knew it was right, I knew it was true,' he recalled. Robert Redford's 1980 Oscar-winning domestic drama *Ordinary People* also stuck amongst his movie memories. Timothy Hutton's Best Supporting Actor turn as the son treading warily through his teenage years must have struck a chord with Pitt. It may also have started him thinking about the acting business a bit more seriously.

The earliest movie Pitt could recall seeing also featured Redford, in *Butch Cassidy and the Sundance Kid* (1969), released when he was six, but it was 1968's *Planet of the Apes* that really impressed him. Seeing the film on late 70s re-release on a family trip to the drive-in, Pitt was perched on the hood of the family car, clutching a Kool-Aid and a tub of popcorn. He was transported to another world, a planet ruled by apes that in the film's shock

Brad with his classmates.

conclusion turns out to be a future Earth. Pitt read into the meaning of the film lessons he was learning from his family's own Baptist religion: 'I think it's actually very accurate to religion in general today. Don't shake the herd.'

Pitt recalled other films that had made an impact on his impressionable young mind. 'I think of the 70s movies, the ones I grew up with. I remember *Dog Day Afternoon*. I remember [*One Flew Over the*] *Cuckoo's Nest* very heavily. I remember *Butch and Sundance*. I remember a movie on television called *The Jericho Mile*: this guy in prison who just ran, and it turned out he could be competing with the fastest men in the world, but that wasn't why he did it...'

These trips to the cinema were important to the teenager. Even if he wasn't consciously planning a career for himself up on the silver screen, he was learning something about the movies, simply by watching them. He saw many movies, but he does seem to recall those that have lasted the test of time and come to be regarded as modern cinema classics. It's as if the actor-to-be had already cultivated.

Brad at a high school prom with his current girlfriend.

a built-in ability to judge good quality material when it crossed his path.

Movies weren't Brad Pitt's only teenage passion – naturally music was a big part of his life too. He'd bought The Who concept album of *Tommy* before he went out to see the film, sitting through it twice to see the pinball wizard section again. The record itself hadn't come easy: 'I had to save up double, 'cause it was a double album.' Having heard the Elton John song 'Daniel', he popped out to buy the *Captain Fantastic* album. Like many teenagers he toyed with being a rock star, strumming a guitar in his bedroom in Springfield.

Pitt had always been popular at school and attracted girls around him from a very early age. His growing sense of the dramatic mixed with his budding romantic side early in his teenage years when he wrote the message 'Hi, Sara' in the snow, next to a giant carved snow heart, as a very public love note to his first serious girlfriend, Sara Hart. She shared his interests in movies and music, accompanying him on weekend trips to the cinema and concerts. The relationship was so strong that many of Pitt's school contemporaries and even his own parents felt they were destined to get married.

Sara may have been Pitt's longest-lasting school days girlfriend, but she was not his first. In Junior High a girl named Kim Bell had won the hard-fought right to be his girl when he was aged 14. Later, as the married Kim Hubbard, she recalled their school days. 'He was a lovely guy. Now my daughter has his pictures all over her bedroom wall.'

Pitt recalled his first encounter with naked women for *Premiere* magazine. 'Somewhere in early elementary school we found a house that was being built, and we found a stack of the old *Playboy*s at the site. Well, I was very impressed. I was just so overwhelmed.' An anonymous friend recalled this epiphany in a British Sunday newspaper supplement profile. 'Brad has been obsessed with women since he was little. The first time he saw pictures of naked women, he went mad. From then on, he was determined to have a girlfriend as soon as possible.'

With the images came the school playground slang and the insistent questions to parents and to those older kids in school who always seemed to be in the know. 'Two kids up the street kept using the word "fuck", and I asked mom what it was, and that's how we got into the whole sex talk. She told me "We don't use that word, this word is slang, but we do use the phrase 'sexual intercourse,' and here it is." With the diagrams. I remember vividly, at that time, being horrified.'

Pitt's youthful horror at the whole idea of sex was short lived, and by the seventh grade his good looks and easy charm had resulted in his basement becoming the venue for the school's frequent 'make-out' parties. A couple of beanbag chairs quickly turned this store-room-cum-freezer-store into a den of iniquity. 'The girls usually overdid it with that flavoured lip gloss,' recalled Pitt. 'But we didn't know it at the time, we thought it was fine!'

But Jane Pitt didn't think it was at all fine and felt the need to keep an eye on the young man surrounded by the adoring school girls in the basement. 'My mom always made a lot of noise before opening the door to the basement. She'd call down, "Brad? Can I come down and get something out of the freezer?" Of course, you had to wonder why mom needed a frozen steak at 10 o'clock at night...'

Pam Senter, who didn't herself have a romance with Pitt, recalled the girls he was involved with. 'There were plenty of them - girls fell all over him,' she remembers. 'He had real charm and a way with women. I made sure not to fall in love with Brad - I knew he'd break my heart. That's just the way he is, he can't help himself. Yet his parents kept him on a short leash. He didn't run wild and he certainly wasn't promiscuous or anything like that.'

Other youthful, short-lived mid-teen relationships followed Kim Bell and Sara Hart. Following Tonya Westphalen, a neighbour in Springfield, was Lisa Stanzer, a girl who caused something of a falling-out between Brad and younger brother Doug. Brad was first to go out with her, but she soon decided she preferred Doug. Brad still sees a lot of her – she married Doug and they now have a young family of their own in Springfield.

All in all, Brad Pitt enjoyed a normal, happy, contented American childhood and adolescence, growing up in a secure and loving environment in the 1970s. What could possibly make this young man suddenly give everything up and flee to Hollywood in search of those most elusive of goals – fame and fortune?

The fact that William Bradley Pitt would go to college was never up for discussion as he was always scoring good grades. It was the expected thing, and thus far in his short life Brad had always done the expected thing without fail. His

Early publicity shot taken in 1988 in Los Angeles.

late teenage years into his early 20s would be no different, believed his loving parents. However, as he got older, Pitt had begun to question his circumstances. He looked twice at his parents' religion, their beliefs and practices. He looked twice at Springfield, Missouri and what it had to offer him. He looked twice at his parents' jobs, their lives, their dedication to their children, and he began to have second thoughts. Perhaps – just perhaps – the expected middle-class American path through life was not for him, after all? He began to develop a feeling for the wider world beyond Springfield. He wanted to get out there and explore it.

Off he went, as the dutiful son, in 1982 to the University of Missouri at Columbia, over 150 miles from home, to study journalism. At least he was getting a taste of the wider world, while still fulfilling his parents' expectations. Having passed his driving test, that adolescent rite of passage in America, Pitt had inherited an old beat up Buick Centurion 455 from his father, giving him independent mobility.

Independence was very much on his mind - although upon arrival at college he quickly began to fit in with the Animal House stereotypes by moving into a frat house and joining the Sigma Chi fraternity. Escaping the supervision of his parents meant a few wild weeks for Pitt, until the pressures of his student work made him quickly pay more attention to his studies. His interest and stated career aim was in doing 'something in advertising,' which was covered by his course, rather than straightforward mainstream journalism. That seriousness didn't stop him, however, becoming something of a well-known figure on campus when he posed, shirt off, for a student calendar. The news of his baby-faced good looks and muscular physique had already spread around the university and Pitt now enjoyed something of a first taste – albeit in a minor way – of the fame that he was to enjoy world wide in years to come. As with his Best Dressed Student award and The Brief Boys antics at school, he was using his physique in a calculated way to his own advantage.

His friend from school Greg Pontious recalled Pitt in action: 'In our first year of college we put on a charity strip show,' he claimed. 'Hundreds of girls paid to watch Brad – he was the hottest guy in the county. We didn't strip completely naked, but the girl's got their money's worth...' Brad Pitt had just enjoyed his first taste of the adulation that could come from performing.

The escape from his parents also allowed Pitt to scrutinise his religious beliefs more closely, away from the hothouse Baptist atmosphere of his home in Springfield. Free to consider what he'd been taught growing up – and to look at alternatives – Pitt decided he'd lost what little faith he may have had. In fact, he doubted he'd ever truly believed anything for himself, he'd instead been following his parents' lead – after all, he was young and didn't know any better. At college, he was surrounded by so many diverse influences and thoughts he could no longer believe in his parents' 'given' faith without question.

'One of the most pivotal moments I've had was when I finally couldn't buy the religion I grew up with,' recalled Pitt of his university-inspired independent thinking. 'That was a big deal – it was a relief in a way. I didn't have to believe that any more, but then I felt alone. It was this thing I was dependent on.'

Examining his religion put Pitt ahead of his parents for once – a few years later Bill and Jane reconsidered their own commitment and left the Baptist faith to join a non-denominational church.

These years at university saw Pitt develop the laid back attitude, his almost Zen-

Even in his first years in Los Angeles Brad could win comparisons with James Dean.

like view of life, that was to stand him in good stead in Hollywood. This developing 'go with the flow' mentality would allow the actor to take chances at the beginning of his career and to not stick too closely to what he knew was a tried and tested formula. His relaxed approach was to be the key secret to his success in Hollywood and to the attraction that emanated from the cinema screen whenever he appeared.

One particular incident during his university period made Brad Pitt aware of his own mortality. Touring the Columbia countryside with a gang of frat friends, he wrote off the Buick he'd inherited from his father in a collision with a huge out-of-control truck. All in the car escaped from the crash with their lives, even though the collision sheared the roof off the strongly built vehicle.

The crash focused Pitt's thoughts on his future, on whether he was really happy in the path he was following in life. Was he going down this road because he wanted to, or was he doing it to please his parents, because it was the expected thing? Pitt couldn't help but recall the words of his father Bill when he'd thrown that temper tantrum while playing tennis: 'If you're not having fun, don't do it.'

The shock of the accident didn't stop him from quickly buying a new car, however, a Nissan he dubbed 'Runaround Sue' after the 60s Dion song. He threw himself back into his studies, working harder than ever before and partying harder than ever before. It didn't work, though – he still had that vague dissatisfaction niggling away at the back of his mind, his disenchantment with a future path that seemed clearly marked out for him growing by the month.

Pitt found his attempts to be creative in his advertising studies were being discouraged by his conservative tutors. 'There were doggin' all my ideas. They wanted the straight thing and it was really boring. You keep finding things in little increments,' said Pitt. 'Each one of those little increments led me to saying, You know what? I don't want to do this. I want to go over there and see what that's all about. I was a paper short of finishing. That's kind of a metaphorical gesture.'

Two weeks before graduation in 1986 and actually two papers short of getting his degree in journalism studies, Pitt loaded up Runaround Sue and disappeared from the University of Missouri heading to an uncertain future. 'It was such a relief. I was coming to the end of college and the end of my degree and the beginning of my chosen occupation.'

Pitt seemed to feel he'd got all he wanted or needed from his college years, with or without the bit of paper at the end of it that said he was qualified. With his interest in a conventional career and a conventional life waning, these life lessons seemed more important than his qualifications. 'I had a great time in college. I learned more about being on my own than anything from a book. It's just as important to find out what you don't want to do as what you do want to do. I decided everyone was either getting married or applying for jobs, and I didn't want to do either.'

The car crash had served to concentrate his mind and made him pay more attention to the voice in his head telling him there was more to life and he had to go out and get it. The crisis of confidence and faith that Brad Pitt faced as he neared the end of his college education was not all that unusual – but his response to that crisis was. His answer to the eternal question of 'What do I want to do with my life' was to pick up sticks and drive from Missouri to Los Angeles with the intention of becoming an actor in Hollywood.

Why acting and why movies? What made this admittedly charming, but not very experienced 22 year old suddenly want to go to Hollywood, to follow in the well-worn footsteps of many would-be stars, most of whom had failed?

Pitt seems to have been inspired by his teenage trips to local Springfield movie houses with girlfriend Sara Hart and his family. The films he saw stuck in his mind, and he'd realised that acting was one way he could use his personality and his good looks to earn a living. Winning recognition from his peers at school and college by being named Best Dressed Student, selected for the calendar and entertaining with a strip show, reinforced his awareness of his physical self. All those factors were combined with a mounting dissatisfaction with the mundane life that seemed to have been mapped out for him, an increasing curiosity about the world away from his family and friends and an almost naive, but refreshing, belief in himself and his unproven abilities. Taken together it all seems to have been more than enough, in May 1986, to propel Brad Pitt westward to the star-lined streets of Hollywood to try his luck.

2 On TV in LA

FROM across the United States, and indeed from across the world, people have relocated to Hollywood for almost a century hoping that they will be the one from all the wannabes that finally makes the big time. For most of them the reality is to join all the waiters, drivers and low-paid service industry workers who harbour unfulfilled ambitions to be a screenwriter, an actor or a director. Initially, for Brad Pitt this hard reality was to be no different.

University had given Pitt a feel for the wider world. He knew there was something more out there than either Springfield or Columbia could offer him. But he also knew that throwing away his religion and his education to pursue some pipe dream of Hollywood stardom would not go down well with his parents, so he decided to not let on to them what his true aim in California was. As far as Bill and Jane Pitt knew, their son was off to Pasadena to continue his studies at the Art Centre College of Design, a perfectly plausible move to follow up his supposed career direction towards the art side of the advertising industry.

Despite his anticipation of the good life ahead, Los Angeles didn't make that great an impression on its newest arrival in 1986. 'I remember being so excited as I passed each state line,' recalled Pitt in *Rolling Stone*. Accompanied on the long trip only by his Led Zeppelin, Jimi Hendrix, Lynryd Skynyrd and Three Dog Night tapes, he stopped off to see some sights on the way, including the Grand Canyon and some spectacular meteor craters. But then: 'I drove in through Burbank, and the smog was so thick that it seemed like fog. I pulled in and went to McDonalds, and that was it. I just thought, "Shouldn't there be a little more?"'

If the city made a disappointing first impression on the 22-year-old, the job options that seemed available to him were even more disappointing. With only $325 in his pockets, Pitt was faced with finding work rapidly in order to afford the basics of life. He quickly joined the ranks of the Hollywood wannabes toiling in the service industry, hoping against hope for that ever-elusive big break.

Pitt started in a world he knew, delivering refrigerators to college students, just like those he'd left behind. It was hard, physical work, but he didn't mind, and it helped keep him in shape. Next on the thankless task list was a stint at telemarketing – sitting on the telephone all day, calling people to sell them things they didn't want and didn't need. It wasn't the back-breaking work of the delivery business, but it was equally frustrating. At least he was paying the rent and finding his feet in Los Angeles.

He soon found himself socialising and enjoying the opportunities Los Angeles had to offer in his spare time. He was not slow in making new friends, and in frequenting gigs and venues where bands played, he was quickly hanging out with a crowd of musicians. However, although he played guitar and dabbled with the idea of actually getting a band together, recalling his teen rock'n'roll ambitions, Pitt didn't want anything to distract him from his main aim of becoming an actor.

Brad Pitt's first performing role in Los Angeles was as a giant chicken,

'He's actually kinda shy.' (anonymous friend)

promoting the Mexican fast food chain El Pollo Loco. It may have been demeaning and far from the kind of performance parts he was hoping to secure, but it was a start of a sort. He'd never performed professionally, never played in theatre beyond the annual efforts at school. He had to get used to doing daft things if he was really going to make it. So, every day he dolled himself up in the yellow feathered costume and became a dancing chicken, welcoming customers into the restaurant at the intersection of Sunset Strip and La Brea Boulevard.

'It was nine dollars an hour,' recalled Pitt. 'That's a lot of money when you're used to making $3.50 for bus boy jobs.' He managed to put up with the insults and jibes that some of the more rowdy customers threw his way, because he felt protected inside the costume. 'I didn't care. They weren't yelling at me, they were yelling at the damn chicken.'

Another of these undemanding jobs was to give him the lead he needed into the real Hollywood world. In the evenings he was putting his driving skills to good use for a strip-o-gram firm. 'That was a good job,' he later remembered in Britain's *Empire* Magazine. 'There were some interesting rides home... I'd drive them there in my car. We'd have a private room. They'd come out and I'd introduce them and play the music – most of them wanted Prince, whatever the "fuck me" songs were – and they'd take their clothes off and throw them my way so guys wouldn't steal them.' It was the first, but not the last, time that strange women would be throwing their clothes at Brad Pitt. At least it beat being a performing chicken.

One of his stripper passengers was to give him his first useful pointer in the right direction. She referred him to a Los Angeles acting coach named Roy London. London was the man who'd given actresses such as Michelle Pfeiffer and Sharon Stone their early career guidance.

Roy London quickly recognised his newest pupil's strong points. He had the good looks that Hollywood liked, certainly at this stage teen idol if not leading man potential, but much more than mere good looks would be required. London took him in hand and guided him in technique. He taught him the basics of the dramatic method and guided him through the duplicitous world of Hollywood agents and casting executives. The young would-be-actor was quick to learn, and he discovered as much about the business side of acting as about dramatic techniques. Soon, Pitt was starting to attend auditions, thanks to London's advice and guidance.

His first exposure to this world was to accompany one of London's other pupils, a young actress, to an audition so he could help her out by reading the male role. The audition was not for a part but to be taken on by a Hollywood agent, the kind of person every young actor needs to fight their corner for them and win them parts. Pitt was relaxed about the whole thing – after all, he wasn't auditioning, he was just helping out a friend. As a result, he was the one the agent wanted to sign, not the actress. His natural abilities shone through because he wasn't really trying. He had set himself a limit of a year in Hollywood. If by then he was not making progress he'd give it all up and head back to the safe, normal life that he knew awaited him back in Springfield, Missouri. That was to be his insurance policy. Now, with an agent behind him, he might not need to call on it.

Pitt started going to auditions more frequently, working them around his continuing bread-and-butter costume chicken and driving duties. Then he started getting second call backs and was beginning to be seriously considered for parts in movies and TV series. His first part was working as a mere extra, but it was a start.

It seems incredible that Brad's first paid acting role was in a huge chicken costume publicising a restaurant.

He appeared in a crowd scene as a preppie standing in a doorway complete with a ponytail and charcoal grey suit in the 1987 movie version of Bret Easton Ellis' nihilistic novel *Less Than Zero*. The film featured several Brat Pack names – young, up-and-coming actors like Andrew McCarthy, Robert Downey Jnr and James Spader. Pitt desperately wanted to count himself as one of them, but a few hours work with the rest of the 'backgrounders' just didn't cut it. For Pitt, though, it was a beginning.

Other bit parts started coming, including a part as a waiter 'in this bad Charlie Sheen movie'. The film was *No Man's Land*, about Los Angeles car thieves; it didn't exactly set the box office alight, but at least Pitt was putting himself about a bit.

After six months in Los Angeles Pitt was making progress. All he needed now was a decent role, something that would get him noticed. His agent and Roy London had suggested TV series as places to develop a good grounding in basic dramatic skills. Guest shots or even a regular part on a series or soap would allow the young actor to try out the business, to see whether he really was cut out for the back-biting world of Hollywood. At six foot tall and with long blond hair and square-jawed face and muscular build, he knew he had the looks to succeed, enough people had told him that, but what Brad Pitt was unsure about was whether he would also have the necessary talent to bring his characters to life.

His first big break came on a handful of episodes of *Dallas*, the high-rating fantasy soap opera that had become a staple of American television in the 80s. Pitt auditioned for a part that was intended to be a short-lived character. He was called back a second time and finally won the role. 'I was in three episodes, probably for about a total of four minutes. I was some reject boyfriend, an idiot. I just had to sit there on the couch and smile and shit,' said Pitt disparagingly of his first TV role.

His character was the brainless but extremely good-looking boyfriend of the daughter of the character played by Priscilla Presley. The daughter's part was

A small part in *Dallas* gave Brad his first widespread exposure and his first serious girlfriend, Shalane McCall.

Brad started getting bit parts within a few months of moving to Hollywood.

played by Shalane McCall, and the fake on-screen romance soon spilled over into a real-life off-screen entanglement. At 23, Pitt enjoyed his first adult affair. However, he wasn't the clichéd predatory actor, bedding his co-stars just for the sake of it. In fact, he appears to have been seduced by McCall, but the relationship only lasted six weeks. Once Pitt finished his part on the show and began again to separate reality from the TV fantasy, he called it off. According to *The National Enquirer*, McCall was devastated by the break-up, having taken the relationship much more seriously than Pitt appeared to have done.

Phil Lobel, Pitt's personal manager from 1987, when he did *Dallas*, through to about 1989, felt the young actor was particularly vulnerable compared with those who had survived the Hollywood feeding frenzy for a few years. 'He fell in love very easily,' said Lobel of his charge. According to the agent, Pitt had a habit of buying his girlfriends numerous, expensive gifts which ate into his meagre acting earnings, and he would finance some of these early infatuations by offering the actor loans to be paid back out of his earnings.

'I've never seen Brad try and get a girl to go home with him,' recalled an anonymous friend in a *People* magazine profile. 'They come to him. He's actually kinda shy.' Like most things in his 23 years so far, romance and women also seemed to come too easily to Brad Pitt. Among those who fell into his bed during his early struggling years in Los Angeles was British pop star Sinitta. 'We only had a brief affair,' she later admitted, 'but it was wonderfully passionate...'

Finally, Pitt was winning enough bit parts to give up the chicken and stripper chauffeuring businesses altogether. He could now pay his rent from his acting income. He had proved to himself he could do it. It was time to call his parents and tell them what he was really up to. 'Yeah, I thought so,' was Bill Pitt's fatherly comment when Brad finally came clean about his acting life. He had been fooling no-one.

He also told some of his old friends at the University of Missouri in Columbia what he was really doing in Los Angeles. 'People at Missouri were really surprised when they found out what Brad was doing,' claimed Pitt's University friend Chris Schudy in *Rolling Stone*. 'But he's always been so charming that it made some sense. The first time my mom met him, she called him a little Roman god.'

Pitt's later fame was to have quite an effect on the population of his old Alma Mater. Four of Pitt's Sigma Chi buddies have followed in his footsteps to Hollywood - although none have hustled as far and a fast as Pitt managed.

Following *Dallas*, Pitt won a week of work in a daytime soap *Another World*, a well-worn proving ground for many young actors and actresses who went on to better things on TV and in movies. He was happy to pay his dues in these parts - they kept him working, earning income and they kept his face and his resumé in front of the town's casting directors.

More short-lived roles followed, including a stint on the sitcom *Growing Pains*, which was later to launch the career of Leonardo DiCaprio. In an episode entitled 'Who's Zoomin' Who?' with Lisa Capp and Kevin Wixted, Pitt played Jeff, a new student at the school where the teen sitcom was set. Playing up his affinity with James Dean, Jeff does his best to seduce Carol (Tracey Gold) away from her boyfriend Bobby (Wixted). The episode included Pitt taking Gold to a screening of Dean's *Rebel Without a Cause* (1955). The episode, originally transmitted on 10th November 1987, featured Pitt in what would quickly become his standard hunky

Brad was determined to break into movies right from the time he left Missouri.

high-schooler TV mode.

The action-adventure series *21 Jump Street* - the series that turned actor Johnny Depp into an international heart throb - also featured a guest appearance from Pitt. In 1988, *21 Jump Street* producer Patrick Hapsburgh prefigured the later thoughts of *thirtysomething*'s Edward Zwick when he recognised Pitt's presence on the show. 'Brad walking into a room was more exciting than most actors doing a scene.'

In episode 33 of *21 Jump Street*, entitled 'Best Years of Your Life' premiered on 1st May 1988, Pitt appeared alongside Cheryl Pollak in a story that explored how the suicide of a popular student - whom Hanson (Johnny Depp) and Penhall (Peter DeLuise) had arrested the night before - leaves his family, fellow students and Hanson in a state of depression and forces Penhall to relive bitter childhood memories of his own mother's suicide. Pitt got to play some lunch room scenes opposite Depp.

A brief part on the TV drama *thirtysomething* followed. 'I had no lines,' remembered Pitt. 'Actually, I think I had one line. It was 'No' or 'Yes'. I can't remember. These are not monumental moments we're talking about here.' His moment on the *thirtysomething* episode entitled 'Love and Sex' (broadcast on 3rd October 1989) may not have been monumental to Pitt, but his presence did impress the TV series creators Edward Zwick and Marshall Herskovitz, who said 'He caused such a stir on the set. He was so good looking and charismatic and such a sweet guy, everybody knew he was going places.' Playing the boyfriend of Cheryl Pollak's baby-sitter character, Pitt got to ride around on a motorbike and wear black leathers. He had a presence in the episode, but the character had next to no dialogue, requiring very little acting from Pitt and a lot more posing. The part, though, made connections forwards and backwards with Pitts career: Zwick was to cast him in the epic *Legends of the Fall* several years later, and Cheryl Pollak, who played the baby-sitter, had also been Pitt's girlfriend in the episode of *21 Jump Street* he had been in.

Although all these jobs were minor efforts, Pitt was very pleased to be doing them, even if he played high school kids in almost all of them. 'I was thinking "This is great!" I come from the Ozark Mountains. We don't have that kind of stuff where I grew up. I move out there [Hollywood] and all of a sudden I'm in the middle of it. Fantastic!' However, while happy to be having some success, Pitt was not so laid back that he was going to put all his career eggs into the Hollywood basket. He may have been hasty enough to leave his university two weeks away from graduation, but he did regard continuing his education as important, just in case the acting thing didn't work out. To that end, Pitt continued during his early days in Hollywood to teach himself about art, architecture and design. At auditions he would often be seen sitting waiting for his call, sketch book and pencil in hand, using his waiting time to productive ends.

Phil Lobel suggested more sitcoms like *Growing Pains* rather than soaps like *Another World*, so Pitt found himself playing for a few weeks in episodes of *Head of the Class*, a high school comedy show. It wasn't the kind of role that he wanted to play any longer, but his romantic instincts led him to an affair with the co-star on *Head of the Class*, Robin Givens. They began a passionate, if short-lived, relationship. Pitt knew who Givens was from the news coverage of her split from boxer husband Mike Tyson, and at the time that Pitt joined the cast of *Head of the*

Class Givens was on the rebound. The pair dated for six months, and Pitt found himself on the roster of subjects making the gossip columns of not only the Hollywood trade press and local Los Angeles newspapers, but national entertainment magazines like *People* and *Entertainment Weekly*. The experience revealed to Pitt that you didn't even have to be a star to make the papers – simply date one and you're there.

According to *People* magazine, Pitt even encountered Mike Tyson during a romantic visit to Robin Givens' home. As the magazine put it 'Givens's fast talking preserved Pitt's profile'. His liaison with Givens gave Pitt a boost up the career ladder – and he hadn't even played a high-profile part either on TV or in a movie yet. He now had a public presence in the entertainment press.

Success seemed to be falling into Pitt's lap. His progress up the Hollywood chain was seemingly effortless. He had swiftly moved from being an unknown with no track record and no experience to being a recognised TV face with a significant handful of sit-coms and soap opera credits to his name. His agents, advisors and Pitt himself clearly saw the next step. He had to make the move away from TV into films, to build on and extend his limited success so far.

3 Making Movies

AS IT turned out Brad Pitt's first feature-length project was for television, despite his desire to get away from the small screen.

A Stoning in Fulham County was a 1988 TV movie starring TV names Jill Eikenberry and Ken Olin (from *thirtysomething*), but to Brad Pitt it was another opportunity to work – and at least it wasn't another one-off TV series episode.

As it turned out *A Stoning in Fulham County* was an above-average example of the TV movie-of-the-week-genre. Directed by Larry Elikmann from an intelligent and provocative script by Jud Kinberg and Jackson Gillis, the film tells the story of how an Amish family whose baby child is killed in an incident of religious harassment refuses to bring the case to trial. Pitt felt familiar with some of the religious issues from his own family background.

Pitt played Teddy Johnson, one of four Fulham County youths engaged in a long-standing local practice of harassing the Amish population. Their stone-throwing ambush on an Amish family in their horse-and-cart results in the death of the family's seven-month-old daughter. A reluctant participant, Pitt's character shows remorse afterwards in a key scene in which he and his mother visit the Amish family. The main thrust of the plot follows the prosecutor's attempt to persuade the family to give evidence in court and so convict the two boys who threw the stones.

The star of the film was Ron Perlman, more famous as the beastly star of the romantic fantasy TV series *Beauty and the Beast*, as the Amish father. Brad Pitt got to work again alongside actor Nicholas Pryor, as the cocky defence attorney, who had featured in *Less Than Zero*. It was a small part, but the film as a whole was a good piece of work for Pitt to be associated with.

He followed *A Stoning in Fulham County* with his first sizeable part in a real film, although 1989's *Cutting Class* was more than likely destined for video hell and drive-in theatres than respectable movie houses.

A cheap and not-so-cheerful horror spoof, *Cutting Class* set out to lampoon the likes of the unfathomably popular slasher movies *Friday the 13th* and John Carpenter's *Hallowe'en*. Horror films in general - whether played for laughs or relatively straight - have proved to be a training ground in movies, not only for up-and-coming actors like Brad Pitt, but also for writers and directors who later then go on to much more significant films, either within or outside the genre that spawned them.

Pitt was happy at the time to get third billing in the credits. Later in his career he preferred to forget the movie altogether and leave it off his official resumé, but these things have a habit of catching up with most Hollywood stars. And while not a brilliant piece of entertainment, there is nothing in *Cutting Class* that should unduly embarrass him.

Directed by Rospo Pallenberg, the film is set in a typical American high school, packed to the rafters with the usual round-up of teenage stereotypes - all just waiting to be bumped off. Pitt plays much younger than his 26 years - something he always found easy to do with his baby-face looks. He stars as Dwight, the all-

American good looking basketball team star with everything going for him. He gets to zoom about town in a fashionable red convertible and is dating the school's prettiest cheerleader - played by actress Jill Schoelen, who had played a more significant horror heroine opposite Terry O'Quinn in *The Stepfather* (1987).

Pitt was simply perfect for the part - and it didn't require much effort for him to fulfil the requirements of the role. He was essentially the hero and the comic relief in the plot rolled into one. Someone in the school is murdering the pupils, and the principal suspect is teen psycho Donovan Leitch. As teachers start to get bumped off the film follows Dwight: fumbling the ball at a crucial moment in a big basketball game, getting drunk with his mates (no doubt drawing on his university experiences for that one) and finally becoming the big hero in the end. Also featured in the movie was veteran actor Roddy McDowall, who'd featured in Pitt's favourite film *Planet of the Apes,* and the chance to work with him might have helped Pitt take the decision to do the movie.

Fangoria magazine described the film in its 'Skeletons in the Closet' section which digs out the early horror movie appearances of today's big Hollywood stars. In a review of Pitt's performance writer Steve Puchalski pulled no punches: 'Pitt's early acting ability consisted of a perpetual doe-eyed stare, perfect for this generic role. Present day fans will see a glimmer of the bigger and better things lurking under the surface. But in truth, the most fun will be had by Pitt detractors who'll get a good laugh from seeing his head stuffed painfully into a shop class vise during the climax. Now that's acting!'

Cutting Class introduced another new woman into Brad Pitt's life, co-star Jill Schoelen. Playing Pitt's girlfriend in the film spilled over into real life, as with Shalane McCall on *Dallas* and Robin Givens in *Head of the Class*. And as with the others, this Pitt romance was short-lived – about three months. The pair split up as they built their separate careers.

Brad Pitt's next effort, 1989's *Happy Together*, was not a great deal better than *Cutting Class*. In his *Annual Movie and Video Guide* Leonard Maltin called the film a 'slight, predictable romantic comedy in which college students Patrick Dempsey and Helen Slater are accidentally paired up as roommates. You can just guess how this one turns out.' Helen Slater had played *Supergirl* in the 1984 film, but there's no suggestion that Brad Pitt found the attractive actress as super as some of the others he'd co-starred with.

Patrick Dempsey played Chris, a would-be writer newly arrived at college in Los Angeles, to discover that his room-mate Alex (Helen Slater) is a girl, the housing department having assumed the name to be male. They make the most of the love-hate situation with all the expected dramatic entanglements. The pair share the same drama class, which also features Brad Pitt as another student named Brian. He starts out as Alex's boyfriend until Chris arrives on the scene. The class exercises tried out in these scenes were probably familiar to Pitt from his days with Roy London. There's even a musical interlude where Dempsey and Slater sing 'Life is a Cabaret', but Pitt doesn't get to take part.

His part in *Happy Together* was far smaller than that he'd had in *Cutting Class*, but Pitt was happy to keep working, to keep his face on the screen, whether it was on TV, videos or in cinemas. He and his manager Phil Lobel knew that was the best way for the new boy in town to get noticed. He would only progress up to

Brad Pitt's 'performance' in a Levi's ad as a young jail-breaker armed with a camera and a pair of jeans brought him to the notice of millions across Europe.

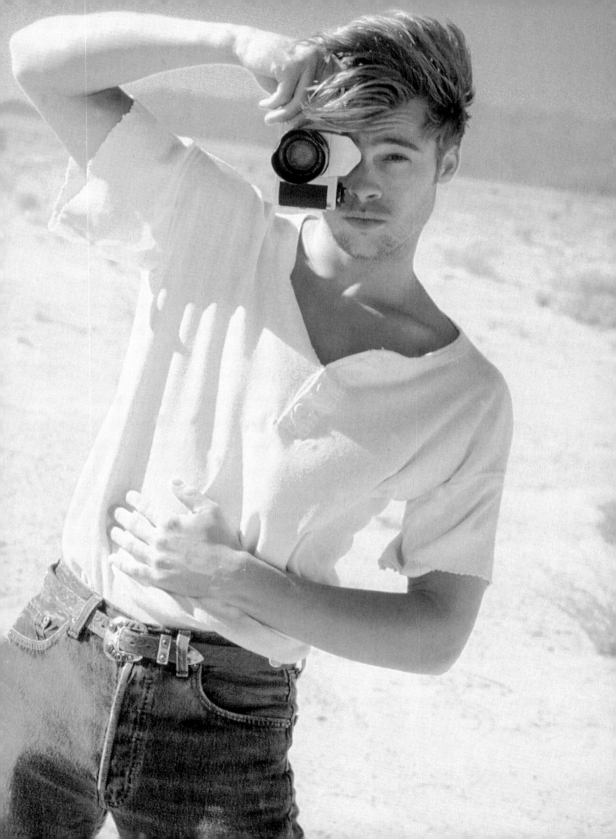

bigger and better parts, get auditions for decent films and get more frequent audition call-backs if he became a familiar face within the industry. Brad Pitt was in too much of a hurry to sit back and wait for casting directors to come to him.

Pitt's biggest role to date came in a 1989 episode of the comic-book inspired Home Box Office (HBO) TV series *Tales From the Crypt*. The series was put together by no less than five high-powered film producers – Richard Donner, Walter Hill, David Giler, Joel Silver and Robert Zemeckis – and drew on the best gruesome blackly comic tales from the 50s DC comic book of the same title. The original idea was that as the series was for a cable station the more liberal rules on sex and violence would allow the producers to do justice to the gruesome tales. The results were rather different, unfortunately.

Each half-hour tale of the macabre was introduced by the cadaverous Crypt Keeper, an animatronic puppet. The script packed each introduction and closing scene with cringe-making, horror-inspired gags, before devoting the remaining 25 minutes or so to pedestrian adaptations of the stories with low production values. Later in 1995 the series was to inspire a duo of spin-off movies, starting with the Billy Zane starrer *Demon Knight* and *Bordello of Blood*.

In the episode entitled 'King of the Road', first broadcast on 18th January 1992, Pitt won his first lead role and his first top billing. He played Billy Drake, a stranger newly arrived in Denver. His tattooed, leather-jacket-wearing drop-out drag racer takes an interest in one of the town's most respectable police officers, Garrett. Drake discovers that Garrett has a secret in his past, namely that he was once a famous drag racer called the 'Iceman', and forces him into a final drag race by kidnapping his daughter.

A very thinly disguised homage to *Rebel Without a Cause*, the *Tales From the Crypt* episode brought Brad Pitt the first of many comparisons with James Dean, making him one of many up-and-coming young actors since the mid-80s, from River Phoenix to Johnny Depp, to have been hailed as the 'new James Dean'.

Happy to be playing a leading role, even if it was only in a 30-minute TV episode, Pitt played up the James Dean connection in his performance, giving just a hint of some of the mean and moody elements he would bring to his characters in feature films like *Kalifornia* and *Legends of the Fall* much later in his career.

Pitt's first flash of fame in Europe was to come not from any of his films or TV show appearances, but from an advert for Levi jeans. His all-American looks resulted in Pitt being chosen for a European advertising campaign. The 30-second spot was an instant hit, with Pitt's smouldering appearance not so much selling jeans as selling himself. He played a jail bird breaking out by removing his 501s and tying them to the broken bars of his cell window, to the tune of Marc Bolan's '20th Century Boy'.

It wasn't the first and it wouldn't be the last time that Brad Pitt's looks alone were enough to turn a woman's head - even the most unlikely of candidates. Later with fame came celebrity friends for Pitt, among them gay singer Melissa Etheridge. 'Brad's effect is far reaching. One night a few of us, shall we say, lesbians were in the hot tub watching the guys play basketball in the pool. We were staring at Brad, and we all agreed he could change a woman's mind,' Etheridge was to tell *Vanity Fair* in 1995.

But Pitt was worried about just relying on his looks, and as a result wavered about doing the Levis advert. This early in what was an acting career that was

The other message that was put across was 'Here's a face to remember.'

growing, albeit slowly, did he really want to be known not for his dramatic work, but for taking his clothes off in a jeans advert? 'It's all just a game, isn't,' he mused on the media's concentration on people's surface attributes. 'It's up to you, if you've got anything more in you, it's up to you to show it.' So he took the part – it was a short work schedule for a good return, and rather than damaging his rising reputation, it might actually do him some good. After all, the campaign was only to run on TV screens across Europe. What harm could it do?

None, as it happened. He found himself to be an instant sex symbol across Europe, where none of his movies or TV appearances had yet been seen. It was the best possible outcome - Pitt could continue to pursue meaty dramatic parts in Hollywood, hoping that when the films reached cinemas in Europe he could cash in on being 'the Levi jeans boy'.

Pitt had achieved his aim, making the cross-over from episodic TV work to feature-length films. Although neither *A Stoning in Fulham County* or *Cutting Class* were star-making projects, they did show that he was capable of handling prominent feature-film roles. While he continued to tackle further TV work in the likes of *Tales From the Crypt* and the Levi jeans advert, he could now direct his ambitions to bigger parts in bigger movies.

Pitt also had a more personal concern on his mind. Since his series of affairs with co-stars such as Shalane McCall, Robin Givens, and Jill Schoelen, Pitt had enjoyed no really serious romantic liaisons. He was on the look-out for a partner to share in his adventures in movie making.

4 Juliette

BEFORE PITT could make the final break with TV he was made an offer the young actor found hard to refuse – his own TV series. That a network thought him worthy of having a TV series built around him was a sign to him and his agents that he'd become a name to be reckoned with. His continued willingness to 'pay his dues' in TV was also to lead Pitt into an unexpected long-term romance.

The Fox TV Network was a long-in-the-planning ambition come true for international multi-media baron Rupert Murdoch. Having started by inheriting his father's newspaper business in Australia, Murdoch had expanded his media interests around the globe. From owning newspapers and satellite TV interests in Britain, to papers and local TV stations in America, to a mid-90s expansion in Asian through the Star TV satellite, Murdoch's ambition knew no bounds. In that context, his plan to build a fourth TV network in America to compete with CBS, NBC and ABC was not at all far fetched. After all, Ted Turner had turned a handful of Atlanta local TV stations into Cable News Network (CNN), a well-respected international 24 hour news broadcaster. With his purchase of the 20th Century Fox film studio and a group of local TV stations, Murdoch had the beginnings of what was to become the Fox Network. The only set back was that because of Federal Communications Commission (FCC) cross-media ownership rules he was forced to divest himself of some of his American newspaper interests, as he was forbidden from owning a TV station and newspaper in the same area. This was not a problem a change of citizenship couldn't solve, however.

By the time Brad Pitt was auditioning for the regular lead role on *Glory Days*, a combination of dramatic series and sitcom, the Fox Network had just completed its first year on air. Although the newest American TV channel could lay claim to some instant hits – notably the animated show *The Simpsons*, the comedy *Married...With Children* and the twentysomething soap *Beverly Hills 90210* – it was four years away from its big breakthrough with the likes of the international mega-hit *The X-Files*.

In an attempt to beat the competing networks and make a bit of a PR splash Fox decided to bring its new season programming for 1990 forward from the traditional September start to midsummer, when most stations broadcast wall-to-wall re-runs. Central to this unique – and ultimately doomed strategy was their new comedy-drama *Glory Days*.

The series was an ensemble piece, following the lives of four friends after they'd left high school. Again, Pitt ended up playing significantly younger than his 26 years, but he could still get away with it. There were echoes from his own life in the character he played, Walker Lovejoy, which cemented his commitment to the part and the series. In the show Walker had quit college in a temper tantrum after having problems with the football team. He was now making his way in the world as a junior reporter for a local newspaper. It was a particularly easy part for Pitt to play, as he could draw on both his college experience and the specifics of his journalism studies.

'He was like, organised to a certain extent, and that was really appealing to me.' (Juliette Lewis)

35

Unfortunately such attention to detail would not be required – *Glory Days* was destined for a less than glorious fate, dying an ignominious death after just six episodes. It is the way of American TV to drop shows quickly if they fail to gather a large audience in a short period of time. Fox was feeling the pressure from advertisers, to whom they would have to refund payments if shows failed to reach a certain level of ratings. With a six-episode commitment to the series, the new station promoted the show heavily, but to no avail. Not sure whether it was a comedy or a drama, *Glory Days* was a casualty of a brutal ratings war that meant that even good shows were not given time to find their feet and secure an audience. The series was, in fact, quite good, something of a precursor for later ensemble youth series, though less of a fantasy, but Fox was quick to drop shows prematurely. They were to learn their lessons, however, allowing *The X Files* in 1993 to weather a low-rated first season and to find its audience through word of mouth. But a more brutal attitude still prevailed for *Glory Days* and Brad Pitt's hopes of TV stardom.

Pitt was upset about the series being cancelled. He saw the show as a chance to reinforce his acting credentials. He had hoped to stay on it for at least one season, then segue into movies on the back of a successful TV series, just as he'd seen other actors do – notably Johnny Depp, from *21 Jump Street*. But it wasn't to be, and Pitt faced a few more years toiling in the world of B-movies and TV movie-of-the-week productions, although to his relief, the quality of the scripts he was being offered started to improve after *Glory Days*.

The chance to work alongside British actor Albert Finney attracted Brad Pitt to a small role in the Home Box Office 1990 TV movie *The Image*.

The drama was a lighter version of Paddy Chayefsky's 1970s film *Network*, about the power of television and those who report the news. Albert Finney played Jason Cromwell, the self-obsessed and driven anchor of a TV show *Here and Now*. Drifting apart from his theatre director wife Jean (Marsha Mason) and into the arms of his researcher Marcie Guildford (Kathy Baker, from TV's *Picket Fences*), Cromwell is under great pressure – he is held to be the most trusted man on American television. Cromwell has a closer relationship with his producer Irv Mickleson (John Mahoney, who now plays Kelsey Grammer's father on the TV sitcom *Frasier*) than with his wife, even though Irv has a tendency to chat to a giant stuffed bear.

Among the stories investigated by the *Here and Now* team are a 'Dr Death' character, a Texan Savings and Loan scandal and a bunch of neo-Nazi skinheads. Things go wrong on the Savings and Loan story, though, when an innocent man accused by *Here and Now* of defrauding the bank commits suicide. After the death of Irv Mickleson in a plane crash, and with station boss Frank Goodrich (a cameo by Spalding Gray) trying to get Cromwell off current affairs and into lifestyle journalism and celebrity interviews, Cromwell sets out to re-investigate the story and right a few wrongs.

On his own in Texas, Cromwell hires the services of a local cowpoke cameraman named Steve Black. Enter Brad Pitt, billed 15th in the credits and on screen for less than ten minutes. However, all his scenes, from their meeting in a car park, to his filming Cromwell's interviews and supplying pizzas and VCRs to the TV anchor, are with Finney exclusively. In retrospect, the part looks like a dry run for JD in *Thelma & Lousie*, with Pitt putting on a Texan accent, ten gallon hat, denim

Brad's resemblance in his early twenties to the young Robert Redford was noted by many, including, to Brad's later benefit, the actor-director himself.

jacket, jeans and pony-tail.

After his two HBO outings in the *Tales From the Crypt* episode and *The Image*, Pitt once again escaped TV movie land in the low-budget cinema feature film *Across the Tracks* in 1990.

The one problem as far as Pitt was concerned was that he was playing younger than his true age yet again. The character of Joe, a high school athlete, was not going to be one that would allow the actor to stretch his abilities. He'd simply be repeating some of the moves he'd made in his previous work. However, this was a real film again, and he wasn't in a position to turn down work, no matter how much he might dislike the part.

The star was Rick Schroder, playing Billy Maloney, and Pitt was cast as Joe Maloney, his younger brother. Their mother was played by Carrie Snodgrass. Billy is the proverbial kid from the wrong side of the tracks, returning home at the beginning of the movie after serving time in jail for auto theft. Pitt's character is the pride and joy of the Maloney family, a good athlete who has kept his nose clean and is bound to make something of his life. With second billing on offer and almost as much screen time as Schroder, Pitt had quickly committed to the project.

In the film, when older brother Billy returns home, he begins to have a distracting effect on younger brother Joe. While Joe concentrates on school and his efforts to win an athletic scholarship to Stanford, Billy is returning to his old criminal ways. When Billy finally cleans up his act and shows Joe he's probably the better athlete, it's enough to make Joe lose heart and almost throw in his struggle to make his life work out.

The part required some physical dedication from Pitt, who was now well out of condition. For all the running and jumping he'd be doing Pitt had to get back into some serious training.

Across the Tracks was shot locally in California, its low budget prohibiting any kind of travel further afield. That suited Pitt as he wanted to stay close to what was now his own turf – he never knew when another audition opportunity might come up.

Shooting in the summer, during school vacation when the production could use a local high school, took its toll on the cast, mainly the major stars who had to perform their athletic feats with the hot sun beating down on them. It was the only minor inconvenience in what was otherwise an easy shoot for Pitt. Joe was so much like his earlier self that the actor was able to draw directly on his own high school and college days – not so much for the emotions of the story which came clearly through from Sandy Tung's script, but for the feel of being a high schooler with ambitions beyond his immediate environment.

Joe Maloney was the biggest role Pitt had enjoyed to date. It meant learning many more lines – although Joe was the first in a long line of Pitt characters who don't say much but communicate better through their eyes than with their words. He was to be on screen throughout much of the film, and, although he had second billing, his character was clearly the main focus of the drama. Although *Across the Tracks* was never destined to be a big hit in the cinema, with no stars to speak of and a less than spectacular story, it was to win a well deserved afterlife on video and TV, where the more intimate nature of the drama worked better. From Pitt's point of view the film was a good calling card to have before the casting directors of

Hollywood. It proved to them that he could hold a performance for the full length of a feature film, after his TV roles and 10 minute stint in *The Image*. It showed he could hold his own up against seasoned performers like Schroder and Snodgrass, and it showed that he was potentially much more than just a pretty face, if he was to be given the right role.

After *Across the Tracks*, Brad Pitt found himself back in TV Movie of the Week territory once again for the issue-based drama *Too Young to Die?*. It was a move backwards, but he was not to regret it, as during the production he was to meet young actress Juliette Lewis.

Juliette Lewis's early life was very different from Pitt's. She was born into a Hollywood family, being the daughter of actor Geoffrey Lewis and Glenis Batley, a graphic artist. Unlike Pitt, who decided to pursue acting almost on the spur of the moment (Pitt called it 'a quick decision that took me 22 years to make'), Lewis had started her acting career at the age of 12, in Showtime's mini-series *Homefires*. However, as Pitt was to do after her, Lewis guest-starred in TV series, and she won a recurring role in *The Wonder Years*.

Again, like Pitt, she starred in a cheesy horror movie spoof early in her career, enjoying fifth billing in 1988 aged 14 in the weird *Meet the Hollowheads*, alongside John Glover and the wonderfully named Bobcat Goldthwait. The same year she won legal emancipation from her parents, not because she wanted to escape the family home but simply so she could be employed to act full time as an adult, giving her exemption from the restrictive child labour laws, and freedom from the requirement of having an on-set tutor.

Bigger and better things awaited her in a star-making turn as the object of Robert DeNiro's desires in the Martin Scorsese thriller *Cape Fear* (1991), leading to parts in Woody Allen's *Husbands and Wives* (1992), *Romeo Is Bleeding* (1994), *Kalifornia* (1994) again opposite Brad Pitt, and in Oliver Stone's controversial *Natural Born Killers* (1994).

Back in 1990, though, Lewis was trapped in TV work alongside Pitt. There were ten years between them - she was 16, Pitt 26, but they were cast as a couple of contemporary characters involved in the drug scene for *Too Young to Die?*.

The movie was drawn from a real-life case that raised the issue of the legal age of responsibility and whether the death sentence could be applied to minors. Lewis played the main part of 14-year-old Amanda Sue Bradley, a teenager living with her mother and stepfather in an Oklahoma trailer park. Abused by her stepfather, she had tried to escape through a short-lived marriage to her high school sweetheart. When it failed, she returned home, only to find her parents gone and herself abandoned.

Hanging around an army base Amanda Sue soon joins up with Billy (Pitt), a local wide boy who gets her hooked on drugs and into his bed. She escapes again, to be taken in by a sympathetic army sergeant who quickly has to give her up when his superiors find out about the underage girl looking after his kids.

After she returns to the abusive Billy, the two of them fall back into drugs and hatch a plot to kidnap Amanda Sue's army sergeant lover. Once they have done that, Billy encourages Amanda Sue to stab him, making her guilty of murder.

This was controversial stuff for a TV movie and Brad Pitt knew when he received the script that he'd be dumb to turn it down. Here was a production that was bound to get a lot of press coverage and be discussed on daytime talk shows. The part of Billy was one that might just bring him the recognition he sought and allow him to branch out from the teens and high schooler parts he'd been stuck with.

The part of Billy in *Too Young to Die?* was a far cry from the sympathetic role he'd played in *Across the Tracks* or any of the other roles he'd previously played on TV and in movies. He was a down-and-out bum living out of a car, involved in drugs and the driving force behind the murder of the army officer, and fundamentally a coward who then tries to blame the whole thing on Amanda Sue. This was not easy stuff for an actor of limited experience who'd previously drawn on his own life to inspire his high school characters. For once, Brad Pitt really had to stretch to find the part within himself.

Although unsympathetic, Billy had to be given some charisma so as to explain why Amanda Sue returned to him and stayed with him. He had to be both disgusting and repulsive as well as attractive to the main character. It was a tall order, but Pitt saw in the role an opportunity finally to exercise his dramatic muscles and prove to himself, if no-one else, that he could handle this kind of complicated role.

After having pumped up for *Across the Tracks*, Pitt quickly set about reversing his athletic physique for the new role. He thinned himself down and grew a straggly, scruffy blond beard. Although he drew his initial inspiration for Billy from the script by David Hill and George Rubino, Pitt brought much more to the role than either the scriptwriters or director Robert Markowitz anticipated. His thinking about the character and his natural abilities brought Billy to life in a way that some other actors might not have. He succeeded in pulling off the tricky combination of characteristics that the part required, but he also displayed something else more unexpected: an emerging star power.

Brad Pitt got more out of *Too Young to Die?* than a mere glimmering of his own developing talents - he also won himself a girlfriend in the shape of Juliette Lewis. 'It wasn't until shooting ended that we realised we wanted to spent more time together,' said Lewis of the way the relationship developed.

During filming Pitt had no real thoughts of having a romance with Lewis – she was ten years younger than him and the theme of the piece was not really conducive to romance. As Pitt said, tongue firmly in cheek, 'It was quite romantic, shooting her full of drugs and stuff.'

However, although neither of them was looking for it, a romance did blossom. The pair did research together and got closer doing the work. 'We got together to look at *Panic in Needle Park* (1971) for research 'cause we had a shooting-up scene,' Lewis told *Rolling Stone* magazine. 'We hung out in this hotel room in Taft, outside of LA, watching this movie. I noticed he had this black luggage, real organised. Matching. I have three different bags from all over. He had a CD case – I hadn't even moved up from tapes yet. He was like, organised to a certain extent, and that was really appealing to me. He was just really authentic.'

Spending two hours driving back to LA from Taft the pair had more time to get to know each other away from the pressures of the movie set. 'We didn't say much,' recounted Lewis. 'We listened to music. After that drive we both knew we liked each other. We didn't even kiss. I was expecting it, because you move so fast these days. But he didn't – he gave me a hug. I tortured my best friend Trish [Merkens, her flatmate] over this for the next three weeks.'

Brad Pitt had to stretch himself to play the part of a druggy down-and-out who
nevertheless exercised a charismatic hold on Juliette Lewis's Amanda Sue.

Brad Pitt spent those three weeks thinking about Juliette Lewis, trying to decide how to handle his feelings for her. He was used to having women around him, and had enjoyed several adult relationships since high school but nothing was as intense as his feelings for Lewis. He was worried, though, about their age difference. It wasn't so much the fact that there was ten years between them, but simply the fact that Juliette was so young. At 16 she still had a lot to learn about life and love. However, Pitt convinced himself that she was mature for her age and decided to take the plunge. He'd thought about how a serious romance would affect his plans for a career in Hollywood, but decided that, as they were both pursuing the same goal, it would be good to share his life with someone he had so much in common with professionally, even if they came from very different backgrounds.

After production wrapped on *Too Young to Die?*, Pitt and Lewis moved in to a one-bedroom rented bungalow in Los Angeles. Soon the small property was cluttered with both their belongings. It was the first time either of them had lived with someone else, and it was a struggle at first getting used to having someone around a lot of the time. In among the usual clutter that any young couple would gather were scripts for forthcoming projects to be read and either committed to or rejected, glossy 8 by 10 pictures of each of them, and invitations to auditions. Both had career paths they were trying to carve out, and it was helpful to have the other one around to bounce ideas off and to get a second opinion on potential scripts.

In a 1991 feature on Lewis, *People* magazine broached the subject of marriage and kids to the couple. Admitting they were 'madly in love', Lewis revealed that the pair expected 'to get married in a few years,' but didn't plan children any time soon.

(Below) Brad and Juliette at home in their small Los Angeles home.

(Opposite) *Too Young to Die* gave Brad the chance to show he could play a scruffy, manipulative character, as well as the clean-cut, athletic types his television work had cast him in previously.

43

Lewis felt she'd struck gold with Pitt. 'He's like a painting,' she told *People*. 'I wasn't looking for that, he just came that way.' Career jealousy was not something that was going to affect them. 'I'd like nothing better than for him to become the next Robert Redford,' she said presciently. 'If he started getting mobbed whenever we go out, sure, that would be annoying. It already is. But he's not turned on by anonymous pretty bodies. They're just bodies...'

As for Brad Pitt's opinion – well, he was going with the flow, off to wherever the moment was to take him. It was a strategy that had served him well so far. Like his decision to give up college and come to LA in search of an acting career, he decided to move in with Juliette Lewis because at that moment it felt like the right thing to do. Living with her became something of an easy-come-easy-go experience. The grungy Hollywood couple that Pitt and Lewis were in the process of becoming in the press was just how they were in real life, not a contrived image manufactured by some PR consultant. 'Maybe it's because we're pigs,' joked Pitt with *The Village Voice*. 'I don't think it's a conscious choice. But I believe in Wallabees [a make of casual shoes] and boxers [shorts], and she's got her own style too. I'm not going to tell her differently.'

Many people in the Hollywood community were surprised by their teaming up, not just because of the age difference, but because they had totally different types of character. Pitt wasn't to be put off by the gossip mongers, though, commenting on the relationship only by saying, 'We surprise me.'

Things had changed for Pitt again. What he'd hoped to be a hit TV series in *Glory Days* had failed to fly, *The Image* had been something of an indulgence, while *Across the Tracks* had more or less disappeared without trace. It was the sentimental movie of the week *Too Young to Die?* that had got both Pitt and Lewis the best notices of their careers to date. Waiting just around the corner, though, was the role in Ridley Scott's *Thelma & Louise* that was once and for all to catapult him into the role of *bona fide* movie star.

Brad and Juliette at the Academy Awards in 1992.

5 The $6,000 Orgasm

IT WAS a casting call like any other that brought Brad Pitt along to audition for Ridley Scott's new movie. In fact, it looked less promising than most because Pitt's chances of winning the role of JD, a hitch-hiker and small time crook looked remote, simply because he wasn't the first choice. The casting director was straight with the young actor – Ridley Scott wanted William Baldwin, one of the Baldwin brothers acting clan, the most successful of whom had been Alec Baldwin. Pitt thought it was worth trying out for the part anyway – and for a good reason. He was going to be auditioning opposite Geena Davis, one of Hollywood's most gorgeous women stars.

'It just sparked,' said Pitt of his audition with Davis, so it was disappointing to know there was no chance of actually winning the role. It was therefore a pleasant shock when he got a call telling him he was going to play JD after all. Baldwin had pulled out of the film at the last moment to take up a bigger role in Ron Howard's all-star fire-fighting drama *Backdraft* (1991) instead.

British ex-pat film director Ridley Scott started his career in TV commercials, before making his feature film debut with the arty drama *The Duellists* (1977), an adaptation of Joseph Conrad's story of an obsessive feud between two officers during the Napoleonic Wars, starring Harvey Keitel and Keith Carradine. Concentrating on the visuals, rather than the story, Scott's work got noticed and next landed him the directing job on what was intended to be no more than a low-budget horror flick.

The story goes that Scott started on this next film and spent the whole of its budget on the first 20 minutes, which he then showed to the producers before asking for more money to finish it off. The low-budget quickie had been turned into something bigger in Scott's hands, and was to make a star out of Sigourney Weaver and a lasting cinematic image out of Swiss artist H. R. Geiger's monster designs.

The resulting film, *Alien*, was the surprise hit of 1979 and launched Scott into the box-office big league. He went on to direct *Blade Runner* (1982) starring Harrison Ford, *Legend* (1986) with Tom Cruise, *Someone to Watch Over Me* (1987) and Michael Douglas and Andy Garcia in the dark thriller *Black Rain* (1989). *Thelma & Louise* (1991) was followed by the historic epic *1492: Conquest of Paradise*, again featuring Sigourney Weaver, and *White Squall* (1996).

'The main reason I chose to do this film,' said the 53-year-old Scott of *Thelma & Louise*, 'was that I've never done anything like it before. This is a film where the emphasis – the driving force, if you will – is almost totally on character, rather than where a spaceship comes from.'

Thelma & Louise is essentially a road movie – a hitherto almost exclusively male genre – featuring two gun-toting women on the run from the law. It was the story and the script that brought Ridley Scott to the project. 'Rarely do scripts come along that are about truth. This one most certainly is and it never deviates from that. It's humorous, it's dramatic, it's even slightly mythical in proportions. That's just about everything you can ask for from a really good story.'

The 'really good story' came from the pen of screenwriter Callie Khouri, a 33-year-old former music video producer. 'I got the idea while sitting in my car outside of my house one night,' recalled Khouri of the project's beginnings. 'What could possibly happen in the lives of two women, two best friends, that would force them to chose between what they had and what they might be able to have? What one event, what mistake perhaps, would make them journey out into the unknown? From there the story just started rolling out.'

The central characters in the drama are Thelma Dickson (Geena Davis), a suburban housewife, married to a male chauvinist pig, Darryl (Christopher McDonald). What Darryl fails to realise about his high school sweetheart, now his docile wife of many years, is that in reality she's had it with being docile. It just takes the right spark to set Thelma off on a course that changes everyone's lives forever.

That spark appears in the form of her best friend, Louise Sawyer (Susan Sarandon), a coffee shop waitress who is having trouble getting her current boyfriend Jimmy (Michael Madsen) to commit to their on-again, off-again relationship. The older of the pair, Louise is also fed up waiting around for her life to begin.

What the women decide they need is a weekend break away from the men in

Thelma & Louise was Brad Pitt's big break. He was only on screen for ten minutes, but his acting in the role of a charming and seductive crook was enough to make a lasting impression

Thelma (Geena Davis) does not realise that JD is more interested in
her money than her body, and is totally taken in by his good looks and easy manner.

their lives. Their aim is to give them some space to look at things, to get some perspective on their current predicaments, but instead the trip turns into a journey to hell and back. During a stop at a roadside bar in Arkansas, the two Texans run into the kind of men they're trying to get away from. Shooting a would-be rapist, the pair end up on the run from a likely murder charge, with the police – led by a sympathetic Harvey Keitel - hot on their tails. Their on-the-road escapades – including meeting Brad Pitt's charming rogue JD – make up the bulk of the movie.

Scriptwriter Khouri saw the film as an allegory, revealing truths and generalisations about life, and not just a women's film. 'As a person, I truly believe that you get more than one shot in life,' she said of her philosophy behind the film. 'Thelma and Louise's road trip is really a passage to some greater journey. As they turn the corner of the highway, they take one more step toward a way of life they never thought they could have - a life where they truly make their own decisions and, in the end, are happier for it.'

Principal photography for *Thelma & Louise* began on Monday 11th June 1990

JD, Brad's character in *Thelma & Louise*, seduces Thelma (Geena Davis) in a motel room. Brad was reported to be very nervous during shooting.

in a tree-lined residential area of Tarzana, California which was to feature in the film's opening scenes as Thelma's small-town Arkansas neighbourhood. For six weeks the production commandeered homes, businesses and public buildings all around the Southern California area, including the Silver Bullet Saloon in Long Beach, where 250 local extras performed a raucous country-western line dance known as the 'Tush Push', and the famous DuPar's restaurant in Thousand Oaks, which served as the coffee shop where Louise works as a waitress.

The company then moved to Bakersfield, where local oil fields and the lush green crops of the San Joaquin Valley served as some of the roadside stops in Oklahoma visited by the on-the-run pair.

During August the cast and crew, numbering about 175 in total, relocated to the former uranium mining town of Moab, Utah. Situated on the banks of the Colorado River, Moab is home to the majestic red rock formations of Arches National Park. Much of south eastern Utah, including abandoned ghost towns like Cisco, was used in the depiction of Arizona and New Mexico in the film.

'During pre-production for the film we travelled the exact route taken by the characters in the film,' said Scott. They decided, however, that it was impractical to

Thelma experienced the orgasm with JD that her chauvinist husband has failed to deliver. It was Pitt who dubbed it the "$6000" orgasm in reference to the money JD stole from her afterwards.

film on that route, despite the attractions of the scenery. 'Southern California and south eastern Utah each provided innumerable locations stemming from one particular base. Although we did shoot at many different sites, logistically speaking it would have been much more difficult to move from state-to-state.' Brad Pitt therefore did not have to travel too far from his home base in Los Angeles.

In the film Louise picks up her life savings from her boyfriend Jimmy. Her $6,700 looks like it'll be enough to see the pair safely on their way to Mexico. However, she didn't count on the sexual attraction the hitch-hiker they pick up would have for Thelma. His outlaw good looks and his tips on how to politely rob a small store bowl over Thelma. It isn't long before the couple tumble into bed in one of the most talked-about scenes in the whole movie. Thelma enjoys her first orgasm courtesy of JD, but she pays the price when the suave thief makes off with the money that she had been looking after for Louise. Pitt himself dubbed the scene 'the $6,000 orgasm'.

Filming the scene was not as easy or as much fun as the finished product looked on screen. *People* magazine reported one crew member recalling Pitt being very nervous. 'He was absolutely charming, very shy and very nervous. His biggest concern was that his mother wouldn't approve.' After all, he had to sweep the woman off her feet and make a big impression on the female audience in the cinema too, if the role was to be convincing. It was a tall order, but director Ridley Scott was sympathetic. 'Ridley would let us play around a lot,' said Pitt of the scene. 'He'd say, "Okay, we got that one. Let's try something else."' Once it was all cut together, the magic of the movies became apparent. What had taken hours to film and had seemed pretty silly, uncomfortable and embarrassing at the time, turned out to be convincing and charged with impact.

In fact, Pitt and Davis got on so well during the filming of that particular scene and on the film in general that rumours swept the set that they were enjoying a real-life liaison. Davis was in the process of separating from her then husband Jeff Goldblum (star of David Cronenberg's *The Fly*, and later a key character in Steven Spielberg's *Jurassic Park*) after five years, so could have been open to the opportunities offered. Maybe Davis was as swept off her feet as her character Thelma was in the film by Pitt's charisma and perfect physique.

Whatever the truth of these tales, Pitt was going to have problems living with the scene. 'I'm having trouble living up to that $6,000 orgasm,' Pitt confided to *Interview* magazine in 1992. 'I prefer to look at the film as about people in dead-end situations, and then an event puts them on a different path. They can become victims of that, or they can take control of it.'

Pitt knew that *Thelma & Louise* would be a good career move: 'I went after the part knowing it would bring me more opportunities.' Working with a cast including Geena Davis, Susan Sarandon and Harvey Keitel – all of whom he shared screen time with – couldn't fail to teach him something about the star business. 'They were fun and exciting,' said Pitt to London's *Guardian* newspaper about Davis and Sarandon. 'It's like when you play tennis with someone better than you – your game gets better.'

After half a decade of jobbing roles in Hollywood, Pitt was ready for the big time. 'I knew that part was going to come along. I can't explain it, but I knew it. Sometimes I was patient, and sometimes I was anxious, but I knew. And then, when it came along, I knew I was going to get it. I read it and immediately I knew. And I

Pondering the possible imminence of fame.

knew this guy to the end,' said Pitt of JD.

'I figured it would be a role like JD. It's something I'm good at – a Southern guy. It basically opened the door for some kind of respect, working with all those great people.'

Pitt was right – it was easy for him to play the role. JD was the type of guy he was familiar with, growing up in Missouri. A much more likeable character than Billy in *Too Young to Die?*, JD was nevertheless ruined Thelma and Louise's chance to get safely away from the authorities after them. He was seductive and smooth with Thelma, but more of his true cowardly and spineless character came through under interrogation by Harvey Keitel's pursuing cop.

Scott's film seemed to hit a raw nerve in American society and on its release it provoked acres of press coverage. Many critics attacked the film as anti-men in a controversy that rumbled in newspapers and magazines for weeks following the film's Memorial Day 1991 opening weekend.

Over those first four days the film took $6.1 million, low for a summer release, but a good performance for a relatively low budget film (set by *Variety* at $18.5 million) driven by two women stars. By the end of a month, the film had reached $23 million. The all-male star-driven *Backdraft* – the film that had gained the services of William Baldwin and allowed Brad Pitt to step into JD's jeans and cowboy boots – took $15.7 million on the same opening weekend, and the psychiatric comedy *What About Bob?* starring Richard Dreyfuss and Bill Murray took $11.3 million.

Under a headline asking 'Can *Thelma & Louise* continue to defy gravity?' Hollywood showbiz bible *Variety* saw the surprisingly high numbers of the opening weekend for such a small film as a sign of things to come. The picture looked set to take on the big studio blockbusters in the early summer of 1991, *Variety* putting its early success down to 'extraordinary reviews and word-of-mouth and the kind of media attention that turns a movie into a cultural phenomenon'.

Audiences were unusually vocal during the film, with women cheering when Louise fires off Thelma's .38, shooting the would-be rapist dead in the car park outside the roadside bar. Men in the audience may have found themselves uncomfortable with some of the points the film made against their sex, but as Susan Sarandon said, 'Only men who wear excessive gold jewellery are going to be intimidated by this film. It's not a feminist movie. These two women still talk about men and still want to be with them, just like Geena and me.'

The male-female 'sex war' issues were always in Ridley Scott's mind while making the film: 'It's two women moving through a landscape where they encounter men, all kinds of men - an uninterested husband, a Peter Pan-type boyfriend, a sensitive cop, a foul-mouthed trucker. This is where the film takes apart the whole male species - one total male being is inferred within the eight men in the film. That is not to say that this film is anti-male or bashes men by any means. It's just an example to show that women are definitely the more vulnerable of the species, not physically or mentally, but emotionally.'

Everyone weighed in with their views on the film, from psychologists, sexologists, academics and countless lesser pundits. Los Angeles critic Sheila Benson accused the people behind the film of betraying responsible feminists by promoting revenge, sadism and the denigration of men. For every critic who wrote

Brad can play smooth and seductive or lost and vulnerable.

of 'female fascism', another hailed the movie as a 'feminist manifesto'. The edition of *Time* magazine which devoted its cover to *Thelma & Louise* trailed its coverage by claiming: 'A white hot debate rages over whether *Thelma & Louise* celebrates liberated females, male bashers - or outlaws.'

The New York Daily News found the film 'degrading to men, with pathetic stereotypes of testosterone-crazed behaviour. It justifies armed robbery, manslaughter and chronic drunken-driving as exercises in consciousness raising.' Another critic, John Leo in the *US News and World Report*, complained of 'an explicit fascist theme, wedded to the bleakest form of feminism, buried shallowly in a genuinely funny buddy movie'. *The Los Angeles Times* saw the movie as 'a sisterhood-bash-a-thon'. Defenders of the film included prominent critics like Janet Maslin in *The New York Times* and Terence Rafferty of *The New Yorker*, who called the film 'a crazily over-stuffed Hollywood entertainment'.

The stars were equally happy about the furore that greeted their work. Criticism that the men in the movie were clichéd and derisory was met by Geena Davis's argument that the positive portrayal of the women characters was a departure as far as Hollywood films were concerned. 'Ninety-nine percent of movies are like: kill the women, slice them open, blow their heads off,' Davis told *The Evening Standard*. 'All Hollywood movies are about letting women be naked, or raped, or abused. The exhilarating thing about *Thelma & Louise* is that you realise you can change your life and get your own power.'

Susan Sarandon took a lighter view of the film. 'We've got this strange effect of having this women's *Odd Couple* in *Mad Max* country.'

Brad Pitt didn't escape the controversy either, with his views on the morality of the film also being solicited. 'I don't think the movie has some big moral the way a lot of people are making out,' he told *The New York Times*. 'I don't find it controversial.'

Controversial the film certainly was, and in among all the hoo-haa, the reviews occasionally found room to pick out Brad Pitt's performance for a special mention. Terrence Rafferty in *The New Yorker* was one. 'Brad Pitt has the sullen handsomeness – and the white cowboy hat – of the country singer Dwight Yoakim.'

The Village Voice's J. Hoberman noted: 'Thelma falls for a boyish hold-up man (Brad Pitt) who, among other things, teaches her robbery etiquette.' *Rolling Stone* threw in it's tuppence worth, too, on the character of JD: 'a hitchhiking hunk charmingly played by Brad Pitt'.

The final word on the film and the controversy surrounding it should be *Variety*'s: 'Despite some delectably funny scenes between the sexes, Ridley Scott's pic isn't about women vs men. It's about freedom, like any good road picture. In that sense, and in many others, it's a classic.' The film went on to win an Oscar for Best Original Screenplay the following March.

At last Brad Pitt stood out from all the other pretty boys of Hollywood, the would-be stars and wannabe heart-throbs. Coverage moved quickly from the film reviews and 'controversy' articles to the pages of the teen magazines. Features on him began appearing regularly, taking the actor by surprise. He'd had a brief taste of this before, when he'd appeared as the hunk of the month in *Dallas*, but he was quite unprepared for the teenage enthusiasm that goes with idol worship.

Juliette Lewis felt the full brunt of her boyfriend's new found stardom when they attended the official premiere of *Thelma & Louise*. 'Everyone was screaming

"Brad! Brad! Over here!" The flashbulbs are exploding in your face. It was like a brainwashing trip,' she recalled, as the effect of the movie on Pitt's profile began to sink in.

Rather than cash in on his new found fame, Pitt refused to play the JD clones that the scripts starting to land on his doorstep required of him. He'd played the part twice before – in *The Image*, where he dressed and acted almost exactly as he was to do in *Thelma & Louise*, and to an extent in the character of Billy in *Too Young to Die?*, although that performance was more like a prototype of Early Grayce from *Kalifornia*. For his next role, he was determined to find something very different.

The Favor was inappropriately titled insofar as Brad's career was concerned, although he did make the most of the poor material.

Before the impact of *Thelma & Louise* was felt by the movie-going public, the word about Brad Pitt had spread through the Hollywood grapevine, and it wasn't long before he was back in front of the cameras, in another role which, despite his best career intentions, capitalised on his sex appeal.

Although made in 1991, *The Favor* didn't get a cinema release, caught up in the problems that plagued producers Orion, Woody Allen's old studio, when bankruptcy loomed. The film was shelved, only to be belated released on video in 1994, mainly on the strength of Brad Pitt's by-then growing star status.

Pitt was cast again in the role of a boyfriend, but with the sex appeal of his *Thelma & Louise* character mixed in. *The Favor* was an ensemble comedy piece about love and romance in the 90s, written by Josann McGibbon and Sara Parriot, and directed by Donald Petrie.

The film focused on the romantic entanglements of four characters. Pitt played Elliot Fowler, a young and successful Portland artist who is enjoying a fulfilling affair with gallery owner Emily, played by Elizabeth McGovern. The pair are friends with a married couple, Kathy and Peter (played by Harley Jane Kozak and Bill Pullman), who seem happy with their routine lives and two kids. Emily discovers, however, that Kathy can't forget about an old school friend that she was infatuated with, but never actually slept with, and has been fantasising about him in anticipation of an upcoming 15th anniversary school reunion. He now lives in Denver, where Emily is about to go on a trip - without Pitt's Elliott because of a fight they have had at a birthday party. Unlikely as it may seem, Kathy manages to persuade Emily to look up her old would-be boyfriend and sleep with him to satisfy her overwhelming curiosity – the 'favor' of the title. Surprisingly, the cast almost

managed to pull off this silly story with straight faces.

Upon returning to Elliott after her fling on the side for her friend, Emily finds herself pregnant, and unsure of who the father might be. Further complications ensue, and things are finally resolved with another trip to Denver for all the major characters.

Bill Pullman probably comes off best in the cast, playing a academic computer science nerd who becomes worried that his wife is having an affair with Pitt. Tom, the object of Kathy's fantasies, was played by Ken Wahl, star of the 80s cult TV series *Wiseguy*.

Pitt did his best with the thin material he had to work with. His character is first seen in bed with McGovern, referencing his *Thelma & Louise* star turn, before he tries to sketch her - based on Pitt's real-life habit.

Pitt had tried comedy before, in some of his TV roles and in *Happy Together*. It was something he felt he should be able to do successfully, but all his comedy film roles failed dismally. Doing *The Favor* was a useful lesson – concentrate on the straight dramatics and forget about going for laughs.

Certainly, the few reviews the film had were enough to hammer home the message to the cast. *People* wrote 'The Favor cannot lay claim to a single plot twist that is at all new or interestingly redone. The cast members, particularly Pullman and Pitt, deserve an audience's deepest, deepest sympathy.'

In the film Pitt does manage to hold his own in a thankless role against experienced performers like McGovern and Pullman. Lightly funny, but ultimately inconsequential, *The Favor* doesn't amount to much as a film and is even less successful as a follow-up to Pitt's breakthrough role in *Thelma & Louise*. As far as Pitt was concerned, *The Favor* could have stayed on the distributors shelf indefinitely.

While Pitt was having his first taste of what it was like to be a real hot property, living with Juliette Lewis gave him a solid base in the weird world of Los Angeles. The pair were devoted to developing their careers, and Lewis, with *Cape Fear*, was rapidly catching up with Pitt in the fame game. With talk of possible Oscar nominations for Lewis, features in major magazines and all the coverage given to Pitt in *Thelma & Louise*, the pair couldn't be happier. There was trouble ahead for them, however, but at the beginning of the 90s they set about enjoying their hard-won success.

For Pitt the problem of keeping his career on the right track after the impact of *Thelma & Louise* was paramount. He'd made a turkey with *The Favor* - but no one was going to see that for a while, giving him time to carve out a niche for himself in distinctive roles. Just such a role was right around the corner in the cult movie *Johnny Suede*. Now it was up to him to turn his 15 minutes of fame into a lasting career.

Hollywood's newest hot property smoulders.

6 The Cool World of Johnny Suede

BRAD PITT's first top-billed, starring role was in a low-budget character piece to be helmed by a first-time film director.

Most actors in his position would have milked the notoriety he'd gained from his brief fling with Geena Davis in Ridley Scott's controversial film for all it was worth. But Pitt had other concerns. He wanted the fame and fortune that being a star could offer him, but he also wanted to stretch himself a bit. The title role in *Johnny Suede* was to be the first film to give Hollywood's newest rising star that chance.

From the beginning, director Tom DiCillo's film *Johnny Suede* had all the elements to make it an instant cult classic. DiCillo himself had previously been a director of photography, working on such low-budget, independent cult films as Jim Jarmusch's *Stranger Than Paradise*. He came from a theatre background, where he'd acted and directed, and it was in the New York acting classes he'd attended that DiCillo had first generated the character of Johnny Suede.

DiCillo came up with his offbeat hero as an antidote to all the run-of-the-mill stuff his fellow students were doing to hone their acting skills. 'Day after day they brought in pieces *à la* Tennessee Williams or Eugene O'Neill, so I said, bullshit! I'm going to come in tomorrow and just start talking, and they're not going to know whether what I'm saying just happened to me, or whether I wrote it.'

'I did a guy who appears to have got everything together, but really hasn't, who keeps stumbling every step of the way. It seemed an interesting sort of hero – the exact opposite to Woody Allen, who I find boring after two minutes.'

His off-the-cuff character went down well enough for DiCillo to invest time and effort developing it further. He eventually came up with enough material to launch a one-man show, all from his initial ten-minute monologue. 'It was immediately accessible to do on stage – it was cheap! My one-man show I mounted for about $3000, way off Broadway!'

DiCillo eventually found his way onto New York University's film-making course, where he struck up a friendship with Jim Jarmusch. 'We were in the same class together at film school and I was assigned, completely arbitrarily, to shoot a student film for him. That led to my shooting *Permanent Vacation* in 1981. That led to me shooting two more films with him after we graduated – at times it was an alternative to painting apartments!'

DiCillo found himself going down a career path he didn't intend, and it took some effort to give it up to strike out in a new direction – making his own movies rather than being known for shooting someone else's. After all, why give away all his good ideas to others?' 'I never studied cinematography and had never planned to,' said DiCillo, 'I guess it was just my eye. I shot *Stranger Than Paradise* [which won Jarmusch the Camera D'Or at Cannes in 1984]. I found myself going down this road that I didn't want to be on. Eventually it became depressing because it created a category for me as a cameraman which is not what I wanted to do. I spent a long time out of the business totally, until finally everything came together for me to make *Johnny Suede*.'

'Brad Pitt plays the sweet, dim pompadoured hero with a charisma that reminds me...of James Dean." (*Financial Times*)

For his film DiCillo returned to his original one man show, which had been entitled 'Johnny Suede: Lessons in Love'. The original play had been extremely sexist, a factor that had worried DiCillo prior to performing it. 'My biggest fear was that some woman in the audience would stand up and yell at me "You arsehole!" but they didn't - they found it fascinating. That's what encouraged me to write the screenplay.'

DiCillo had some help in developing his script from an unexpected source - the actor Robert Redford. Redford had set up the Sundance Institute, an organisation based around the annual Sundance Film Festival of independent films with the aim of promoting independent, non-studio film production in America. Promoting new talent was a major aim. 'The script was invited to the Sundance Institute,' recalls DiCillo. 'They paid for me to stay there two weeks and film some scenes from it. For all its faults, Sundance is the only place in America where they allow you to genuinely play around. That's one of the most important, creative things you can do, to say, I'm gonna try this...whoops, I just fell flat on my face in front of 100 people. And then to try again.'

With a script ready to go, the next task facing the neophyte director was finding the funding for his film. 'I hit everyone I knew for money, but it was always a dead end street. I probably had the worst experience a first-time director could have with financing.' The National Endowment for the Arts came to his rescue, kicking in $25,000, which attracted the rest of the finance he needed. 'The money came from a Swiss producer who liked the script and the fact that it was not much money - $500,000. I had intentionally kept the locations simple, mostly interiors. It has basically the same structure as the play, though it is an expansion.'

As with the stage version, DiCillo was keen to play the lead character of Johnny himself, as well as writing and directing the film - a real Orson Welles-style debut. He thought better of it, however, deciding to cast someone else in the role - but it had to be an actor who wasn't too well known and who would not bring any baggage from any other roles.

He first tried auditioning in New York, a process DiCillo found fruitless: 'All these guys coming in and acting goofy,' was his pithy account of the process. He switched to Los Angeles, where pickings were richer. However, he still wasn't finding what he was looking for in those who auditioned. 'It was unbelievable how many "hot" young American actors missed the point of what the part was about. I wanted an unknown, and I was looking, I realised, for someone a bit like Jon Voight in *Midnight Cowboy* – innocent and a bit stupid, but not Latin, not ethnic. From Middle America.'

Onto the scene came someone who looked interesting from his picture. Brad Pitt had on his CV an as-yet-unreleased film called *Thelma & Louise*, and DiCillo had never seen the young actor in action. 'Brad Pitt came in, a bit nervous, very Southern,' recalled DiCillo. 'I asked him to do Johnny's monologue about suede – "rough but soft, strong but quiet" – and he took off his cowboy boot, looked at it with love, and spoke with that gentle quality which showed he understood that, underneath, the character is absolutely terrified. He'd got it just right.'

DiCillo was impressed by Pitt's ability, out of all those actors who had played before him, to get right to the heart of the character. He had found an actor on the right wavelength able to pull off the character in the script and bring him to life on the screen. 'Brad was the only one that showed that this love for this shoe he was

Brad's portrayal of the fundamental innocence of Johnny Suede's fifties-obsessed romantic helped the film achieve cult status.

holding was genuine and came from a fear and insecurity in himself: that he had to love this shoe, because he had no other identity without it.'

For Brad Pitt the role of *Johnny Suede* was ideal. It allowed him to build on his *Thelma & Louise* teen idol credentials without simply repeating the young stud stunt. Instead here was a really different character, a unique soul and he was the perfect person to play the part. 'I want to keep the work interesting,' Pitt said.

There were other attractions in the part. The fact that Johnny Suede was an aspiring musician appealed to the actor who'd shelved any musical ambition he may have been nurturing. There were other, deeper, reasons for taking the role. Without knowing it, DiCillo had in his personal creation come up with a character that shared a lot of basic similarities with Pitt in real life. 'It's almost about self-discovery,' Pitt told Alison Powell in *Interview* magazine. 'You know, how you try to emulate this or that, and then you wake up one morning and realise what an idiot you've been?'

At its heart, *Johnny Suede* is a romance, even if it's a little twisted and off-the-wall. Suede, not so much played but incarnated by Pitt, is a huge Ricky Nelson fan who sports a gravity-defying pompadour. He has an image, with his 50s cool chic and his black suede shoes. Although seemingly contemporary and filmed in out-of-the-way New York locations, the film could be timeless and set in any grim American metropolis. Johnny gains his suede shoes as if they were gifts from the Gods when they fall out of the sky one day. Believing this means his success as a rock star is assured Suede deludes himself, as he does in his relationship with girlfriend Darlette (Alison Moir). Convinced he's a great musician and an even better lover, Suede is spectacularly incompetent in both departments. What he does boast is an overwhelming sense of bravado and an unbelievable innocence that seems to carry

Johnny Suede and the woman he meets in an alley (Cheryl Costa).

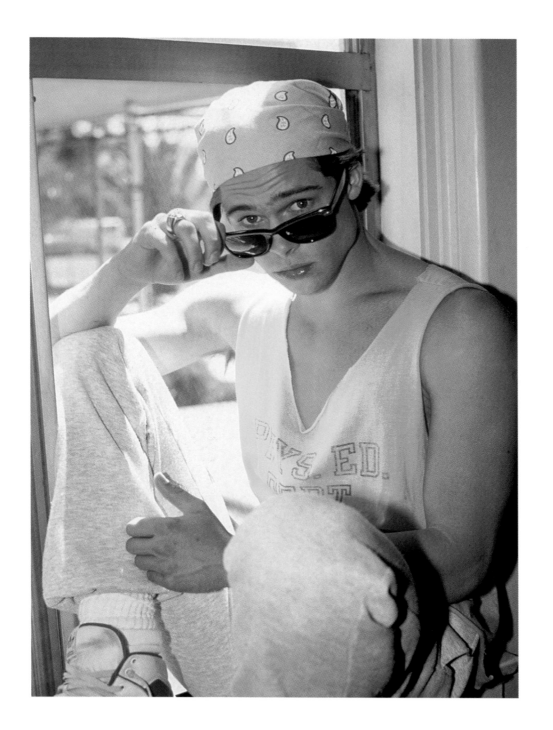

him through most situations unscathed.

The shoes from heaven are his reward for rescuing a woman from a seeming gang-rape as the film opens. They complete his outfit, his all-important image. The rest of the film is a series of picaresque adventures, during which Darlette dumps Johnny, returning to her ex-boyfriend, a violent photographer curiously named Flip Doubt. Soon, Johnny has a new, if unlikely, girlfriend in the form of Yvonne (Catherine Keener). She is more down-to-earth than any other character in the film and she manages to drag Johnny kicking and screaming to some sense of reality by tossing away his beloved black suede shoes.

'There's something humorous about someone who believes so strongly in his own self-image,' said DiCillo of the character he created. 'An identity drops on Johnny's head like the suede shoes - an identity that fits him perfectly. I was fascinated to start peeling back those layers. I see *Johnny Suede* as a kind of art comedy about a man's slight glimpse of himself.'

Hardly strong on plot, DiCillio's debut film was certainly strong on style. Saturated in colour and boasting stylised performances from all the principals, *Johnny Suede* became an immediate cult success. Getting there wasn't easy, though, as the making of the film was no bed of roses.

Brad Pitt was a leading man on a film at last, and he intended to make the most of his situation and the power that came with it. That flexing of his star muscle was to bring him into conflict with the writer-director. 'The making of *Johnny Suede* was a very long, detailed process. It wasn't peaches and cream. I didn't want any fucking ad-libbing,' said DiCillo of his leading man. 'If you ad-lib words like "Hey, you know?" and "Got me?", it doesn't work. I said, "Brad - just say the words."'

Pitt's sin – after winning the part by standing out at the auditions because he displayed a strong understanding of the role – was to play the part too literally in 50s style, throwing in then-hip catchphrases not in the script. His approach showed an actor still unsure of his craft, unwilling to trust wholly to the script or the director. He was beginning to become convinced of his own star potential. Being a prima donna on the set was not to gain him many friends.

DiCillo was to gain his revenge three years later in 1995 in his second film *Living in Oblivion*. A clever and witty comedy set behind the scenes of the production of a low-budget film, *Living in Oblivion* starred Steve Buscemi as a frustrated director and James LeGros as a prima donna film star named Chad Palomino. Palomino is forever throwing tantrums and tossing his tuppence worth into the creative process. Calling LeGros the 'Brad Pitt of independents', *People* magazine asked: 'Are the rumours true that LeGros' no-brains pretty boy actor is actually based on Pitt?'

LeGros said: 'Chad's an amalgam of different actors I've worked with – three in particular, who shall remain nameless. Brad's a handsome devil ... ' He denied that the part was a send up of Brad Pitt, while Pitt himself claimed he wanted to play the role in *Living in Oblivion* with his *Johnny Suede* director, but couldn't due to other commitments.

Whatever the on-set friction between the rising star leading man and the frustrated independent director, DiCillo still believed that Pitt was the only actor capable of bringing *Johnny Suede* to life the way he envisaged the character. He had other reasons to be grateful for Pitt's participation. As the filming was completed, *Thelma & Louise* was released and Pitt's star had arrived.

Brad Pitt, in Johnny Suede pompadour, discusses his role with director Tom DiCillo. The pair had different views of the way the part should be played.

'Miramax bought the US rights to the film without even seeing it, based on three things,' said DiCillo. 'We'd just won the first prize at the Locarno Festival [the Golden Leopard award], it had got a great review in *Variety* and it starred Brad Pitt.'　However, signs of director–star jealousies remained in DiCillo's complaint about the film's distribution. 'Miramax is now trying to capitalise on Brad,' he said when the *Thelma & Louise* controversies were in full swing, 'which is a little annoying – I would like them to create an identity for the film too...'

Pitt was keen to credit the limited success of *Johnny Suede* to Tom DiCillo: 'That film was all DiCillo. Someone should cut open his head and lay it out. I think it would be very entertaining. *Days of Thunder* it ain't! There will be a group of people out there who will appreciate it. I want to try a wide variety of things before I get stuck in some corner. I want to show what I can do. I've got big plans, big goals,' announced Pitt, aware that his time had now come.

Pitt's Baptist parents turned out to be the biggest critics of *Johnny Suede*. 'I like it,' Pitt told Britain's *Empire* magazine, 'but my folks hated it. I always know. I talked to them on the phone and they said, "We're going to rent *Johnny Suede* tonight" – these movies don't make it to where I grew up. And a month went by and I realised they hadn't mentioned it...' Later, in another phone call Pitt's grandfather told him he'd finally seen *Johnny Suede*: 'We saw that movie of yours. Betty? What was the name of that movie we didn't like...?'

The reviews were kinder than Pitt's own family. The *Variety* review – one of the three factors that sold the movie sight unseen to Miramax for American distribution – was particularly good. 'Brad Pitt, fresh from stealing scenes in *Thelma & Louise*, gives Johnny the right kind of innocent appeal, and the rest of the cast surround him with loving care,' read the write-up.

In *The Village Voice*, J. Hoberman pointed out the cult film's most successful feature: 'It is DiCillo's good fortune to have Brad Pitt play his sincerely self-absorbed hero. Indeed, for a stylish exercise in cool, *Johnny Suede* is extremely well acted. *Johnny Suede* may look like a cartoon, but it is deep enough to leave open questions...'

Upon the film's British release in June 1992, the critics were also quick to claim Pitt as a new cinema icon in the making. David Robinson in *The Times* called Pitt 'a striking young actor, [who] effectively catches Johnny's absurdity, dumb cunning and unselfconscious sensuality.' Derek Malcolm in *The Guardian* saw versatility in Pitt's first leading man performance. 'Pitt's slow burn performance – totally different from his portrait of the ne'er-do-well lover in *Thelma & Louise* – is memorable because he never camps it up too much.'

Alexander Walker in *The London Evening Standard* joined many who picked up on Pitt's *Thelma & Louise* notoriety before predicting big things for the actor. 'Pitt is a personable performer. He has the romantic-loner look of James Dean. Rediscover Brad Pitt before his face is everywhere.'

The Financial Times film critic made the same comparison: 'Brad Pitt plays the sweet, dim pompadoured hero with a charisma that reminds me - indeed has reminded everyone to judge by the American press quotes - of James Dean.'

The inevitable James Dean comparison had risen again. Brad Pitt had played pastiche Dean in his *Tales From the Crypt* episode, and he was touted alongside other young actors as the 'new James Dean'. 'I don't think about it much,' said Pitt, then aged 27, three years older than Dean when he died. 'They have to compare you to something at the beginning, but I'll prove myself on my own terms as I go along. Don't get me wrong - it's a very nice compliment.' The 'compliment' was made so often after *Johnny Suede*, that Pitt began to tire of it, especially when asked if his Dean resemblance was deliberate. 'Why would anyone pattern themselves after a dead person?' he once snapped at a reporter who made the suggestion.

The combined press coverage of *Thelma & Louise* and *Johnny Suede* did go to Brad Pitt's head, though. *Johnny Suede* was not to be the last time that Pitt would have clashes on film sets with directors and co-stars. Both *Legends of the Fall* and *Interview with the Vampire* would become subject to Pitt's egotistic demands.

The Village Voice film critic may have compared *Johnny Suede* to a cartoon because of its hyper-reality, but Pitt was next to star in a real cartoon-live action hybrid, director Ralph Bakshi's *Cool World*.

A controversial Hollywood figure, Ralph Bakshi was the maverick cartoon genius behind the animated X-rated *Fritz the Cat* (1972), as well as other animated features like *Wizards* (1977), *American Pop* (1981) and an unfinished version of J.R.R. Tolkein's lavish epic fantasy *The Lord of the Rings* (1978).

Cool World started development two years before Bakshi began serious shooting in May 1991 in a meeting he had with producer Frank Mancuso Jr.

Mancuso had produced the *Friday the 13th* films as well as the thriller *Internal Affairs* (1990), starring Richard Gere. The two men discussed a project about a man who becomes trapped in a cartoon world he created. Bakshi suggested combining live action with animation as a way to tell the story.

Development began on this reverse version of *Who Framed Roger Rabbit?* (1988) with Bakshi expecting the project to be his most technically challenging effort. His previous animated features had all tested the limits of techniques and technology and he saw *Cool World* as a chance to do the same. He was also itching to get back to film-making after an eight-year hiatus during which he'd studied painting.

The film would require a brave team of actors who would be willing to act opposite characters who were not there in the studio, but would be added by a team of animators afterwards. The first star to be attracted to the project was Kim Basinger, interested in the role of Holli Would, a cartoon character who longs to become human. 'Holli's a great girl,' said Bakshi of his creation. 'She wants more than she has. She wants to be real, which is admirable, and she does everything she

Playing opposite Gabriel Byrne as the cartoonist Jack Deebs in *Cool World* was lot easier than shooting scenes with absent animated characters who would be added later.

can to become real. She's a girl who wants to get the hell out of where she is – and there are girls like that in Brooklyn [where Bakshi grew up] that want to get out and go to LA.'

It was clear from early sketches of the character that Bakshi and his animators were already basing Holli on Basinger well before she showed interest. Having starred in the Sean Connery 1983 Bond comeback movie *Never Say Never Again* (1983) and in the steamy *9 1/2 Weeks* (1986) opposite Mickey Rourke, Basinger had featured in *Batman* (1989), *Final Analysis* (1992), *The Marrying Man* (1991) and *The Getaway* (1994), the last two opposite her husband Alec Baldwin. Producer Mancuso believed the production enjoyed a stroke of luck in actually managing to secure her for the role. Booking her immediately raised both the profile and the budget of the project. What was originally intended as a low-budget version of *Who Framed Roger Rabbit?* was now on its way to summer blockbuster territory.

The cartoonist who creates the animated *Cool World* of the title was played by Gabriel Byrne, an Irish actor who was best known to American audiences for his gangster role in the Coen Brothers' film *Miller's Crossing* (1990), and later for his part as one of *The Usual Suspects* (1995). Byrne described his character, Jack Deebs, as a conjuror who has brought his deepest fears to life. 'It's a real journey for him,' he said of Deebs's trip into the animated domain, 'with a beginning place to an end place and he really doesn't know where he's going.'

The film follows Deebs as he experiences his life unhinging when he finds himself in the two-dimensional world he created. Holli Would is one of the characters he encounters; she is a doodle who has sprung fully formed from his mind, and she desperately wants to be human. The only way the cartoon characters can become real is by having sex with a real human – a typically adult twist from Ralph Bakshi.

The only other human to have entered *Cool World* is detective Frank Harris, the part played by Brad Pitt. A tortured young victim of a tragedy, Harris is a World War Two veteran who seeks solace in the animated world to which he has escaped.

'Harris took some hard knocks in life, so he checked out,' said Brad Pitt of his troubled character. 'Now he's here in *Cool World* and it's really grand here. It's fantasy time.'

Because of his performance in *Thelma & Louise*, Pitt was the actor that Frank Mancuso wanted for the unusual role. 'Harris is one of the most complex characters of *Cool World*. He stayed in *Cool World* because he was frightened [of the real world]. Now he's stuck in an unreal world.'

Ralph Bakshi was attracted to the project because of its potential for groundbreaking animation work and because of its semi-adult approach to animation, not surprising considering *Fritz the Cat*. 'Animation for too long was basically just for children, and I think that was its biggest drawback. Not that children's films weren't beautiful, just that animation can do more. So this film represents the outer limits of animation.'

The tone of the script was difficult for Bakshi to define. 'There are three or four genres running through it,' he admitted. 'It has horror moments, it has *film noir* detective pulp moments, and it has pure cartoon moments.' Moreover, while Deebs is a contemporary character, Pitt's detective Harris sports 40s suits and spouts post-war lingo.

In *Cool World* Brad's Detective Frank Harris is one of two people who enter a cartoon world populated by doodles who want to become human.

The major problems were technical – how to combine the live action and animation elements successfully on a tight $16 million budget. For a solution Bakshi went back in time, to 1937 when the Disney studio developed the multi-plane camera, which mounts layers of artwork on glass plates, giving a 3D style depth-of-vision. This allowed the drawn backgrounds for the animation to also be used for the life-size live action sets.

'Economically, it was impossible for us to construct huge sets in the traditional manner,' said Bakshi. 'I came up with the idea of blowing up the animated backgrounds as photographs and constructing these to form the sets. We have turned the entire set into a live action multi-plane camera – a concept which is bound only by the size of the stage.' This breakthrough allowed the film to be produced cheaply and gave a bizarrely surreal 3D look to the 'real world' scenes.

Principal photography began with three weeks in the larger-than-life city of Las Vegas for all the live-action sequences and as the setting for the 'real world' portions of the film. Las Vegas was also the basis for the *Cool World* fantasy land.

'There is no better place in the world to serve as a cartoon city,' said Mancuso. An additional six weeks of shooting took place on soundstages in and around Los Angeles.

A specially designed facility was needed to accommodate the new animation technology being used. Bakshi hired a mix of veteran animators and newcomers, some of whom were still on their studies at the California Institute of the Arts. It took two months to complete a final edit of the live action material which was to be combined with the animation elements, a process which took a further nine months work by over 300 background artists, technicians, editors and animators. It was touch and go for the film to meet its scheduled opening date of July 1992.

The pressure on the stars, director and producer was great. The concept of *Cool World* was a difficult one to communicate to studio heads and publicists, never mind actually successfully pull off in the film itself. In the end, the project seems to have become too large for its individual elements to add up to something that made much sense.

'There's no question that this is a movie that's causing Ralph and me to stretch to places we've never been to before,' Mancuso admitted to science fiction TV and movie magazine *Starlog*. 'Ralph has never done live action before, and I've never been involved in animation. It has been taxing and, in a sense, alienating.'

The producer and director were not the only ones alienated from the production. The actors were having trouble coping with the unreality of what they were doing, with experienced film stars like Basinger and Byrne adrift from their normal reference points. The experience wasn't as bad for Pitt, who was just setting out on his cinematic adventures and was still open to new ways of working, but when asked about 'blue screen' work after the production his response was concise: 'Never again'.

Within the production staff it often seemed as though the right hand didn't know what the left hand was doing, resulting in a bizarre hodge-podge in the final film. Production designer Michael Corenblith was landed with the job of trying to knit the bits together into something that seemed consistent. 'We've drawn on a far broader range of comics, cartoons and contemporary art styles than we normally would,' he confessed to *Starlog*. 'We're dealing with so many different factions who each have their own method of doing things. I spend a lot of my time as a negotiator between the animators and illustrators. I make sure that both sides don't forget that there is a live-action movie going on here – and that things have to be created to a precise scale to accommodate live actors and stunts.'

The major problem with *Cool World* was precisely that the production seemed to loose sight of the human element. The actors – Basinger, Byrne and Pitt – simply became extra elements to be moved around in the mix. Bakshi seemed to miss his first opportunity to direct real actors. As it was, it was left up to the actors themselves to come up with characterisations. Pitt had more to work with than the others in his character and seemed to come off best in the film, but the entire project seems to have been doomed to be a brave experimental failure rather than a mainstream *Roger Rabbit*-style popular hit.

Paramount's marketing department was faced with the unforgiving task of selling the confused and confusing film to the movie-going public. They had an asset in Kim Basinger, as well as Pitt's rising star to hang the film on, but found the concept of cartoons who become real and humans hiding in cartoon worlds too complex to get across easily.

Someone, however, came up with the bright idea of draping the famous Hollywood landmark sign with a 75ft likeness of the *Cool World* cartoon Kim Basinger as a promotional gimmick. Receiving the odd request from Paramount to pop Kim Basinger's animated counterpart atop the letter 'D', the Parks Department agreed as Paramount was the only Hollywood film studio still actually located in the Hollywood area, the others having long since relocated to other parts of Los Angeles. Paramount didn't have to pay for the privilege, but they did make a donation of $27,000 to the sign maintenance fund and paid a further $27,000 to the post-1991 LA riots fund, Rebuild LA, as well as footing the bill for a two-man 24-hour guard.

The plan was not to the liking of the Hollywood Home-owners Association, who went to court to try and stop Paramount from pulling off their stunt. 'Los Angeles is the only city in the world that would take its most prominent monument and turn it into a common billboard,' complained Chuck Welch, president of the Association. 'I don't think you can rent the Eiffel Tower for a billboard, or the Tower of London, or the Washington Monument...'

The Association failed in its campaign and Paramount won millions of pounds worth of free publicity. It was all to no avail, however. The film still flopped, although it enjoys a healthy cult life on video – just like *Johnny Suede* before it. As for the Hollywood sign, it would appear that Paramount are destined to be the first and last organisation to get to tamper with its letters.

Released in July, *Cool World* suffered dismal reviews in both the United States and Europe. *The Village Voice* tried to outline some of the film's problems, laying the blame firmly at Bakshi's feet. 'He directs the badly synched actors so poorly,' wrote James Hannaham, 'that they pale against his crazed animated methadone clinic of wired wolfhounds, screaming telephones and cute yet megalomaniac bunnies.' Although clearly struggling with the material, Pitt came in for particular criticism from the *Voice*: 'Brad Pitt fails in every world suggested by the film...his performance is uncomfortable and mush-mouthed...'

Having boosted Pitt's career and per-film asking price with its glowing review of *Johnny Suede*, *Variety* was merciless in panning *Cool World*. Again, Hollywood animation rebel Ralph Bakshi was the main target. *Variety* called the film 'an ordeal...in the form of trial by animation. Bakshi has let his imagination run wild with almost brutal vigour, resulting in a guerrilla-like sensual assault unchecked by any traditional rules of storytelling.' Put more simply, in the words of *The New York Daily News*: 'Bakshi's skill as an animator continues to outshine his judgement about subject matter.'

In Britain the film fared a little better, with critics being kinder about Brad Pitt's role. *Sight and Sound* regarded him as the sole redeeming feature of the piece: 'The opening sequence, in which Brad Pitt as Frank suffers a motorbike accident, is the only well-directed live-action segment, while the *Cool World* sections are swamped by numerous irrelevant characters running or flying across the screen. Pitt and Gabriel Byrne struggle against the odds, though, unfortunately, the same cannot be said of Kim Basinger,' wrote critic Jeremy Clarke.

With many critics comparing *Cool World* unfavourably with *Who Framed Roger Rabbit?* and drawing comparisons (again unfavourably) between the Kathleen Turner-voiced Jessica Rabbit and Basinger's turn as Holli Would, *Cool*

World was on a hiding to nothing, despite its seasonal Christmas 1992 UK release.

Recalling that some of his family had not liked *Johnny Suede* much, Pitt was not too surprised to their unanimous reaction to *Cool World*. 'They all hated that one,' he recalled. 'It was dog shit, wasn't it? I like bad movies, 'cause I like to yell at the screen at home,' he joked.

In reality, though, starring in a flop was a bad experience. Quite apart from seeing a lot of invested time and effort go to waste as a film fails, it's not something that actors can easily recover from. 'I had my fears,' said Pitt of the troubled production. 'I wanted to see it, to see what went wrong, not like it's a big surprise. You see, the studio [Paramount] toned the script down because they wanted a PG, and in doing so they left all these holes. And of course new studio heads came in. They're not to blame, but if there was a chance to improve the film, they sure didn't take it. There's politics involved, which to me is the craziest thing, because it's anti-art. Ralph's too good a person, and it makes me mad.'

Pitt found himself on something of a personal and professional plateau in the early 90s. He'd suffered two mainstream flops in a row with *Johnny Suede* and *Cool World*, and it was a losing streak the actor couldn't afford to maintain. His bankability – and so his castability – would suffer if his next film failed. The search was on for a suitable property to give him the next boost up the Hollywood ladder.

His life had become far more complicated than it had been before, but in his laid-back, spaced-out way Pitt was coping. 'I honestly see things as very simple,' he said. 'When things get out of hand there's a simple answer. Some people are good at finding it quickly, some never find it.'

Despite the flops, he was famous, and was intent on enjoying his fame. 'I'm not surprised,' he told *Interview* magazine about his success; after all he'd worked for it. 'A whole lot of new steps come with it.' He was now in a position to sit back, during 1992, and mull over his feelings about Hollywood. 'This place has been good to me, but everyone makes judgements about it from afar. There are people, including me, who thought happiness was the place. This is why I left Missouri. I've found happiness is a way of travel.'

All was not perfect, however, in his private life. Pitt and Juliette Lewis had been spending a lot of time apart, pursuing their individual film careers. And the distance was putting pressure on the relationship.

7 The Road to Stardom

BY THE beginning of 1992 Pitt had already come a long way with what had seemed to be very little actual effort on his part. 'I've had it too easy,' he later admitted in a 1995 *Vanity Fair* interview. 'I'm starting to believe that anyone who's successful in these little circles has got to feel that way. That's why a lot of them don't survive it. You know, people want to be famous, but you have no idea what you're getting into. It just happens and the happening is big.'

The big break on *Thelma & Louise* had made him a recognised name and face in Hollywood. *The Favor* had done him a favour by vanishing, and he'd stuck to his guns by not simply repeating the JD role in a string of sex-themed movies, despite being offered many opportunities: 'Right now I have to prove there's more here than a pretty face, that there's substance,' he claimed. 'People will always try to pin you down and define you, but they'll always get it wrong. You're the only one who knows where you're really heading. And you're the only one who knows who you really are...'

Pitt was offered a host of parts, some of them to co-star with Juliette Lewis again. Jonathan Demme's follow-up to *Silence of the Lambs* was announced as being *Crazy for You*, a film about a mental patient who befriends an outcast in his ward. Pitt was up for the main role, which would have pre-figured his part in 1995's *Twelve Monkeys*. Pitt and Lewis were offered roles in Frank Military's courtroom murder mystery *Beyond a Reasonable Doubt*, which was turned down, as was a starring role for Pitt in *Baboon Heart*, later made as *Untamed Heart* (1993) with Christian Slater. Pitt also considered a role in *Devil's Advocate*, the tale of a hotshot lawyer entering a law firm, only to discover that it's run by the Devil. Al Pacino was talked about for the role of Satan and Joel Schumacher was down to direct, but the film didn't happen.

Whatever he did do next, to be taken seriously as an actor he would have to take risks to show his genuine, albeit developing, acting abilities. But, also, he could not afford another flop like *Cool World*.

At 55, Robert Redford was a mature Hollywood heart-throb who had gone through the experience that Brad Pitt was enduring. Cast initially for his pretty boy looks, Redford had triumphed over typecasting in front of the camera. He'd branched out from mere acting to writing and directing films, expressing his own political and environmental views in the process. He'd set up the Sundance Institute and Film Festival to promote new, young, independent film-making talent, and he already had a connection with Pitt, having played a hand in the script development of Tom DiCillo's *Johnny Suede*.

Having starred in the likes of *The Great Gatsby* (1974), *Butch Cassidy and the Sundance Kid* (1969, one of Brad Pitt's earliest film memories) and *All The President's Men* (1976), Redford's output had slowed down through the 80s, culminating in the big-budget flop *Havana* in 1990. He followed that with a starring role in *Sneakers* (1992), a high-tech computer thriller with an all-star cast

'Pitt is a revelation, shedding his teen heart-throb image and turning in a
layered performance that anchors the entire movie.' (*Empire*)

75

that included Sidney Poitier, Dan Aykroyd and River Phoenix.

Redford's director's credentials were good, having won an Oscar for directing *Ordinary People* in 1980, but he had not been behind the camera since 1987's *The Milagro Beanfield War*. *A River Runs Through It*, Norman Maclean's autobiographical tale of a father and two sons who can only communicate through their shared passion for fly fishing, was close to Redford's heart, and he was determined to film it. 'This film is about a deeply loving family that did not understand each other. It's about how the ethic of pride affected them, and how to help someone you love before it's too late.'

Casting the roles was his greatest problem. He'd secured Craig Sheffer for the older MacLean brother, Norman, and had signed Tom Skerrit to play the father, but the role of Paul, the younger brother, a character who was both clever and doomed, was proving harder to fill.

One of the names that had come to mind for the part was that of River Phoenix, Redford's young co-star in *Sneakers*. Phoenix had enjoyed an unprecedented success as Hollywood's latest young pin-up during the late 80s. The young actor was ideal magazine feature material, with his bizarre south American childhood and unconventional upbringing by hippie parents. Phoenix had auditioned for Redford and was keen on the role, but doubtful that he would be cast. 'It's a great script,' he said. 'I auditioned – me and a thousand other guys. I had a good meeting with Redford, but I think he's gonna find the guy. The guy who is just that image – the Montana mountain boy, fly-fisherman image...' It turned out that 'the guy' was to be Brad Pitt.

Pitt was not yet such a big star that he could be cast in major roles without an audition. Unfortunately his first audition for the part of Paul Maclean had been, in his own word, 'shit'.

What looked to be the biggest and most challenging role of his career to date seemed to be slipping from his grasp. Determined to have another go, Pitt and his actor friend Dermot Mulroney – co-star with Bridget Fonda in *The Assassin* (1994) and later an investor/co-producer and star of Tom DiCillo's *Living in Oblivion* (1995) – got together with a video camera and taped a few scenes from the movie together. Pitt sent the tape off to Redford as a kind of unsolicited second audition. 'I think it kept me in there,' said Pitt of his unusual taped showreel.

Robert Redford had, in fact, been keeping close tabs on Pitt's growing reputation, especially because several commentators had already commented on the uncanny similarity in looks between him and Redford in his younger days. The older actor-director had discussed Pitt with *Cool World* director Ralph Bakshi, not once but three times, to determine whether he was worth hiring. Three times the answer came back, definitely yes! Having had his hopes independently confirmed, and having seen the tape, Redford was now prepared to cast him as the self-destructive younger brother.

Redford had no intention of featuring in the film himself, but one of the undoubted attractions of casting Brad Pitt was that the young actor could function as a surrogate for the director in the film, the way Woody Allen would later use John Cusack. Redford says he chose Pitt because he could embody the 'golden boy' aspects of Paul Maclean. 'There's no signs of trouble in his face,' said Redford, but Pitt also had the acting skills to capture the darker side of the character – the drinking and obsession with gambling that were to prove his downfall.

Fly fishing is both the main relaxation and a test of character for the Maclean family in *A River Runs Through It*, and Brad Pitt worked hard at mastering the techniques.

Robert Redford directs Brad and Craig Sheffer as two brothers in early 20th-century Montana in *A River Runs Through It.*

Four months before production began, Norman Maclean died. Redford had known the author for over five years, during which time he had struggled to convince him to release the cinema rights, sometimes in competition with other actors interested in the property, such as Oscar-winner William Hurt. Of Maclean's initial reluctance to have the film made, Redford said: 'I think he knew that in a small way he'd done something perfect. With it came all the pain and anguish of that time. Why risk all that by having it butchered on screen?' Following the author's death, Redford felt even more duty-bound than before to do the work justice.

Making the film presented a series of problems – many of which were inherent in the material. 'I thought this was a book that would be almost impossible to do,' admitted Redford. 'It has two elements – it is very literary and very lyrical. Film is not a literary medium, obviously, and in America at least, such things don't go down very well. Lyricism in film is treated with a great deal of cynicism. There were two hurdles right there.'

Shooting the film on location in Montana was important to Redford who was keen to capture, as much as possible, the feel for landscape from the original story. 'We couldn't use the original Big Blackfoot river, which is a very prominent river in the north west of Montana, near the town of Missoula, where the story took place,' lamented Redford. 'The idea was to film it on the actual river where Norman spent every summer of his life from childhood onwards. It was totally polluted from mining, the indiscriminate abuse of industry.'

It was impossible for a film that concentrated on fly-fishing for the principal actors to escape having to learn how to fish properly. Pitt threw himself into

Paul and Norman Maclean with their Protestant minister father (Tom Skerrit, centre).

learning the craft – he wanted to look authentic on screen. After all, Paul was supposed to have a God-given gift for the sport, so he couldn't afford to look as if he didn't know how to fish for real. Opportunities to practise were few and far between, however, until he got to location. He'd try out his technique high atop Hollywood buildings. Occasionally he'd pop over to his friend singer Melissa Etheridge's house to use her swimming pool as a fly-fishing try out venue, a place to practise his casting technique in relative safety.

On location in Gallatin, 200 miles away from the Big Blackfoot River, Pitt was able to absorb the panoramic perfection of the landscape into his character – an important tip given to him by Redford. Pitt also got to play with antique collectors item fly-fishing rods – but only for close-ups. It was deemed too risky to have the neophyte fly-fisher let loose with the real 8ft Montague bamboo rods, originally used in the Montana of the 1820s.

Robert Redford enlisted the help of expert John Bailey to instruct his cast in the fine art of fly-fishing. While he came away from the film with more than a passing acquaintance with the sport, Brad Pitt got much more out of working with Robert Redford. He became aware that it was up to him to make sure other people knew what he was capable of. Redford offered advice, which Pitt took to heart. 'Hollywood is a business. It's very clear about what it is, very mercenary, and you have to work in that or around it. Once you understand that, you'll have a much better time.'

A River Runs Through It was welcomed by most critics, although many had reservations about its ability to draw a big audience given its limited-interest subject matter. However, most were pleased to see a film based on characters rather than slam-bam action.

In *The New Yorker*, Terrence Rafferty wrote of Pitt's character: 'Paul is mysteriously gifted at catching fish and mysteriously inept at living; the narrator tries, and fails, to connect the two mysteries.' *The Village Voice* played up the

Most of Pitt's scenes in *A River Runs Through It* are with his elder brother Norman
(Craig Sheffer), the narrator of the autobiographical story.

similarities between Pitt and Redford for all they were worth, suggesting that
Redford's motives in casting Pitt were almost entirely narcissistic. 'A very clear line
runs between Redford and Brad Pitt's golden boy,' wrote Georgina Brown. 'Wearing
vintage suits, suspenders and fedoras, Pitt is a dead ringer for the young Redford of
The Sting (1973). The camera dwells so lovingly on his toothpaste smile, manly jaw
and sky blue eyes it seems that some narcissistic impulse is the true motive here.'

In Britain the reviews focused more on the film than the story's relatively
obscure literary origins, and many hailed Pitt's performance as a significant
breakthrough. *Empire* magazine, in particular, was full of praise. 'Pitt is a
revelation, shedding his teen heart-throb image and turning in a layered
performance that anchors the entire movie. It's a part Redford knows well and 20
years ago he would have played it himself.'

Others were as fulsome, with *The Independent*'s Adam Mars-Jones
commenting 'Brad Pitt gives a particularly good performance'; *The Daily
Telegraph* claimed that 'Brad Pitt is uncannily like a cross between James Dean and
the young Robert Redford'; and Derek Malcolm in *The Guardian* thought 'it is well
acted by Pitt in particular'.

'That was a beautifully crafted movie,' said Pitt of *A River Runs Through It*.
'Chiselled, you know. I'm not as satisfied with that performance as much, but the
movie is so well done, it is bigger than any one performance.'

The press comparisons with the young Robert Redford seemed inevitable. 'It
doesn't amount to much,' said Pitt of the constant references. 'Just what we need,
hey, another sex symbol...Brad Pitt symbolises sex? I don't think so. They've never
even been to bed with me...If that was all that I was known for when it's all said and

done, I'd be disappointed. But hopefully I have more to offer than that...'

Although there was no sex in *A River Runs Through It*, Pitt was playing his by now standard clean-cut character, accentuating his good looks. If he was not entirely happy with his performance, perhaps it was because even Robert Redford was concentrating on how he looked and how he was lit, rather than on his acting and performance. Pitt didn't get to explore or display Paul's darker side as much as he would have liked – he had to wait to play Tristan in *Legends of the Fall* for that kind of part.

Although *A River Runs Through It* was certainly a step in the right direction for Pitt's career, at the end of it he found himself still confronting the same issues – how could he get the chance to surpass and escape his looks? Could he find a role that didn't depend on how he looked, but allowed him just to act, to show what he could do?

After Redford's film Brad Pitt made it clear to his agent that he was seeking something different, and his agent duly obliged, sending him a copy of a script entitled *Kalifornia*.

'I asked for it,' said Pitt of his decision to play the controversial role of serial killer Early Grayce. 'I picked the hardest one I could find. You take a movie because there's something it brings to you that you want to investigate. After *A River Runs Through It* I got this big label stuck on me and you want to remind the people that there's a little more going on than that. You can't go on doing the same thing over and over.'

This constant search for challenging material was to drive his career forward

A River Runs Through It is as much about growing up in a land still between wilderness and civilisation as it is about relationships.

from this point on, but Pitt hasn't looked at his career like his contemporary Johnny Depp. While Depp has pursued roles simply to please himself, almost deliberately carving out a quirky, box-office-avoiding career, Pitt has realised the importance of the business side of the film industry, something he'd learned from his old drama coach Roy London as well as from Robert Redford. He has known he has to alternate hit movies with films which might be more personally satisfying, but not such box office blockbusters. *Kalifornia* was his first step on that road.

The movie was to be a character piece, a showcase for four actors playing very different parts. The drama in this off-kilter road-movie-to-hell is kicked off by the character of Brian Kessler (played by David Duchovny, later to win international fame as Fox Mulder in the TV series *The X Files*). Kessler is a writer who is pleased – not to say self-satisfied – with his pet thesis on serial killers, which looks upon them as people to be pitied and helped, not condemned and jailed. His girlfriend Carrie Laughlin (Michelle Forbes, best known as the rambunctious Ensign Ro, one of Patrick Stewart's sparring partners in the TV series *Star Trek: The Next Generation*) is a photographer who takes sexually explicit pictures. Tired of their big-city life in New York and longing to move to California, the pair get the idea that they can combine their talents to produce an illustrated book on serial killers, the research giving them the opportunity to travel across the country. On the way they intend to stop off at infamous sites, the homes of serial killers or the venues of the

Kalifornia provided Brad Pitt with a different kind of part, that of Early Grayce, a serial killer with no redeeming features.

killings, take some pictures and notes for the text. The only problem is that they need to share the costs with two other passengers. Enter Early Grayce and Adele Corners, a real-life serial killer and his girlfriend who burst Brian's death-fantasy bubble by bringing a much-needed dose of down-and-dirty reality into his life.

Kalifornia was the feature film debut of director Dominic Sena whose previous film-making experience had been in the world of music videos. He'd directed clips for such acts as David Bowie, Sting, Elton John and Fleetwood Mac, as well as adverts for Estée Lauder perfumes, Coors, M&Ms, Lincoln Mercury and Chic Jeans. He started working with Tim Metcalfe's script in 1990, attracted by the main character. 'What caught my attention immediately,' said Sena of the screenplay, 'was the character of Early Grayce, this strangely likeable guy who just happens to be a serial killer.' Sena's producing partner Aris McGarry agreed: 'The most appealing characteristic of Early is his lack of consideration for the future, for the ramifications of his actions.'

Brad Pitt didn't see his as the leading part, though, feeling that all four characters were important to how the film was to work. '*Kalifornia* is like a musical quartet,' he said. 'Each character is integral to the whole as any other, and each must play in tune.'

Sena had to spend about 18 months working on the script, in between directing music videos, until he felt the characters were developed enough for him to decide to make the movie. 'While Early and Adele were pretty well drawn,' recalled Sena, 'we wanted to flesh out Brian and Carrie. Carrie needed more drive, so we made her a photographer gung ho on getting her boyfriend out to California. With him a writer and she a photographer, their collaboration on a book bonds the two and gives the stops during their road trip a purpose.'

Sena found his two leads for *Kalifornia* when viewing a videotape of *Too Young to Die?* the 1990 telefilm that had brought Pitt and Juliette Lewis together, professionally and personally. 'I was so excited when I saw her,' said Sena of Lewis. Part of his excitement came from the fleeting thought that he'd discovered a new talent. 'This was Adele – and better yet she's my discovery!' But he soon discovered that Martin Scorsese had beaten him to it by casting her in *Cape Fear*. Although fearing that she would now be outside the production's price range, Sena took a risk and sent her the script.

For some time Pitt and Lewis had been looking for another project to do together. Every time one or other was in a film the pair were separated for long periods of time – and the strain was beginning to show. Pitt had been in Montana for *A River Runs Through It*, while Lewis had been working with Scorsese and with Woody Allen on *Husbands and Wives*. Their careers were both well on track, but their personal lives were suffering. The way to deal with the problem was to work together on a film, just as they had done on *Too Young to Die?* It seemed that *Kalifornia* was the ideal opportunity, especially as the characters of Early and Adele were almost a reprise of the parts they'd played previously.

'Adele is like a ten-year-old girl,' thought Lewis of the character she was to play. 'She doesn't want to confront the severity of circumstances that surround her, so to maintain her innocence she sings songs, whistles, plays with her yo-yo, does anything to prevent her world from being overturned. She loves Early as someone who will be around her. He protects her.'

Sena had first seen Brad Pitt in *Thelma & Louise*, and coming across him in

Kalifornia gave Brad and Juliette Lewis the opportunity to work together again after three years of being forced apart by their different commitments for much of the time.

Too Young to Die? alongside Lewis gave him a ready-made serial killer couple. *Kalifornia* seemed to take as its starting point what might have happened to the characters of *Too Young to Die?* if they had not been caught at the film's climax.

Although his character was to be very different from anything else he had ever played, Pitt had two things to draw on. Firstly, although not as extreme, Billy Canton in *Too Young to Die?* had laid some of the basic groundwork for Early Grayce and, secondly, Pitt had known characters just like Early in his youth. 'Early Grayce is an animal,' Pitt said, simply. 'He's a little kid, a beer drinker. I've been familiar with guys like him. They kick cats around or stick firecrackers in their mouths. What drew me to this script was the questioning of why he does what he does.'

This character's look was very important, both to Pitt personally and to the production generally. Keen to escape his pretty boy image, Pitt was happy to get down and dirty for Early Grayce. He grew his hair long and added a scruffy beard. An accident also added to his appearance – he chipped one of his front teeth trying to crack open a bottle of Mountain Dew. Something most Hollywood stars would regard as a disaster and which would result in an emergency call to their orthodontist was actually welcomed. The 'defect' remained uncorrected until after the *Kalifornia* shoot was over and became part of Early Grayce's appearance.

Costume designer Kelle Kutsugeras, who had worked with Dominic Sena on

Brad Pitt grew his hair and a straggly beard for the part of Early Grayce, and had a tattoo and scars made up each day.

music videos for many years, had a clear view of the characters through their costumes: 'Early is dressed in trailer trash maximus,' joked Kutsugeras. 'His clothes come from whatever the workplace provided – mechanic pants and shirts. Adele wears polyester – it's built to last. Most of what she wears are 70s hand-me-downs, tube tops, floral dresses and wedgie cork shoes. Brian and Carrie, on the other hand, are very utilitarian – a lot of black, white and grey.'

Like Robert DeNiro in *Cape Fear*, Pitt also had to suffer some temporary body modification for the role. 'Brad didn't want his body to be clean,' recalled make-up artist Michelle Buhler, 'so he came up with this great tattoo idea for his forearm – a heart with the name that was once in it carved out.' Similar scars, wounds, burns and tattoo were placed on his body daily during production.

Production designer Michael White chose Atlanta as the location for the film because of its versatility. 'Atlanta has become an incredibly popular place to shoot lately, probably because it's a production designer's dream, with every type of location from worn-out urban decay to lush farmland.'

With the cross-country road trip taking the foursome of characters to some offbeat venues, White had a few challenges ahead. He avoided the usual method of hiring props from film studios, though, buying much of what was needed for the film's locations from thrift stores in the Atlanta area. 'Every place – Early's trailer, the diners, the motels, the mines, the abattoir – has either been forgotten or ignored. There's an uneasy, unsettling feeling about them.'

The five-week stay in Atlanta was taxing on the cast and crew. With much of the action taking place outdoors, weather became very important. High temperatures and higher humidity plagued the production, with record amounts of rain falling on the city during their stay.

Pitt viewed the film as 'something different...cops and robbers, and rubber guns and fake blood'. Taking childish delight in getting to play 'cops and robbers', Pitt got somewhat carried away. In his first big shooting scene, he had to blast away at a couple of policemen who are unlucky enough to stumble across the foursome. Take after take the sound man complained that there were weird noises on the tape. Eventually the problem was tracked down – every time he pulled the trigger on the prop gun he was using, Pitt was going 'Bam! Bam! Bam!'. 'I had no idea,' he said. 'I was like a little kid.'

Despite the 20 extra pounds he piled on, his long, lanky unwashed hair and scruffy beard, Pitt was still the centre of attention for many women on the set during production. Talking to *People* magazine, director Dominic Sena commented of Pitt: 'This guy just gets through to women, no matter what!'

The final four weeks of shooting on *Kalifornia* took place in the high deserts of California, where the temperatures reached 120 degrees F (49°C). While shooting in Barstow at 5am, a huge earthquake rocked the state, registering 7.4 on the Richter scale. The crew's location was only 40 miles from the epicentre, but no one was injured. Aftershocks, however, continued for weeks, unsettling many in the cast and crew as they wrapped production.

Having embarked on this risky role, Pitt found himself criticised by the movie press. Why didn't he stick to tried and tested roles? When was he going to play another JD? Did he take his clothes off in the new movie? Tired of the questioning, Pitt attempted to lay out what it was about the character of Early Grayce that had caught his attention, and he tried to explain why it was important personally to him

Early Grayce gets tough with Kessler (David Duchovny) in *Kalifornia*.

to play the part. 'Taking on a physically unappealing role was a help. Early was very far away from my own character and that was somehow easier.'

His choice to play such an unredeemed villain left many confused, just when they thought they'd got Pitt pigeon-holed. 'He doesn't have any redeeming features,' admitted Pitt of Early Grayce. 'But I like him. He's a killer but, you know, you can hear about someone who does something really horrible, then you begin to understand a little bit about where they came from. Some can overcome bad beginnings and become lawyers and doctor and have good families. Other people take great offence and shut off. This guy, Early Grayce, would have loved something in the beginning and been completely slammed down – where he gave up and had no feelings – so that killing someone meant no more than killing a bug. That's the way I saw him.'

There were some aspects to Early's character that audiences for *Kalifornia* didn't get to see, according to Pitt, either because they were cut from the film in favour of action material or were scripted but never shot in the first place. 'There was a scene that Early has with his father that I think we needed, even though it was the standard story of coming from a bad home. And in the original, there was more about his attraction to Carrie. We had such a low budget that we couldn't do it all.'

While pleased with the finished film, Pitt was not averse to seeing its problems. 'It's definitely a flawed movie,' he said, 'but it was a good time, too.' Release was limited, with its not coming out in Europe until two years after it had been shot, just like Pitt's earlier film *The Favor*. In America it came and went, making little impact on the box office. 'I went to bed one night and it was out, and I got up the next morning and it was gone!' Pitt joked. At least for Pitt big box office wasn't the point of *Kalifornia*. He'd had his chance to play against type and stretch his talents.

Many critics realised the unique look of the film and praised the lighting and direction, as well as the central performances. Despite those good points, though, most found the concept of the central character being a serial killer too discomforting to accept.

For Pitt the gamble had paid off, with American critics paying special attention to his against-the-grain performance. *The New York Times* noted: '*Kalifornia* confirms that Pitt is an interesting, persuasive actor,' while show business bible *Variety* felt moved to comment: 'the charismatic Pitt explores his character with quiet resolve, venting both horror and darkly comic implications'.

When belatedly released in Europe in 1994, *Kalifornia* received a mixed reception. Although seen as too pretentious for its own good, the film was recommended for its performances, particularly Pitt's. Typical was *Sight and Sound*. Criticising the film for its requirement that the viewer bring along a 'cultural studies primer', it nevertheless praised Pitt's performance: 'Not that Brad Pitt doesn't put in a show-stopping performance as Early Grayce, with an accent as thick as a mouthful of chewing tobacco and body language straight from *A Streetcar Named Desire* Brando. That is precisely one of the film's major problems – it is such an over-the-top performance that Early simply dominates the film and its other characters, making them little more than fellow passengers caught in his murderous tail-spin.'

Kalifornia was something Brad Pitt had to do. That the film was not a huge hit didn't matter – to those that were interested, particularly casting directors, *Kalifornia* was a calling card that presented a different side to Pitt's talents.

Work on *Kalifornia* was finished before *A River Runs Through It* hit cinemas, and confirmed Pitt as a rising Hollywood star. However, before the Hollywood machine totally took over Pitt had one more brief indulgence up his sleeve.

Following the success of *Reservoir Dogs* Quentin Tarantino found in 1993 that one of his screen plays that had been sold previously but not produced was being rushed into production. *True Romance* attracted a bunch of top stars to cameo roles because Tarantino was one of the few writers in modern Hollywood who provided speeches for actors to perform and dialogue they could get their teeth into. Hence people like Christopher Walken, Gary Oldman, Dennis Hopper and Val Kilmer all had small, but significant roles in the film.

Attracted to taking part in a project whose success or failure did not rest on his shoulders alone, Brad Pitt was quickly in contact with Tony Scott to see if there was a part in the movie he could play.

Christian Slater and Patricia Arquette were the leads, an unlikely on-the-run couple who have eloped with a suitcase full of stolen drugs which they aim to sell in Los Angeles and get rich on the cash. On arrival in LA, Slater's character Clarence

Brad's part as a dope-head in *True Romance* was only a cameo, but given the film's
high profile it greatly enhanced his reputation.

Worley looks up his best friend. Playing the best friend's permanently stoned
roommate named Floyd was Brad Pitt.

For the role Pitt spent his entire time lying about on a couch spouting variations
on surfer and valley speak, appearing at times to be involved in conversations
entirely different from those of the rest of the cast. It was a small, but showy role,
something most actors would positively jump at. As it was, Pitt – almost literally –
slept through the part. As various characters in the film came and went from the
house, Floyd's space oddity would offer them some drugs or the chance to watch a
bit of TV.

'That was fun,' reckoned Pitt of his brief star turn, 'but I was only there for a
few days.' Having read the script and told Tony Scott he liked it, the part was his,
no effort involved. Pitt particularly liked his role 'because he gets everyone killed'.
Pitt brought much to the character himself. 'I said, "Can I make him a stoner? A
pothead?" and he [Tony Scott] said, "Do whatever you want!"'

The laid-back atmosphere of the production, and the fact that the responsibility
of the film wasn't his, all added to Pitt's engagingly goofy performance. 'You know
Brad has a sense of mystery and a darkness, I think it comes from the chequered
life he had before,' Tony Scott said. 'That's a character that he knew and hung out
with at his house, this guy came for a week and stayed for two years – a pothead
who never got off the sofa.'

Pitt indeed had a real-life model to base the character on, a friend of his who'd
come to stay with him in Los Angeles for a short while, only to remain for many
months. Asked by *Empire* magazine if his friend had seen the film, Pitt answered:

'No, he's in an asylum, actually.'

Pitt's pothead friend may not have seen the movie, but many millions of others did. The combination of Tony Scott directing and Tarantino scripting, along with the all-star roster of cameos and Christian Slater as lead, was enough to ensure success. Even in his bit part, critics singled out Brad Pitt.

Variety highlighted the 'dopey fun in Brad Pitt's space cadet'. In among the cameos, *The Village Voice* commented that Brad Pitt 'almost steals home,' no mean feat up against well-known scene-stealers and scenery-chewers like Dennis Hopper, Christopher Walken and Gary Oldman. Writer Manohla Dargis noted a subtext in the film missed by many reviewers who chose instead to concentrate on the violence. 'If nothing else, the preponderance of pretty guys [Slater, Kilmer, Pitt] makes obvious that the film's real romance isn't between men and women, but men and men. Working the same homoerotic turf as *Reservoir Dogs*, Tarantino and Scott test the limits of fear, desire and masculinity with razor wit and surprising heart.'

In Britain it was the violence, rather than any sexual subtext, that grabbed the headlines, with many Conservatives clamouring for it to be banned following the withholding of *Reservoir Dogs*. Critics were no better disposed, calling it, variously, 'a bloody farce' in *The Independent on Sunday*, a 'pernicious' movie in *The New Statesman*, a movie that boasted a 'full compliment of fashionable violence' in *The Sunday Telegraph* and a 'noisy, vacuous fantasia' in *The Times*.

Some, however, did take a shine to the cameo performances, with Sheila Johnston in *The Independent* highlighting Pitt in 'a funny, unexpected role'. Hugo Davenport in *The Daily Telegraph* noted Pitt's 'perpetually stoned room-mate' and *The Guardian* mentioned 'Brad Pitt playing flat out (quite literally) as an LA space cadet, advanced grade'.

Whatever the reception of the role, Pitt wasn't in *True Romance* for the critical plaudits. Playing the part was a breeze and featuring alongside all those other actors in a prestigious and popular film like *True Romance* was not going to harm anyone's career. More importantly, his few days on the *True Romance* set, at the start of 1993, gave him the chance to come to a decision he had been putting off for sometime.

Kalifornia and *True Romance* were calling cards that Brad left with the industry to show that he could portray characters far removed from his normal image.

8 Playing Legends

HAVING wrapped up on *True Romance*, in February 1993 Pitt had finally decided to call off his long-lasting relationship with Juliette Lewis.

Pitt and Lewis had epitomised the then-fashionable grunge chic ethic, dressing down for film premieres and public appearances. But no matter how good (or bad) they looked together, Pitt and Lewis had spent much of their three years actually far apart from one another. Now Pitt was home from *True Romance*, Lewis was preparing to leave to shoot another Tarantino screenplay, Oliver Stone's *Natural Born Killers*.

They had, in fact, both been offered the lead roles, Mickey and Mallory, but Pitt hadn't been as interested in the material as Lewis. He had two reasons – he did not want to do another Early Grayce so soon after *Kalifornia*, and having just completed *True Romance* he was wary of doing another Tarantino script in quick succession.

During all the separations Pitt and Lewis had grown apart. Pitt was approaching 30, while Lewis was just still under 20. The age difference, which had not seemed so apparent before, was becoming an issue. There were other pressures - Lewis was keen to get married, and Pitt wasn't ready for such a serious commitment. 'She became very intense about their relationship,' a friend of the pair commented to *The National Enquirer* about their break-up. 'Brad became scared when Juliette started to tell friends that they would soon marry.'

Juliette was 'extraordinarily intense' according to another friend who spoke to *People* magazine about their split, 'but Brad is really the most laid-back young star I can think of.' Pitt had his own take on their doomed relationship: 'We were trying to be Sid and Nancy or something,' he said.

The pressures of work and the desire of one partner to get married and of the other to simply drift along, as he had done for most of his life, would be enough to strain any relationship to breaking point, especially one in the Hollywood spotlight. However, what was to drive the final wedge between them was Scientology.

The Church of Scientology had been found by 50s pulp science fiction author L. Ron Hubbard. The 'religion' claimed to be able to help people on the road to success, to be able to determine the negative emotions that hold someone back by 'auditing' them and then 'clearing' them. The courses involved in this process which the individuals have to undergo typically cost in the region of $300 to $400 per hour – a nice little earner for the Church and those that run it.

Healing the psychic scars caused by trauma in the present or in a past life is done with a device called an 'E-meter', invented by Hubbard. Students are then indoctrinated in the ways of the Church in a series of courses, with those who reach the higher levels learning of the secret mystery of Scientology. In something that sound like one of Hubbard's horrendous SF plots, according to the cult's theology (which only those in the upper hierarchy are supposed to know) an evil alien being called Xenu imprisoned other aliens under volcanoes on Earth 75 million years ago. The imprisoned aliens were then zapped by Xenu, leaving their spirits (or 'thetans')

Filming of *Legends of the Fall* produced strong differences of opinion between Brad Pitt and director Ed Zwick over the interpretation of Brad's role, Tristan.

to wander the Earth, attaching themselves to humans, thereby causing all sorts of psychic ills which could only be purged by Hubbard's patented 'technology'. Fiercely litigious, the cult has used the law and the courts to try and suppress its 'secret knowledge', a battle that continues in the 90s in cyberspace across the Internet.

It had been an aim of founder L. Ron Hubbard to recruit celebrities to his bogus operation as a way of spreading the message as early as 1955. According to John H. Richardson's exposé of Scientology activities in Hollywood in a 1993 issue of *Premiere* magazine, Hubbard had created something called Project Celebrity. A list of targets, including Orson Welles, Danny Kaye, James Stewart, Greta Garbo and Walt Disney, was drawn up and disciples were told to try and recruit them. Forty years later, after the establishment of the Celebrity Centre International on Franklin Avenue in LA, Hubbard had his wish.

The Hollywood honour role of recruits included John Travolta, Kirstie Alley and Tom Cruise. Cruise and his wife Mimi Rogers were both Scientologists, but his greater devotion to the cult was a factor in the break-up of their marriage (the prime one being their failure to have children). Other well-known names involved in the cult included Karen Black, Anne Archer, Kelly Preston and Nancy Cartwright, the voice of Bart Simpson on *The Simpsons*. When Michael Jackson's shock marriage to Lisa Marie Presley, Elvis Presley's daughter, was announced many thought it a Scientology plot to recruit Jackson, as she was an evangelical member.

Juliette Lewis had first become involved in the cult in the late 70s and early 80s through her father. She then became more active in the early 90s; for Pitt it was the last straw in their deteriorating relationship. 'Oh boy,' he exclaimed when the subject was raised by Britain's *Empire* magazine. 'Don't get me started! I'd go on for a couple of hours about that. The 30-second version is: I'm not big on anything that tells you how to live your life.'

Brought up by his Baptist parents to be tolerant of others, Pitt had tried humouring Lewis. He'd even attended some of the Scientology classes in Hollywood in an effort to get to the bottom of it, but he drifted into and out of the religion in short order. He was in good company. Others had taken this suck-it-and-see approach before quickly rejecting the creed, including Patrick Swayze, TV comedian Jerry Seinfeld and the late *Top Gun* producer Don Simpson, according to Richardson in *Premiere*.

Pitt's own struggle with his parents' religion had shown him the dangers of blind obedience, which seemed to be a key facet of Scientology's approach. It wasn't Lewis's involvement that Pitt disapproved of – it was just that he wanted to distance himself from anything that echoed his childhood religious experiences.

Since university Pitt had broken free from the people in his life who had tried to arrange his future for him – although they'd always done it with the best of intentions. In going unexpectedly to Hollywood, he had struck out in a direction that was truly his own, not dictated by his parents or by the expectations of his local community or peers. More importantly, he'd succeeded. He wasn't about to step backwards into a lifestyle where rules and regulations would govern his life once more. He was too independently minded for that.

Keeping it in the family is common in Scientology – Travolta married fellow cult member Kelly Preston; Cruise's second wife, Nicole Kidman, was also a member; while actor brothers Charlie Sheen and Emilo Estevez had been the target of recruitment attempts through their girlfriends (the same Kelly Preston in Sheen's case). But despite their relationship, Lewis did not try to recruit Pitt into the cult. 'I wasn't under any pressure at all,' he said. 'You've got to see what's going on if your love's into it, because you've got to respect your love.'

Pitt was happy for Lewis to go her own way, and if that meant getting more involved with Scientology, so be it. By his own ethics and standards, he felt he couldn't interfere, although he didn't approve. He said: 'Whatever helps you sleep at night, whatever helps you get up in the morning. As much as I don't want anyone telling me how to live my life, I can't tell someone how to live theirs.' For Pitt, Scientology was not his thing. 'It's bad for me,' he admitted, 'but I know it made my girl feel better.'

Their three years together now over, Pitt and Lewis vowed to remain friends and possibly even work together again in the future. 'I'd work with her again in a second. You could have some powerful stuff out there. I still love the woman. There's some real genius there. I had a great time with her,' Pitt told *Vanity Fair*. 'She has her own views. It was one of the greatest relationships I've ever been in. The problem is, we grow up with this vision that love conquers all, and that's just not so, is it?'

It took a long time for Lewis to get over the break-up, and even in 1995 talking with Quentin Tarantino in *Details* magazine she still felt strongly about the end of their affair. 'From 16 to 20, I was with one person and truly, truly in love,' she said, 'and then all these elements in his life and mine were changing, and those are enormous years as it is...'

One of the major problems for her was that the pair didn't so much break-up as continue to drift apart until they simply stopped being together. Their relationship lacked a final dramatic closure. 'It wasn't cut and dried, it wasn't totally breaking up, so I lost myself there for a second,' Lewis said. 'I felt bad about myself, and the thing about doing movies when you're going through personal stuff is that you've got to feel good enough to be in front of a camera. It's a distant thing now, but a couple of years ago it was a huge change, and I had to remember that I had once lived alone, and had my own pride and my own ideas. There was much more to it than the relationship, it was also where I was in my life. It's old now, and I actually care about Brad and I think he and Gwyneth are cool. I think he's found a good girl.'

Following his break up with Lewis, Pitt moved out of their shared home, packing all his stuff into the back of a car, including his antiques, his huge and disorganised CD collection, his cherished espresso machine and his equally cherished guitars.

Moving into a temporary rented apartment, Pitt couldn't seem to settle down. He wasn't used to living alone - for years he'd either been on film sets or at home with Lewis. There'd always been company around. Out of work and out of Lewis's life, he was at a loose end and he found it difficult to occupy himself. Never a big reader, he'd while away the evenings watching indifferent movies on TV, or else he would find himself heading out into LA in the evenings, driving around and stopping off in bars. He was candid about that period: 'The main reason I used to go to bars was to pick up girls.'

During 1993 Pitt was offered a variety of roles which he turned down, in addition to the lead in *Natural Born Killers*. He also turned down an approach from his *Thelma & Louise* director Ridley Scott to take part in his proposed film

Pancho's War to play a 1916 Mexican revolutionary who is a munitions expert delivering guns to General Pershing. The film was scrapped as it was in competition with another similar film, *Tom Mix & Pancho Villa*, to be directed by Scott's brother Tony. Eventually neither film was made.

Producer Edward Zwick easily recalled Brad Pitt's impact during his one guest shot appearance on the TV show he was producing. Pitt's brief monosyllabic turn in *thirtysomething* had not only been noticed by audiences, but the young actor's early performance had stayed in Zwick's memory.

An Emmy-award winning TV writer, producer and director, Ed Zwick had ambitions in the cinema. He began his feature film career with *About Last Night...* (1986), a teen movie adaptation of David Mamet's play *Sexual Perversity in Chicago*. He followed that with *Leaving Normal* (1992), a sort of imitation *Thelma & Louise*, featuring Meg Tilly and Christine Lahti. Zwick's own strong interest in American history led to *Glory* (1989), a Civil War epic starring Matthew Broderick and Denzel Washington, who secured the Best Supporting Actor Oscar for his performance.

Since reading Jim Harrison's novella *Legends of the Fall* in a 1978 edition of *Esquire* when he was 26 and studying at LA's American Film Institute, Zwick had harboured ambitions of one day making it into a movie. 'Reading it was a very moving experience,' recalled Zwick. 'It has held its power over me all these years of trying to turn it into a film. It's a big, dark, beautiful and generous family chronicle. At once a great story, and also a kind of meditation on the humility and dignity of man.'

'I called the agents and publishers,' said Zwick of the beginning of his 17-year fight to bring the story to the screen, 'but I was still in film school and they laughed at me and told me the rights were owned by other people.'

Harrison's short novel tells an epic tale – that of the Ludlow family in the early years of the 20th century. The father and three brothers live an isolated existence on a ranch in the foothills of the Rocky Mountains. Col. William Ludlow had retreated there after he left the US Cavalry in protest at the authorities' treatment of the Western tribes of American Indians. Separated from his ambitious, city-living wife, Ludlow tries to raise his three sons in the country away from the madness of the times.

Alfred is the eldest brother, and the most dutiful and reserved, while Samuel is the impetuous, idealistic youngest of the trio. In between comes Tristan, a wild, untamed spirit, full of animal passion and wise in the ways of the Indians, having come under the tutelage of his father's old Cree Indian scout, One Stab.

The three brothers were inseparable growing up, but with maturity come challenges, both personal and professional, and the trio do not know what trials the modern world they are unprepared for will throw at them. Beginning with the outbreak of the First World War, the story follows the lives of the three and their involvements with one woman, Susannah. Epic in scale, but personal in nature, *Legends of the Fall* was ideal material for Zwick to follow *Glory*.

The main challenge for Zwick was casting the central role of the middle brother, Tristan. It was one he answered easily, as Brad Pitt leapt immediately into his mind. Since he'd had experience of working with Pitt early on in his career, Zwick had followed the actor's developing Hollywood persona, and was convinced he was right

'Brad had a very strong, intuitive understanding of his character.' (Edward Zwick)

for the role.

Zwick had sent Pitt an earlier draft of the script two years before the film was ready for production, hooking the actor's interest in the project. 'He'd not even done *Thelma & Louise* then. Not many people know that he'd done two days' work on *thirtysomething* and we started to meet and talk about this role while his career began to unfold.'

Pitt committed in principal to playing the part when Zwick finally got the project off the ground. The family saga had struck a chord with him too. 'A lot of the elements are very strange,' felt Pitt of the *Legends of the Fall* story, 'western, war, love triangle, family, killings – right? It's bold, it's big, like a great bottle of wine or something.'

'He was quite passionate about it,' said Zwick of Pitt's interest. Zwick was intending to defer his salary until after the film started earning from box office receipts in order to get it made, and he managed to persuade Pitt also to defer part of his $3 million salary, even though as his career sky rocketed, so did his asking price. 'One way we got this movie made was for me to defer a significant part of my salary and for Brad to become my partner, doing that for himself as well. As I struggled to get the movie made, I was able to see his work as it began to emerge. It's a very difficult thing to embody the kind of lifeforce that this character has and you had to be willing to take certain emotional risks and certain challenges. I knew the toughest role belonged to Tristan, but how do you send out a casting call for a force of nature? It became obvious Brad was the right choice, but the studio was hesitant, and it wasn't until I got Anthony Hopkins [as the father, Col. Ludlow] that they gave us the go-ahead. I think, frankly, it was Brad's involvement that encouraged them, and Tony's that cemented it.'

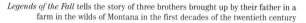

Legends of the Fall tells the story of three brothers brought up by their father in a farm in the wilds of Montana in the first decades of the twentieth century

Tristan, the middle in age of the three brothers and the one played by Brad, is the pivotal character of the film. The others are played by Aidan Quinn (left) and Henry Thomas (second right) with Anthony Hopkins (second left) as their father

'I've always thought that there would be someone better for most of the roles I've taken,' said Pitt candidly. 'But I knew I was the best one to play Tristan. I knew it the minute I read it. I knew the corners, I knew the bends in the road, knew exactly where it went. My difficulty was in trying to get others to see it the way I did. Films are very exhausting to make, so you'd better pick something that means something to you, and this one did.'

For Zwick, Pitt and Tristan had much in common. 'Brad had a very strong, intuitive understanding of his character. I think there is a great deal of Tristan within him. I know he has challenged himself to explore some of the darker aspects of his character as well as the more romantic qualities.' Yet, their instinctive feeling for the material and their admiration for each other were not to prevent Pitt and Zwick later disagreeing over exactly how the emotions of the story should be filmed.

During his long struggle to get the film underway, much had happened in Zwick's life. He had married, had children, enjoyed professional success and failure and lived through his brother's death. It all fed his determination to make this family saga his way. 'I relate to a man's life being defined by his losses and grief as well as his victories. Tristan is a wish-fulfilment for all of us, someone who expresses the most primitive of thoughts we all have, and acts on them, unbound by convention.'

Once production on the tightly budgeted $32 million project was underway, filling the other leading roles was easy work. One of Zwick's coups was to audition a young actor named Henry Thomas, who had sprung to fame as Elliot in Steven Spielberg's magical *E.T.–The Extraterrestrial* (1982), the little boy who befriends an alien stranded on Earth. 'I was auditioned for the role before anyone was cast beside Brad,' recalled Thomas. 'Then I heard Aidan Quinn was in it, and I thought "Oh, it's getting better and better.' Then I heard Anthony Hopkins, and I was like, "Oh wow, I hope I get this." And then finally, after they cast Julia [Ormond], they cast me, and a week later rehearsals started.'

With Thomas as younger brother Samuel, rising British actress Julia Ormond as his fiancée Susannah, and Aidan Quinn as eldest brother Alfred alongside Hopkins and Pitt, *Legends of the Fall* was ready to roll. Pitt and Zwick had flown to London on a red-eye flight to tape a hurriedly arranged screen test with Ormond, who had become a hot property on the back of a stage performance of *Wuthering Heights*. After *Legends of the Fall* she went on to star as Guinevere opposite Sean Connery as King Arthur in *First Knight* (1995) and opposite Harrison Ford in the title role of *Sabrina* (1995).

After the casting, the next hurdle awaiting Zwick and his team was finding the right location to shoot the film. Some scenes were filmed on location in Vancouver, British Columbia, but the majority were shot on the Stoney Indian Reserve outside Calgary, Alberta. One of the reasons for shooting in southern central Canada – apart from saving the production $2 million due to an advantageous exchange rate – was the weather. The area is traditionally one of the driest parts of the country. However, the weather decided to break with tradition as the *Legends* crew arrived to begin filming. It turned out to be fortuitous. 'Of course, the movie wouldn't be as beautiful if we didn't have that extraordinary weather,' recalled Zwick. 'Everything you see in the movie is before a storm hit or just after one hit – but it certainly made things tough. For every beautiful cumulus cloud you see, you don't see three hours of us huddling under these awful tarps with lightning striking the dolly.'

So it was that in the summer of 1993 Brad Pitt found himself spending a gruelling, rainy three months in Calgary, throwing himself heart, body and soul into the role of Tristan. He rented a cabin in the foothills of the Rockies and every Saturday night, as an antidote to the stresses of playing his character and to the tensions beginning to develop between him and Zwick, bouts of silliness would break out. 'We re-created the *Blazing Saddles* scene around the bonfire a few times,' laughed Pitt. 'I must say, Aidan Quinn, he's quite impressive. A lovely little Indian girl who worked on the movie, named Sekwan, dubbed Aidan "Wind in his Pants". Then we dubbed her "One Who Sniffs the Wind".'

Rumours flowed from the location filming to tabloid newspapers that Pitt – who was, after all, well-known for romancing his leading ladies – and Ormond were more than mere co-stars. Both denied that sharing the rented cabin during production indicated any deeper relationship.

Legends of the Fall was intended to be a blockbuster from the beginning and Brad Pitt had a huge task ahead of him. Although sharing the spotlight with the two other brothers and with Oscar-winner Anthony Hopkins, it was Pitt who was to carry the film. His character is the centre of the drama. His actions – or lack of them – affect the lives of all around him. Although he was not present in every scene, Tristan's spirit suffuses the film, and it was important that when he was on screen that he had an impact. For Pitt, this performance would require all of his skills and all of his experience. He would draw on every role he'd played to date, combining the squeaky clean good looks of Paul in *A River Runs Through It* with the darker aspects of characters like Early Grayce or Billy in *Too Young to Die?*.

It may have been the pressure of the performance, or simply the fact that Zwick

Several scenes of *Legends of the Fall* were shot in Jamaica, covering for
New Guinea, Africa and the South Seas.

101

had committed many years of his life to the project, but early on it was clear there was going to be a major difference of opinion between the director and the star over the interpretation of Tristan. When he realised he had a conflict with Pitt, Zwick couldn't simply recast the role as he might have done with any other hired actor. He'd interested the studio on the back of Pitt's name, the star was his partner in the production, he was genuinely friendly with Pitt and he needed his presence to pull in the mass audience he hoped for. He had no choice but to manage what was to become a difficult situation.

Filming during the first week of shooting included a scene important to the climax of the film in which Susannah visits Tristan behind bars. There was another reason too: Pitt had already committed to another movie, *Interview with the Vampire*, and to be ready to start on time his scenes in *Legends* had to be shot early in the production. It was too early for Pitt, however, who didn't feel the scene was ready to be committed to film. 'The jail scene wasn't right, wasn't written right, didn't fit in,' he said. 'When we shot it I said, "This is a mistake."'

Zwick, however, mindful of his tight schedule, was loath to get behind and miss this opportunity to clear what he felt was an easy scene to shoot. He believed that Pitt hadn't reached the right point emotionally to play the scene, not that it was badly written. 'You have to be quite careful finding your stepping-stones, because it's all out of order,' said Zwick, sympathising with his star's quandary.

According to *Premiere*, though, this encounter turned violent, prompting the crew to clear the set. Furniture was said to have flown through the air. 'If a chair or a stool was thrown,' said an on-set source, 'it certainly wasn't thrown at anybody...' The scene was filmed, but Zwick told co-producer Marshall Herskovitz (his partner from *thirtysomething*) that he would have to find time later in the shoot to film the scene again, as neither director nor actor were happy with it as it currently stood.

'Brad had to internalise an enormous amount to express a scene's truthfulness,' said Zwick. 'The explorations he's asked to make in this part are difficult. Sometimes when I'm directing, I feel like an interpreter at the United Nations. Sure, we went at it, and that too is part of the process. Certainly by the next morning we were contrite and desperately eager to make up, not hold onto it, and go on to the next thing.'

Pitt was equally diplomatic after the incident. 'Yeah, Ed and I had a tough day that day, which is good. It's good if two people care. Have at it, 'cause at the end you're going to come up with something good – and that was the result in the jail scene we got now. This time it was written right, it was done right.'

Although that particular dispute was resolved, it was not a good start to the production. There was a widespread fear among the crew that tension between star and director would rear its ugly head once again and might even continue on through the coming weeks of heavy production.

The Hollywood rumour mill went into overdrive as the first stories of on-set disputes filtered back to the LA film community. 'There was all this press that came out that we were not getting along, these rumours in Hollywood that it's not going right,' said Pitt of the early production period in Calgary. 'You know, this is a gamble, and even TriStar's gambling on me, putting me in this kind of movie. So people want to hear it's going bad. I find myself having to defend Ed, 'cause these rumours are going around. But that hasn't been the case; it's been pretty easy-going.'

Pitt seemed to get on better with the other members of the cast than he did with his director. He worked particularly closely with Julia Ormond, the woman around whom the lives of the three brothers revolve, and with whom he was sharing the rented cabin. 'We've had a lot of dying and crying on this one,' said Pitt. 'Julia has this kind of timeless class that I haven't seen anywhere else. The shooting was in a remote spot. At night, the guys all just sat around a campfire and Henry [Thomas] played his guitar. Julia brought a whole library of books. She read, and wrote, all the time. She wrote a diary of the filming.'

Pitt had pushed Zwick to cast Aidan Quinn, whose work he had admired, in the role of his older, more down-to-earth brother. 'It's probably the toughest part in the movie,' felt Pitt. 'It could easily have gone wimpy. We needed somebody who'd be equal to Tristan, bringing nobility and strength to the role, and sexiness, of all things, and that's Aidan.'

For his part, Quinn saw a maturing of Brad Pitt during filming. 'I happened onto some dailies that were on tape, and saw him at that grave, and he was just devastating.

Julia Ormond was rumoured to have had an off-screen relationship with Brad, as well as an on-screen one.

Brad's got a very traditional, manly kind of persona, so to see that man fighting the emotion and not winning – there was stuff he was adding that wasn't even scripted – was just so powerful, watching it spill out.'

Thankful to his co-star for getting him the part, Quinn was not above making light of the areas where Pitt, quite literally, fell down. 'I'm not a horseman, but I never fell off my horse, like some people who shall remain nameless,' he said of Pitt. 'He actually called the studio to get me hired. They wanted a bigger name, but he wanted me.'

Inevitably, *Legends of the Fall* provided another love scene for Pitt – this time with Julia Ormond. Conditions on the set were, however, not at all conducive to the action. 'It's not the most romantic setting, y'know,' said Pitt of shooting on a plywood set in the middle of a Calgary curling rink. 'Very anti-erection...'

To get in the mood, director Zwick allowed Pitt to play his choice of music on the set – hence he and Ormond attempted to convince the movie-going public of their passion for one another while Toad the Wet Sprocket's 'Fear' played on a nearby ghetto blaster. 'You throw a little music on and you try to forget about all the people staring at you,' said Pitt of his approach to love scenes. It was a technique he'd been using successfully since playing JD. 'I got that, actually, from Ridley [Scott], because he let us play music during that Geena Davis scene.'

In fact, using music is central to the method in Brad Pitt's acting. Far from hailing from the Method Acting school, epitomised by Marlon Brando and James Dean, Pitt claims to be intuitive in his skills and talent. 'I don't know much about acting. I don't know what the hell I'm doin'. I just don't.'

One thing he does know, though, is how to use music to get him into the mood of the character he's playing. 'That's what works best for me,' he claimed, citing Stevie Ray Vaughan as inspiration on *Legends of the Fall*. (Pitt was to consider playing Vaughan in a proposed biopic in 1996.) For his next film, *Interview With the Vampire*, Pitt would get into character by playing bits of Mazzy Star and The Doors, as well as some Blind Melons and Smashing Pumpkins. Early Grayce in *Kalifornia* was a different matter: 'That was more heavy metal...'

Pitt strives to avoid assuming any kind of identification with his characters – he doesn't want to absorb or take home from the set any of the characteristics of the people he plays, a problem many Method actors suffer. 'Somewhere in the third or fourth week, you respond to things a little differently, like your character would respond. I don't like it,' he told *Vanity Fair*. 'I can't wait to get my own clothes back on, listen to some good music, eat what I want to eat. Movies are very complicated. You don't realise what it takes to get a good movie. Sitting home in Missouri, I sure didn't. It's fun for a little while. Then I'm ready to get back into my own boxers...' However, avoiding being taken over by a character was not always to be easy, and was to become a problem in *Legends* and even more so during the production of *Interview With the Vampire*.

Despite the jibes of Aidan Quinn, horse riding was a key skill required in *Legends of the Fall*. It was something Pitt had never done before, but he was required on screen to look like someone who'd ridden horses all his life. He threw himself into learning how to deal with horses properly, refusing to cheat through editing and swift cutting or by using a double. If the script called for Tristan to mount a horse, Brad Pitt was going to learn how to do it convincingly. 'Listen, you just grab the pommel and kick,' he said.

His new found easiness with horses came in handy during the shoot when the young actor playing his son took fright at having to ride one of the beasts. Pitt sat down with him and told him: 'Look, we took this job, we have to do this scene, but you don't have to do anything you don't want to do. If you don't want to ride on the horse, you can ride in the car. But I'm going to ride on the horse, because I like the horse.'

Pitt's approach was in marked contrast to that of other members of the crew, and was enough to convince the young actor onto the animal. According to Pitt: 'What they were doing to him when I walked up was going, "But don't you want to ride on the horse. It's a magic horse! Na-na-na-na-na." Talking to him like a moron, y'know. That's when we went for our little walk and I told him, "You don't have to do anything you don't want to do." It's that simple. You can always find a way to make something feel right.' Pitt had clearly absorbed some lessons from his own father's thoughtful treatment of him while younger.

The epic sprawl of *Legends of the Fall*, both in geography and through history, had to be captured on a very tight budget. 'I used all my experience in TV of how to stretch your dollars a long way – that's something I take pride in... My background is in theatre, where suggestion is important. We had 800 people one night during a war scene, but then only 300 the next night and then the other two nights we had 100 people. Yet the size seemed much larger because we kept the frame alive.'

Zwick also stretched his budget-busting skills to their maximum extent to film scenes in which Tristan tries to escape his grief and responsibilities by adopting the life of a sailor. 'We went to Jamaica for three days and in that time we made Jamaica be New Guinea, Africa, and the South Seas in a boat. We did all this with little things created only in one direction for the lens to see and you and your imagination to fill out,' said Zwick. However, his less-is-more philosophy led to some of these scenes not making the final cut. 'There is almost a way in which this movie was deliberately illustrated like a book, with one strong image rather than a five-minute sequence.'

At the end of his taxing time in Calgary, and after the battles with Zwick over the direction of his character and the role he would play in the film, Pitt was satisfied with his work – and up to this point, he had been his own harshest critic. 'This has been a good deal,' he told *Premiere* as the shoot wrapped. 'It's been the hardest thing I have tried to tackle, and as I look back, finishing up, it's been good – to work hard.'

Pitt's opinion changed somewhat when he saw the final cut. The tensions that had been exhibited during the shooting of the jail scene and that had rumbled on during production came to a head. The film he watched was not the one that he felt he'd made. 'Our process was not without tensions, passions,' said Zwick of Pitt's problems with the finished film. 'Brad has great artistic impulses, great instincts. But in the acting world, he skipped a lot of steps. He's no less emotional, but he's less obviously expressive, and the role required real self-revealment. Where he's from you keep that stuff to yourself...'

Pitt objected to the scenes featuring his character's descent into madness being cut from the film. The actor felt that they were necessary to show the process by which Tristan eventually reaches redemption. Zwick claimed the scenes were cut to give space to the other characters in the film. That wasn't how Pitt saw things, though. 'By taking out so much as they did, the movie becomes too mushy, 'cause there's no space in between the mush,' claimed Pitt. 'If I'd known where it was going to end up, I would have really fought against the cheese. There are moments where, if it was reduced to that, if that's all we were going to see of him, I would have whittled it down. I wouldn't have shown so much.'

Zwick simply accepted Pitt's intense nature and need to contribute to the development of his character. 'Of course he's intense,' said the director. However, he felt equally strongly that it is the director's right to call the shots, to decide what gets used and what doesn't and how, exactly, the characters should develop and how he should get the performance he wants from his actors. 'As a director you learn to communicate with the individual actor according to his individual needs – and God knows, Brad and I spent a lot of time getting to know each other, trying to understand each other's process.'

Pitt was more open about his side of the dispute: 'People want to hear that we were not getting along. You read things in scripts and envision them. I didn't want

my character to show his cards so blatantly and Ed did. So you've got two people who care about the film and the character and we had different views. Fortunately, something good is going to be squeezed out of that...'

Generally, critics agreed with Pitt that *Legends of the Fall* - after the struggle between star and director over the films direction - turned out to be better than merely 'good'.

It was released in December 1994, a month after *Interview With the Vampire*, which he filmed immediately afterwards. The critics either loved it or hated it. Ben Greenman in *The Village Voice* was definitely in the former camp: 'The real focus of the film is Pitt's Tristan. Deeply divided – lover and loner, brutal warrior and spiritual introvert – Tristan toes the line between rugged hero and a man whose appetite for solitude borders on the pathological. While Pitt was anaemic in *Interview*, he proves here that he can inhabit a character without sacrificing his own charisma. With the physicality of the young Brando, he dominates not only the screen but the audience, and even the clutter and cliché of the film's final hour cannot dim the power of his performance...'

People magazine tried to hedge its bets: 'It either sweeps you up in its rapturous wake or ... you just sit there and snicker.' Others concentrated on Pitt's performance. 'Star making,' said TV critics Siskel and Ebert, while *Rolling Stone* announced: 'Pitt carries the picture. The blue-eyed boy proves himself a movie star stealing every scene he's in.'

Released in Britain in April 1995, the film was received in similar fashion. *Sight and Sound* critic Ben Thompson got quite caught up in the overblown spirit of the movie: 'An epic performance from Brad Pitt. The first time we see him riding across the plains as a full grown adult, his brother tells him, "You smell". He doesn't just smell, he positively reeks – his machismo all but fogs up the screen...Brad Pitt is a god on horseback. He ropes steers, he steers ropes, he prowls the high country in a selection of beautifully starched fabrics. And when things go wrong for him emotionally, he does what all men long to do: he grows his hair long, and goes out into the world to kill things...'

As far as British critics were concerned, Brad Pitt was the main reason for going to see *Legends*. *The Daily Mail* didn't mince its words: 'Brad Pitt is Hollywood's fastest-rising sex symbol and here he chooses to follow in the footsteps of James Dean, with a sprawling family saga which is even bigger than *Giant*.' Even *The Financial Times* got caught up in Pitt-mania: 'Brad Pitt is eminently watchable as he portrays this youthful energy smashing against the rocks of a tumultuous world ... his performance is shot through with a barely controlled passion...'

Legends of the Fall was the first major film where Pitt was to be the main draw. His casting had to, in Hollywood parlance, 'open' the film - attract a big enough audience in the first few weeks of release to ensure that the picture was deemed successful, at least economically, if not also artistically.

The period between *True Romance* and *Legends of the Fall* had been a difficult one for Pitt, after the break-up of his long relationship with Juliette Lewis. Although he initiated it, the split had thrown him into a depression from which his work had rescued him. More work was just what he needed, and before embarking on *Legends of the Fall*, he had made the commitment to the film version of Anne Rice's *Interview With the Vampire*. Before donning the fangs, though, Brad Pitt had to make room for a new woman in his life...

Brad had little time to relax between the end of the shooting of
Legends and the start of *Interview with the Vampire*.

9 The Reluctant Vampire

BRAD PITT's solitary existence after his split from Juliette Lewis had come to an end during his days of cruising Los Angeles bars. Attending a party he'd struck up a friendship with a 24-year-old actress named Jitka Pohlodek, who claimed to be from Czechoslovakia 'by way of Arkansas'. Hitting it off – Pitt nicknamed his new girlfriend Yit – the pair were soon living together in Pitt's newly bought home.

Having taken his time to find just the right property after splitting with Juliette Lewis, Pitt had settled on a 1910 Craftsman house high in the Hollywood hills. It featured terraces and balconies all around, with a pool and a pond, as well as a man-made cave which Pitt kitted out with an Oriental rug, and also boasted a rooftop recreation area which Pitt kitted out as an alfresco bachelor pad, featuring a sofa, a coffee table and a CD player. 'It gets rained on,' said Pitt of his high up hideaway.

Music being central to Pitt's way of working, it is also key to his relaxation. His haphazardly arranged collection of CDs was spread throughout the house, and choosing music tended to be a random lucky dip. 'It's kind of ... you're on the search. You just find the right one for the needed moment.' Except when Yit moved in with him, Pitt got organised and attempted to catch up on some Rolling Stones stuff. 'This woman that I'm kinda hanging out with, she thinks Mick is it!'

Pitt and Yit were never going to be a long-term deal, and it seems both knew it when they moved in together. Working on both *Legends of the Fall* and *Interview With the Vampire* back to back didn't allow Pitt much time to spend with her.

When she moved in, though, Yit brought a new addition to Pitt's menagerie of animals. Her two bobcats joined his three dogs, all anointed with unusual names. 'This one is Todd Potter, this one is Saudi - she's a pound dog, she loves the love – and this one is Purty, 'cause he's so damned purty,' he explained to *Vanity Fair*. 'I buy my dogs chocolate treats, chew bones, all that kind of stuff. I love it when they can smell what it is and they rip all the wrapping paper off.'

The newest additions to the Pitt animal menagerie brought associated problems. 'Believe me, one of our biggest concerns is keeping the bobcats completely free. Not caged in like a bird, which blows my mind, cutting its wings,' said Pitt. 'I do not understand that. Cutting a dog's tail off for the way it looks. In fact I'm going to start a cause, Save the Tails. All us young actors, we have causes, that's going to be my cause, Save the Tails.'

Inside his new home, Pitt installed copper walls embossed with leaves and the furniture consisted of big old wood-and-leather sofas and chairs, some guitars for jamming on and built-in glass cabinets, crammed with CDs. Out in the back area of the building, he did have some animals in cages – 40 chameleons, kept in Chinese-lantern-shaped boxes.

For his next film, straight from wrapping *Legends of the Fall*, Brad Pitt brought his own chameleon-like attributes to the fore. He was to play a reluctant vampire in the movie version of a book that enjoyed a loyal and vocal following.

The story of the film version of Anne Rice's novel *Interview With the Vampire* is

'I saw everything he'd done and he is just absolutely captivating.' (Neil Jordan).

109

a lengthy and tortuous one. Rice, who also writes soft-core pornographic fiction, wrote the first of her vampire novels in 1976, shortly after her five-year-old-daughter, Michele, died tragically of leukaemia. In reaction to this personal tragedy she set about exorcising her demons and her anger with the world by creating a cast of vampire characters. She dreamed up a lost soul in the character of Louis De Ponte Du Lac, a 19th-century plantation owner in New Orleans, who, in despair after the death of his family, succumbs to the seduction of the charismatic Lestat de Lioncourt. A vampire, Lestat offers Louis a release from his earthly suffering by turning him into a blood-sucking creature of the night.

Even that is not enough to relieve Louis's suffering, and he begins to tire of merely being Lestat's creation. Lestat responds by turning a small girl, Claudia, into a third vampire to function as his companion.

Publishers steered clear of the novel, finding it too dark and disturbing to publish, until the prestigious Knopf Books decided to take the risk. The book struck a chord and went on to become a best-seller, spawning a series of sequels which attracted a cult following.

Naturally on the back of a successful book came talk of making it into a film, but it took over 18 years to go from option to production. The movie rights were, in fact, optioned for $150,000 even before the book went to press.

The hottest Hollywood actor of 1976, John Travolta, was pencilled in for the part of Lestat. However, it wasn't a good time to be considering a new vampire movie as the market was already saturated: Frank Langella was playing the title part in *Dracula*, while George Hamilton played the same role for laughs in *Love at First Bite*. In the face of this competition, Paramount decided to hang fire on *Interview With the Vampire*, anticipating a second novel they could incorporate into the script. This book, *The Vampire Lestat*, however, didn't appear until 1985, almost a decade later.

In the sequel Lestat had become a rock star. Paramount was unhappy with this and dropped its option. The right to both books passed to Lorimar Television, who planned to produce them as a TV mini-series starring Richard Chamberlain. That version didn't get off the ground either, and other formats were considered, including a musical by Elton John to star Sting and Cher in the lead roles.

By January 1989 Warner Brothers had purchased Lorimar, and with the company came the rights to the Anne Rice books. Producer and record mogul David Geffen had a production deal with Warner and was a big fan of Rice's books. It wasn't long before he became the latest Hollywood producer to try to turn the material into a film.

Geffen's first step was to throw out all the previous script versions and to return to the source, Rice herself. Hollywood is notorious for not commissioning authors of novels to script the film versions of their work, but Geffen was not a typical Hollywood producer, and sticking to convention was not one of his habits.

Rice was thrilled and jumped at the chance to work on the movie of her book. A forthright and opinionated person, she was not backward in telling Geffen how she thought the transfer should be handled. She even had a series of suggestions for potential directors: David Cronenberg (*The Fly, Dead Ringers*), Ridley Scott (*Alien, Blade Runner*) or Neil Jordan, who had directed the fairy-tale-inspired *Company of Wolves* (1984), a film Rice loved.

Jordan, the Irishman behind a series of low-budget British thrillers such as

Mona Lisa (1986) and the controversial box-office hit *The Crying Game* (1992), had suffered two previously disappointing Hollywood experiences with *High Spirits* (1988) and his remake of *We're No Angels* (1989). On the back of the success of *The Crying Game* Geffen signed him up.

Jordan's first step was to rewrite Rice's script, bringing the film more into tune with his ideas, but alienating Rice. 'The story didn't work – nobody got the script right – so I had to get the script to work, to make it kind of beautiful,' said Jordan, justifying his revision. 'I had to bring the moral dilemma to the forefront, Louis's whole question of is he evil or is he good? Or is he beyond evil?'

The first of several behind-the-scenes production fights began over the screenplay. The final on-screen credit read 'Screenplay by Anne Rice, based on her novel', but only after Writers' Guild arbitration, whose rules indicated that a director and writer must have contributed over 50% original material to the screenplay to justify a credit. Jordan had beefed up the screenplay by injecting more material from Rice's own novels, so his painstaking work on the script was not deemed to be 'original'.

The next battle was over the casting. Neil Jordan was set on having Brad Pitt play the troubled Louis from the beginning: 'I saw everything he'd done and he is just absolutely captivating,' said Jordan. At least this decision seemed to be welcomed by Rice. Then came a flood of suggestions from Rice to Geffen and Jordan of who she would like cast as Lestat. Her suggestions ranged from the ridiculous, like Rutger Hauer, her original model for Lestat in 1976, but now too old to really do the part justice, to Jeremy Irons, John Malkovich, William Baldwin, Ralph Fiennes and Mel Gibson. Jordan had other ideas, and pursued Daniel Day Lewis.

All hell broke loose, however, when Neil Jordan announced his choice of Tom Cruise. 'It's just that the guy is kind of amazing,' Jordan said. 'After Daniel [Day-Lewis] turned it down I made a list and Tom was at the top. I thought, "If he goes the distance, if he could go where his character went, it would be really great."'

Hollywood is no stranger to controversies when strong-willed creators or fans take on producers over the casting of favourite characters. Michael Keaton as *Batman* and Tom Hanks as Sherman McCoy, Bruce Willis as an alcoholic British journalist and Melanie Griffith as McCoy's mistress in *Bonfire of the Vanities* had been the most recent examples. It was no real surprise to Geffen nor Jordan, then, when Rice's fans and even Rice herself began to disapprove volubly of the casting of Cruise. They were surprised, however, by the way in which the controversy became something of a *cause célèbre* in the film press.

In an interview in *The Los Angeles Times* in August 1993 Rice made clear her objections: 'I was particularly stunned by the casting of Cruise. He is no more my vampire Lestat than Edward G. Robinson is Rhett Butler...I'm puzzled as to why Cruise would want to take on the role. He's a cute kid, on top of the world and on his way to becoming a great actor, but I'm not sure he knows what he's getting into...He should do himself a favour and withdraw.'

Cruise, the biggest movie star of his generation, was not about to do any such thing. As far as Geffen and Jordan were concerned, he was capable of playing the role and – almost as important – was a form of box office insurance. The combination of Cruise and Brad Pitt would be enough to ensure that the film could enjoy a healthy opening few weeks.

Louis De Ponte Du Lac is a lost soul, who agrees to be turned into a vampire so as to end his grief over the deaths of his family.

The casting of Brad as Louis was straightforward, but that of Tom Cruise (right) as his vampire mentor Lestat caused considerable controversy.

Neither Geffen, Jordan nor Cruise were about to rise to Rice's bait, even if she continued to up the ante. At a Halloween rally of her supporters, she continued to vent her frustrations: 'I wanted to call David Geffen and say "How the hell could you do this?"'

Cruise was more measured in his reaction to the controversy: 'She was opposed to me being Lestat based on the other characters that I've played. She had created Lestat and feels great affinity for this character because of her family, her daughter and what occurred. It was very important to her - but it hurt me.'

In fact, Rice felt that Brad Pitt would make a better Lestat than Tom Cruise. After all, Lestat is described in the novel as 'an overpowering person...very tall, very blond, very athletic, very full.' Brad Pitt down to a tee.

'They should have reversed the roles,' confirmed Rice. 'Brad Pitt would have made a wonderful Lestat. He did that wonderful thing with his hips in *Thelma & Louise*, remember that? And *A River Runs Through It*...this is a guy who could play Lestat.'

Rice was right in as much as the role of Lestat was certainly going to be a stretch for Cruise, best known for playing squeaky clean good guys. In *Interview With the Vampire* he would be playing a bitchy, decadent vampire who had to exude sexuality and menace at one and the same time.

Escaping all the controversy was Brad Pitt. He'd received the script for *Interview With the Vampire* at the same time as that for *Legends of the Fall*, and quickly committed to both films, meaning a punishing shooting schedule. His restricted shooting period on *Legends of the Fall* led straight into the filming of *Interview With the Vampire*. He went from the gruelling, physically demanding production in the wide-open spaces of the Canadian countryside, to a largely interior-based, dark, twisted romance. It was something of a dramatic change. 'I did *Legends of the Fall* for four months,' recalled Pitt, 'a very tragic character, very tormented, and this guy's [Louis] even more tormented...'

For David Geffen, Pitt was perfect in the role: 'In *Interview With the Vampire*, Brad's character is very passive. You need an awful lot of charisma to be in a movie where someone else does all the action. And Brad has it.'

Casting was completed with the addition of young actress Kirsten Dunst in the pivotal role of Claudia, the young vampire who eventually teams up with Louis to rid the world of Lestat. Despite achieving the dream of teenagers the world over and getting to kiss Brad Pitt, in interviews Dunst would maintain a distinctly unimpressed facade. Other vampires were played by Jordan regular Stephen Rea and rising Hollywood heart-throb Antonio Banderas.

The problems with *Interview With the Vampire* were not over just yet. Cast in the small, but pivotal role, of the interviewer – the character who talks to Louis in modern-day San Francisco about his vampire life – was rising young actor River

Louis (Pitt) shelters the young girl (Kirsten Dunst) Lestat has
turned into a vampire to act as his companion.

Malloy (Christian Slater) interviews Louis about his vampirism in modern San Francisco. Before his death River Phoenix was cast as Malloy.

Phoenix. With a reputation for clean living – Phoenix and his family were New Age-type evangelists for vegetarianism and healthy living – and a dedication to his work, as well as a strong, ever increasing, fan following, Phoenix was the ideal choice.

Tragedy struck at the end of October 1993 when Phoenix collapsed and died outside Johnny Depp's Hollywood nightclub The Viper Room on the corner of Sunset Boulevard and Larabee Street. Declared dead on arrival at hospital, Phoenix's sudden and unexpected death was attributed to a cocktail of drugs. The clean-living myth was blown wide open as stories of Phoenix's drug abuse hit the headlines for months following his death.

Pitt had his own view of drugs in Hollywood, a scene he'd never really been seriously involved in. 'The drug thing is out. I've experimented with all kinds of lifestyles, but you either quit drugs or you die. I'm smart enough to learn from other people's mistakes. River Phoenix was the best of all the young actors. He was getting deeper and deeper into his roles – and then, nothing. His death threw a damper on *Interview With the Vampire*. It woke up a lot of people.'

River Phoenix's death left the producers and director with a problem. They were due to start shooting and were now without an interviewer. Among the replacements mooted were Leonardo DiCaprio and Stephen Dorff, but the role went to Christian Slater, who managed to get six days away from shooting his thriller *Murder in the First* (1994). Slater donated his $250,000 salary to two of Phoenix's favourite environmental charities: Earth Save of Santa Cruz and Earth Trust of Malibu.

Interview With the Vampire finally began its production schedule with 40 days of night shooting near the bayous of Louisiana. The first few days, mainly close-ups of the actors, were scrapped when David Geffen decided the vampire make-up was too heavy. These shots were eventually picked up on a British soundstage where the production team recreated the bayou backdrops.

Production for the studio shot scenes switched to London, with the stars flying over amid something of a media feeding frenzy. Tabloid newshounds and photographers would try every trick under the book to infiltrate the set and snap the much-sought after first photograph of Pitt or Cruise in full vampire regalia. Such was the paranoia that a covered walkway-cum-tunnel was built to cover the route from the dressing rooms to the sets from prying eyes. 'It's not a tunnel, it's a canvas passage,' a publicist helpfully informed the waiting press.

But Jordan's precautions were in vain after a British tabloid paper managed to snap the eagerly awaited photo of Tom Cruise.

Security wasn't the only problem. Making *Interview With the Vampire* was one of the worst experience working on a movie that Brad Pitt had ever endured – not physically, but psychologically.

'I hated doing this movie. Hated it. I loved watching it. Completely hated doing it. My character is depressed from the beginning to the end. Five and a half months of that is too much.'

The security at Pinewood, where the film was being shot, wasn't enough to stop Pitt cruising the streets of Notting Hill, searching out pie restaurants or pubs with good pints of beer and the inevitable journalists to give interviews to. 'I wake up and feel good,' he told Chris Heath of *Empire* magazine, 'and I got to go to work and feel bad. I gotta find a comedy next, man, or I'll break out the razor blades...'

Committed to playing the part – it was too good an opportunity to miss – Pitt didn't manage to overcome his problems on set simply by playing music or sketching as he'd done on films in the past. 'You gotta understand,' he explained, 'My character wants to kill himself for the whole movie. I've never thought about killing myself. It was a sick thing. I don't like it when a movie messes with your day. "You are the devil! We belong in Hell!" Do you know how hard it is to say lines like that?'

As in *Legends of the Fall*, Pitt found himself being subsumed by the character he was playing. The strain of demonstrating the angst experienced by Louis, who sucks the blood from rodents to avoid killing humans, was spilling over into his everyday life, making his stay in London a lonely and tormented one. 'This person is a very reactive role,' said Pitt. 'I understand why women complain a lot about their roles, because that's it right there.'

Part of Pitt's problem was his lack of preparation time for the film. 'I never made it through the book,' he sheepishly admitted.

Neil Jordan was watching his star closely. 'He's never played a part where he has to deal with a huge amount of speech; he's very much played himself. Brad has no technique. He didn't come up through the theatre. He's a movie actor *par excellence*. Louis is a deeply empathetic human being, which is what Brad is. He identified so strongly with the part that halfway through the film, he was having a lot of trouble with his character. He didn't realise it, but he was eating, drinking, sleeping and living that character. Brad is all emotion; Tom plays all aggressive, an individual who's all icy.'

Dealing with the travails of his character was not the only problem Pitt faced.

(Top picture) *Brad Pitt* and Tom Cruise, as rival leads in the film, were wary and distrustful of each other throughout the shooting of *Interview With the Vampire*. (Lower picture) Lestat (Tom Cruise, left) and Louis (Brad Pitt), creatures of the night, feed on a lady of the night.

He also had to cope with the petty jealousies and rivalries of his co-star Tom Cruise, who seemed to feel threatened by Pitt's presence.

Although one of the world's biggest film stars, Tom Cruise has never been renowned for his acting ability and the part of Lestat was regarded as difficult for him, not only by Anne Rice, but by many people involved in and outside of the production. More practically, Cruise was shorter than his six-foot-tall co-star. Rumours emanated from the troubled set that Cruise's voice was proving to be too high, but Cruise himself was felt to be too short to be credible opposite Pitt. Platform boots were quickly ordered up to make the co-stars of more equal stature, according to the rumours. Not so, sources on the production said, claiming that Cruise's period boots, which were merely part of his costume, happened to have the happy side-effect of making him taller.

'You're not going to get me to talk about that,' said costume designer Sandy Powell of the height controversy. Powell was not allowed to retain any of her drawings or sketches from the production for fear that some of five-foot-nine Cruise's secrets might leak out.

Pitt was sanguine about the whole fiasco. 'It's something people want to make a big deal out of. He wanted his character to be more physically dominant. It does make sense...and then, it doesn't.'

That wasn't the end of the problems between the stars though. They may have passed the time recreating Cruise's *Days of Thunder* in go-cart races, which Cruise invariable won, but the rival leads were wary and mistrustful of each other. They had been forced together on this movie by the logic of Hollywood packaging deals, but they were rivals for the same crown and they both knew it.

'You gotta understand, Tom and I are...we walk in different directions,' claimed Pitt of their on-set rivalries. 'He's North Pole. I'm South. He's coming at you with a handshake, whereas I may bump into you, I may not. Y'know.'

In the 90s, Pitt's laid-back sex appeal was surpassing the aggressive, controlled and calculated star image crafted carefully by Cruise throughout the 80s. Faced with the rival who was chasing his tail, it seems clear that Cruise forgot some of the usual niceties of star communication. Stories of bitching on the set and hours spent comparing trailer sizes and privileges leaked to the waiting, hungry press from Pinewood like water through a sieve.

'I always thought there was this underlying competition that got in the way of any real conversation,' was how Pitt summed up the situation afterwards, putting a diplomatic gloss on his childish spats with Cruise. 'It wasn't nasty by any means, not at all. But it was just there, and it bugged me a bit. But I tell you, he catches a lot of shit because he's on top, but he is a good actor and he advances in this film. He did it. I mean, you have to respect that.'

Cruise was generous about Pitt's acting ability, pinning down the secret of the actor's success: 'His emotions are all right there on the surface.'

The battle royale between the stars was only the last in a long line of troubles that had dogged *Interview With the Vampire* for over 18 years. Thankfully, there was a silver lining when near the end of post-production a videotape of the film was sent off to Anne Rice to solicit her opinion. The result was double page advertising spreads in *The Los Angeles Times*, *The New York Times* and Hollywood's in-house newspaper, *Variety*, in the form of an open letter from Anne Rice declaring how much she actually appreciated the movie. 'I loved the film from start to finish, and

Kirsten Dunst, who played Louis's young female companion Claudia, was one teenager unmoved by kissing Brad Pitt.

I found myself deeply impressed by every aspect of its making...The charm, the humour and the invincible innocence of my beloved hero Lestat are all alive in Tom Cruise's courageous performance; the guilt and suffering of Louis are poignantly portrayed by Brad Pitt...I think you will embrace this film as I do...See this film, guys, see it!'

It was quite a dramatic about-face after Rice's earlier vehement statements about what she saw as horrendous mis-casting. The cost of placing the advertisements would be pretty close to $100,000. All suggestions that Hollywood commerce had won out and that Anne Rice had been in receipt of a not inconsiderable sum of money to endorse the film were all rejected out of hand by all parties as false and malicious.

David Geffen was well pleased with Anne Rice's Road-to-Damascus-like conversion to the film version of her work: 'The movie and the performances were beyond her wildest expectations. She thought Tom was incredible.' The next test to be faced by the film would be the international press critics.

Neil Jordan was particularly concerned with how the critics would react to his film. He had more to worry about than most film-makers. Anne Rice's earlier intervention in the production of the film had been widely noticed, perhaps even more so than the pages proclaiming her support for the film. 'I think it damaged the critics' reaction,' said Jordan of Rice's first batch of publicity, 'because there had been so much public talk about it. It won't affect the audiences. She said the movie was great. She didn't say "I'm sorry," though.'

The critics were reserved. David Denby in *New York* magazine found the film 'boring...and remote', while *Rolling Stone* was 'Dazzled, but unmoved', and *The New Yorker* claimed that Jordan's 'virtuosity cannot hide the movie's emptiness'.

British critics were less harsh but here ambivalent about the performances of both Tom Cruise and particularly Brad Pitt. According to *The Daily Mail*, 'Pitt remains a whining, monotonous killjoy...', while *The Sunday Express* felt 'Brad, as the reluctant bloodsucker Louis...is far more suited to the role of scrubbed sexual magnet in more gentle films such as *A River Runs Through It*...' Other publications were kinder. According to *The Independent*, 'Brad Pitt wanders the centuries looking elegant and melancholy, which is a relatively easy task given that vampirism in this version isn't disturbing.' *The Guardian* pegged Pitt's Louis as 'far from a grim cardboard cut-out. [Cruise] is more than equalled by Pitt, who tells his story of descent into hell...'

Interview With the Vampire opened at cinemas shortly before *Legends of the Fall*, and together the films were make-or-break time for Brad Pitt. Their fate was now out of his control. All he could do now was sit back and wait, relax and have some fun with Yit while reading new scripts. His intention now was to find something less taxing, something lighter that would allow him to relax a bit during the shoot, something that would be based closer to home.

Offers came which he declined, such as a starring role in a film being developed by James Cameron entitled *The Crowded Room*, based on a true tale of someone who suffers multiple personalities. More high-profile was the chance to star as a lawyer in a big-budget version of John Grisham's thriller, *The Chamber*. His character would be defending an ageing racist killer incarcerated on Death Row. Pitt went for the role but then pulled out when the original director, Ron Howard, left the production. In its place he considered going the swashbuckling route in a remake of *Captain Blood* for Chuck Russell, director of *The Mask* (1994).

Instead, he spent time at home, enjoying the tranquillity of not having to subsume himself in another character. For a while Pitt got to be himself. Every so often he'd head downtown, to a club like the Luna Park, perhaps to see his actor friend Dermot Mulroney's band The Sweet and Low Orchestra play a gig. Mulroney and Pitt would hang out afterwards, shooting the breeze, discussing Mulroney's recent trips to Europe.

Before embarking on a new film, though, Pitt found himself living alone again. Rumours of a dalliance with actress Thandie Newton on the set of *Interview With the Vampire* had reached Yit, the final straw in a relationship that was never that strong to begin with. Tired of Pitt's constant absences and the tales of yet another film-making romance, Yit packed up her bobcats and moved right back out. For Pitt it had been brief, but fun. After Juliette Lewis he was not ready for and was not looking for another head-over-heels long-term romance. He felt free to play the field and see what came along. After all, if the two films about to unspool at cinemas around the world were hits, he would be spoilt for choice.

Interview With the Vampire allowed Brad to hone the riding skills he had learned for *Legends of the Fall*.

10 Sin and Redemption

THE PUBLIC voted on *Interview With the Vampire* by buying tickets to cinemas, with the film taking $38.7 million over its first weekend. The film was placed fifth on *Variety*'s list of all-time biggest openings though by the end of its run, the movie was expected not to gross much more than a very respectable $110. *Legends of the Fall* was even more successful. It was the number one film at the American box office for four straight weeks, taking in excess of $60 million during that period. The first big hit of 1995, it eliminated any remaining doubts about Pitt's ability to successfully tackle a leading role and open a big-budget drama. Its success according to Lynn Snowden in American *Premiere* magazine, was 'thanks almost entirely to Pitt's sex appeal…'."

Brad Pitt could now feel that he had made it. He'd been around in Hollywood for just over eight years and had climbed the slippery slope from dressing as a chicken on the streets of LA through low-budget cult movies like *Johnny Suede*, *Cool World* and *Kalifornia*. Now he'd arrived at the destination he'd set out for: Hollywood's A-list. With the box office successes of *Interview With the Vampire* and *Legends of the Fall*, he was now first choice for many of the most high profile roles in town.

Now he was in that position, he could be choosy about what he committed to. He didn't have to be constantly in work, he was financially secure. The only real consideration was to build solidly on the success he'd achieved, to be careful to maintain his bankability and at all costs avoid a flop movie.

With that in mind he passed on many of the films offered to him. The dross he dismissed out of hand, but some high-profile films were also rejected. *Model Daughter*, a comedy about a divorcing couple fighting for their child's love, would have allowed him to explore a more emotional character than he'd attempted before, but he turned it down.

Pitt struck up a friendship with Ben Stiller, a young writer-director he felt a strong bond with. Stiller had enjoyed a modicum of success with *Reality Bites* (1995), a Generation X comedy-drama starring Johnny Depp's ex-girlfriend Winona Ryder. The young director was planning a film about the Rolling Stones which piqued Pitt's interest, as he'd got into their music through his relationship with Yit. It says much for his new star power that his interest alone was enough to put the film into development and his later withdrawal was enough to cause the project to be quickly scrapped.

Politics beckoned in *City Hall*, a drama about political corruption in New York, which also passed across Pitt's desk. The film was eventually made with John Cusack (in what would have been Pitt's role), Al Pacino and Bridget Fonda. He considered other options, like an action movie. A side-step to action hero territory was a well-worn method of enjoying some variety and still staying at the top of the Hollywood tree. It had worked for Keanu Reeves in *Speed* (1994), but it wasn't a route that attracted Pitt, so he opted out of *Tears of the Sun*, an adventure set in the Amazon rainforest to be directed by John Woo. He was more interested in character-based parts than muscle-based ones. Crime and punishment didn't appeal either, so *Last Dance* had to find another star.

One role Pitt did take up was on audio tape, not film. He recorded the audio book version of *The Crossing* by Cormac McCarthy. Although he didn't read a great deal, he considered McCarthy his favourite novelist. According to *People* he was the ideal person to have tackled the book. '[His] twangy stoicism perfectly reflects the novel's tone.'

Making a decision about what to do next became a problem. He had to make the right choice. Doubt about the likely fate of the finished film prompted him to follow Mel Gibson in turning down the lead role in *The Saint*. To those around him, his advisors and agents, maintaining their client's new-found bankability became the main object of their concentration.

That bankability was ensured when in January 1995 *People* magazine named Pitt the 'Sexiest Man Alive'. The accolade brought acres of good publicity, but it also confirmed him as public property. 'I think that was a cruel thing to do to me,' said Pitt of the award. 'It was some cruel and heinous joke. A friend of mine said they misspelled it – it was supposed to be the "Sexiest Moron"!' *Speed* star Sandra Bullock was named Sexiest Woman.

Later in the year he was to be annointed with an altogether different label: one of the world's smelliest stars. Along with Keanu Reeves, Pitt was dubbed one of tinseltown's 'hygenically challenged'. A London tabloid claimed that he was tired of being fussed over by make-up and wardrobe people on shoots and often went for days off-camera without changing his clothes. Apparently, Pitt followed this charge with a shopping spree, spending $1,000 on Clavin Klein underwear, suggesting that he thought the paper might have a point.

Contemplating future roles, Pitt also had other considerations in mind, remembering his gruelling schedule on his last two films, as well as the heavy emotions he'd had to deal with. 'Right now I'd like to play a guy who just wants to fuck everybody so I can have a damn good time,' he claimed.

He was looking for something more uplifting than *Interview With the Vampire* and something less physically taxing than *Legends of the Fall*. He was also having doubts about his own abilities to carry strong emotions on the screen. During the making of *Interview With the Vampire*, the mother of one of the workers on the set had died. 'I was thinking, we do death every other day in the movies, you know, but you'll never be able to do it to the full impact of what it is to have someone die. It's pretty much bullshit, really, what we do. I was sitting there on the set and someone was dying in front of me, and I was supposed to be tormented by it, and I'd see him – the person whose mother died – and he was going through something much more, and I felt like a phoney.'

From now on he couldn't afford to fail, and merely impressing or surprising the audience with the revelation that the pretty boy can actually act was not going to be good enough either. 'I'm smart enough to know that this is the start, and I'm also smart enough to know that this is the end of surprising people. From now on it's expected of me.'

However, his next move was surprising, turning down one of the leading roles in the true-life space-age thriller *Apollo 13* (1995) opposite Tom Hanks, instead signing on to star in a new low-budget thriller called *Seven*.

'The script had been around for over four years,' Pitt said of *Seven*. 'At first description, I thought it was just another cop-buddy flick, but upon reading it, I knew it was different. People are going to love it or hate it, but they'll be talking about it.'

Andrew Kevin Walker was the man who had put the words down on paper. The 31-year-old from Pennsylvania concocted his devilish mix of *film noir* and horror shocker while working in New York City.

'I lived there for about five years,' he said of New York. 'I was miserable just about every minute of every day. I just couldn't adjust to living in a big, angry, loud city. It was a reaction to that. New York is an amazing place, but it's a cauldron of unpleasantries. You see it everywhere from the projects and parks to the subways and street corners. I was working for a low-budget film company that made exploitation horror films. The seven deadly sins seemed easily encapsulated.'

Walker had previously scripted the Jeff Goldblum thriller *Hideaway* (1995), based on a Dean R. Koontz novel, and *Brainscan* (1994), an ultra-low-budget flick about a killer computer game. He put together his screenplay for *Seven* over a six-month period in 1991. 'It by-passed a lot of the bigger studios, probably because the subject matter was too dark.'

Seven is about as dark as they come in mainstream, star-driven cinema. Initially seeming to be a police procedural thriller, the latter third of the film turns into a psychological horror film, focused on Pitt's character.

Pitt was cast as Detective David Mills, an ambitious, keen-as-mustard young detective who has secured a posting to the big city. Born and raised in the country,

Obsessed with his own self-image, Detective Mills fails to make real contact with the older Lieutenant Somerset, unlike his wife who wants to get to know the person, in *Seven*.

like his beautiful young wife (Gwyneth Paltrow), he feels out of place in the city, but is determined to make a success of his opportunity. He's partnered with Lieutenant William Somerset (Morgan Freeman), a philosophical old timer who is one week away from retirement. Having tired of fighting a losing battle against the tide of crime on the streets, Somerset is looking forward to turning in his badge and gun in order to move out to the country.

During the week that the film covers, Somerset and Mills investigate a series of bizarre and gruesome murders, each one of which is labelled by the murderer with one of the seven deadly sins. Despite the illicit help of FBI moles, the pair are not able to crack the case, until John Doe (played by *The Usual Suspects* star Kevin Spacey in what was a surprise cameo) walks into the station and gives himself up. It's then that the real descent into horror begins for Mills.

After by-passing the major studios, Andrew Kevin Walker's script for *Seven* came into the hands of producer Arnold Kopelson, responsible for such films as Oliver Stone's *Platoon* (1986), the big-screen remake of *The Fugitive* (1994) inspired by the 60s TV series, and *Falling Down* (1994), a controversial portrait of life in modern Los Angeles that starred Michael Douglas.

'I grew up in Brooklyn and rode the subways. I saw danger every day of my life. This was a script that was so brilliantly conceived, it grabbed me and shook me. Very few writers have been able to do that,' recalled Kopelson.

Kopelson approached David Fincher to persuade him to direct. Fincher, a graduate of the music video industry, had withdrawn from film-making after a bruising experience making the third in the *Alien* series.

Alien3 was his first feature film and he had jumped at the chance to make it. The problem was that he inherited a script that had been through so many hands that it had become an incoherent blend of drafts and treatments compiled by such luminaries as SF writer and cyberpunk godfather William Gibson and acclaimed New Zealand film-maker Vincent Ward. The responsibility of maintaining a hit series of films was also a daunting task. Heavily criticised upon release, *Alien3* has aged better than most critics in 1992 expected. His dark take on the *Alien* saga is reflected in *Seven*, but this time out, Fincher had total creative control and a cracking script to work with.

'I didn't know what was going to happen at the end,' he said of his first reading the script. 'I liked the fact that the movie was so ruthless. All of a sudden it took this turn and I found myself getting more and more trapped in this kind of evil, and although I felt uncomfortable about being there, I had to keep going...'

Fincher knew that if he could capture even a fraction of that spine-tingling frisson on screen, he'd have a film the likes of which had not been seen since the mid-1970s release of *The Exorcist*. First, though, he had to fight with the producer over the film's bleak ending.

'I called my agent and said "This movie, are they going to make this? I mean, have you read this thing?" and he said, "Yeah, I read it,"' Fincher told *Empire* magazine. 'And I said, "There's this fucking head in the box at the end, it's just amazing. Are they really going to do this?" And he said, "No, you've got the wrong draft." So they sent me the right draft, and it had this big chase at the end to get to the bathroom where the wife is taking a shower and the serial killer's crawling through the window...'

The pat Hollywood version was not the one Fincher wanted to make. He was

Pitt is cast as the novice detective David Mills who thinks he has little to learn from the about-to-retire Lieutenant William Somerset (Morgan Freeman).

The atmosphere of *Seven* is predominantly claustrophobic and threatening.

keen to make the original draft of the script, the head-in-the-box ending, even though he thought he'd never get away with it. He was due for a surprise. 'I went to talk to Michael [De Luca, New Line head of production] and said "The head-in-the box, that's the cool ending," and he said, "Yeah, I thought so too, let's go make that version".'

Serial killer movies were ten-a-penny in the 1990s, but no one had seen a film as gritty and downright nasty as *Seven* in a long time. One reason such films weren't being made was that since the heyday of the pre-*Star Wars* mid-70s American cinema, producers, directors and stars had become more and more unwilling to take risks with the audience, with the narrative and with their own public images.

For Pitt, the chance to change his image, lop off his long hair and play a cop who doesn't enjoy a happy ending was too good to pass by: 'You have to find something you are interested in, so you'll bring some truth to it. It may be interesting to me, but I don't know if it's going to be interesting to others. I have a vision going in of what I'm after. Then I look at how I end up once it's done. I think we got what I was looking for in *Seven*.'

While Morgan Freeman was easily cast by David Fincher as Somerset, the older cop, he didn't have a clear idea of who could play Mills. He needed someone who could not only draw an audience, but was also able to handle the drama of the role, and who could be afforded within his overall budget of $20 million. Brad Pitt was not his first choice, as he felt that the role required a more grungy, down-to-earth presence than Pitt seemed to offer.

An accident Pitt sustained to his hand in shooting *Seven* adds to David Mills's
appearance of vulnerability in the closing stages of the film.

Mills and Somerset investigate another murder labelled by the killer as the punishment for one of the Seven Deadly Sins.

Informed of Pitt's interest in the script, though, Fincher was only too happy to meet with the young star, well aware of his marquee value. The pair had lunch and Fincher discovered that Pitt was as wildly enthusiastic about the film – and the head-in-the-box ending – as Fincher himself was.

'He was incredibly enthusiastic,' Fincher recalled, 'and I told him, "This is not a major thing. This is a minor movie for everyone involved – and that's how we've got to keep looking at it. It's a little, tiny, minor movie..." and he was like, "I'm in. I want to do it".'

'Brad helped to get the movie made,' Michael De Luca admitted. 'When he came aboard, people got a lot less insecure about the film. It was very brave of him. I love when people go against type. To come off pictures like *Legends of the Fall* and *Interview With the Vampire* and play a homophobic, bigoted, neo-fascistic cop with a crew cut – it was a very cool thing for Brad to do.'

Although his character is put through the mill by the end of the film, part of the attraction for Pitt was playing someone more down to earth and ordinary than either Tristan Ludlow in *Legends of the Fall*, who was a force of nature incarnated as a man, or the morose reluctant vampire Louis in *Interview with the Vampire*. 'Cop chasing a bad guy – complete genre. I figured I'd give that a try. The guy's got no problems, that's the key thing,' admitted Pitt. 'Just have some fun. Just see if I can say those lines, get the killer...'

After casting Pitt, Fincher's next problem was finding an actress who could play the part of the young cop's wife. He required someone who could hold her own opposite 'the world's Sexist Man' and garner a great deal of audience sympathy during her brief time on screen – sympathy that was required to make the climax of

Brad at the London premiere of *Legends of the Fall*, after finishing *Seven*.

the film work to its full effect. It was a tall order, and Fincher saw over 100 candidates.

His first choice was Gwyneth Paltrow, having seen her in the little-known film *Flesh and Bone* (1995). Pitt had also recommended the actress, whom he'd met casually through a mutual friend a few months earlier. He'd also remembered her auditioning for the Julia Ormond role in *Legends of the Fall*. Fincher, however, felt the chances of her accepting the role he had to offer were slim to non-existent, a feeling reinforced by those around him.

'She was my first choice, and everybody said "You'll never get her – she's too picky, she doesn't want to play the cop's wife, she's not interested in doing this stuff, this is too dark." Finally Brad called her and asked her to come in, not to read, but to meet, and I remember telling Arnold [Kopelson, producer] to watch this girl. He hadn't seen *Flesh and Bone* and she came in and sat down for about two seconds and said, "Do you have a rest room?" and she walked into the rest room and closed the door and Arnold said, "She's perfect..."'

In being instrumental in engineering Paltrow's casting in *Seven* Pitt was unknowingly giving her a large role too in his private life. When time came for the pair to work together in December 1994, it was clear that there was something between them was much deeper than what was required for screen husband-and-wife. It was clear to those around them, too.

'The chemistry between them was real,' according to Morgan Freeman. 'I've always been floored by [her mother] Blythe Danner. And here she comes – she had the gift.' But he didn't see Paltrow throwing the young actor off his laid-back stride. 'He's a real settled young man, considering the whirlwind that goes around him. As

Gwyneth Paltrow plays Detective Mills's beautiful but essentially homely young wife, recently moved to the big city from the country.

The casting of Gwyneth Paltrow as Pitt's on-screen wife quickly led to a real romance. Their relationship went public at the British premiere of *Legends of the Fall*.

Brad and Gwyneth after a David Bowie concert.

far as you can tell with anyone, he's calm like the eye of the storm...'

Both Gwyneth Paltrow's parents work in the media. In addition to her actress mother, her father is TV producer Bruce Paltrow, the man behind hospital drama *St Elsewhere*. As well as her part in *Flesh and Bone* alongside Meg Ryan and Dennis Quaid, Paltrow had appeared as Thomas Jefferson's daughter in *Jefferson in Paris* (1995). She'd previously dated actor Robert Sean Leonard (*Dead Poets Society*, 1989) and Donovan Leitch, Pitt's co-star in his early film *Cutting Class*. Aged only 22 when she took the role in *Seven*, Paltrow was almost ten years younger than her co-star. That fact didn't put off Pitt, although it had been one of the reasons for the end of his relationship with Juliette Lewis – maybe he'd finally grown up himself. 'It was love at first sight, as far as I was concerned,' said Pitt.

Overcoming the publicity that surrounded Pitt, Paltrow was able to put aside any intimidation she may have felt at getting involved with him. 'I don't know who that Brad Pitt is,' she said of the *People* magazine label. 'I know a very grounded, peaceful and wise person. And besides, he has three dogs. People who have dogs are usually good!'

Producer Arnold Kopelson noted the attraction that built between the two stars on the set of *Seven*. 'They are very much in love. The chemistry between them is obvious. Gwyneth is very confident. She is a strong woman who is not threatened by the attention that Brad gets.'

'It was love at second sight,' said Paltrow, modifying Pitt's claim and recalling her previous meeting with her new partner. 'When I was 15 I saw *Thelma & Louise*, and I thought "Who is that gorgeous guy?" And years later, here I am living my dream. I don't think either of us was expecting love or looking for it and it came as a shock to both of us. We went to an Italian restaurant in Los Angeles for a wonderful meal and the romance grew from there. I was charmed by his intelligence and sensitivity, his closeness to his family and the way in which he was completely down to earth.'

Acting the part of Mills's wife became an easy call for Paltrow, who simply acted out the feelings that the pair were really developing for each other. 'The scenes were really sexy and sweet. I mean, it's not hard kissing Brad, so I had a lot of fun.'

While the romance developed, the pair still had a film to shoot. To make their roles as convincing as possible Pitt and Freeman undertook a depth of research neither had tackled on any film before. During pre-production the unlikely pair were taught in the ways of the modern, urban police force by Sergeant Ed Arneson. 'It's our job to make them look as realistic as possible,' said Arneson. 'If they come across as real policemen who have handled weapons their whole careers, are fluid in their motions, and talk like real policemen, then we've done our job.'

For Pitt this process involved firearms training. 'He was very receptive to our input,' recalled Arneson. 'He focused on tactics, and his intensive training will come across looking quite realistic on screen.'

Pitt was no stranger to guns, having grown up around them in Missouri and never having been without one all the time he'd been living in Los Angeles. 'I grew up with firearms, more shotguns and rifles than handguns. But I hung out with some detectives who took me around and taught me a little respect for their job. They taught me how to deal with handguns, clearing corners, what your focus is on in order not to get shot. These guys have a hairy job.'

When he was a teenager, Pitt's father had taught him how to use weapons. It was simply part of life in the South – guns were not seen as unusual or out of the ordinary. The habit of having a gun around stayed with Pitt in the urban jungle of Los Angeles. Unapologetically stored at his Hollywood home are two 12 gauge shotguns and a handgun. While hoping he'll never have to use the weapons, he seems prepared to if he has to, according to an interview in *Rolling Stone*. 'Damn right, if someone comes into my house in the middle of the night, I'm going to shoot.'

Seven's look was dictated by Pitt's availability. Although he had wanted to take a back seat, Pitt found himself capitalising on his current position to secure further work, and he agreed to appear in a featured role in a new film to be directed by Terry Gilliam. The schedules meant he had a short period of time in which to wrap *Seven*.

As a result, according to Fincher, the film's rain-soaked atmosphere came about because of 'a pragmatic decision based on the fact that we had Brad Pitt for 55 days and then he was going on to Terry Gilliam's movie [*Twelve Monkeys*] – there were no ifs, ands or buts about it. So, it was raining in LA at the time and we knew we'd have to match in the exteriors stuff that was being shot as interiors. Also, it was a way to kind of make it not look like Los Angeles, 'cause Los Angeles is always seen in the sun.'

Much of the work had to be completed in a rush. That led to people getting careless – prime among them was Pitt himself, who suffered an injury during the filming of the movie's central chase scene. 'I was running across the tops of the cars in the rain, and I went through a window and cut all along my forearm. I'm looking at bones in my arm that you're not supposed to see,' he recalled. 'I cut one tendon, I abraded another and I cut some nerves. I didn't even think of that when I first saw

The two policemen are constantly taunted by the mysterious serial killer in *Seven*, even when they think they have tracked him down.

it. It's pretty good now, though. I've got almost all the feeling back, but not quite.' Pitt hoped that his accident would have been caught by the camera and could be used in the film, but it wasn't to be. He fell over out of the camera's sights, but not out of earshot: 'They missed it, the bastards. But I could hear it. I went ass first.' The accident and injury meant on-the-spot script changes, putting Mills's arm in a sling for the rest of the film. The rest of the production was managed without further incident.

The moral context of the film – or rather the lack of a clear moral direction – was criticised by some people when *Seven* was released, but to the director and his cast they were reflecting life as it is. Fincher saw a message in the film: 'It's the context for the ideas in the movie that are important. It builds and lulls you into thinking there is some kind of sense and order to things. And then the final act of the movie is revealed to contain just as much chaos as everyday life. That's a horrifying realisation for an audience. It compromises their expectations of entertainment...'

Fincher is the first to admit that although he tried to capture true horror, real life has a nasty habit of constantly outdoing cinema: 'I think it's true that evil both attracts and repulses, and I think the film has a lot of evil in it. We live in a society where the most drama people have in their lives is from other people's tragedy. The film really plays on that, and punishes it, too. But there's nothing in it that's more disturbing than those two kids beating a baby to death on a train track. There's nothing in it that's as horrifying as a husband and wife who have been videotaping, raping and killing girls for years. Truth is now always more horrifying than fiction...'

For his part, Brad Pitt agreed with his director: 'I don't see anything more in this film than I see in the news everyday, as far as violence goes. It's more about the telling of the story and then your mind goes from there. This film is a thinker. Listen, I admit it's sick. It's cruel and it's brutal, but it's brutally honest. I think there's a fascination with an understanding of that, and I actually think the film is smart about it. The film doesn't justify the killer's actions by any means, but the guy has got a point...'

For Morgan Freeman, the moral debate was surplus to the purpose of the movie: 'I don't want the audience to get a message. I just want them to get their money's worth.'

With both Fincher and Pitt expecting *Seven* to be a 'small' thriller, they were bowled over by the positive critical reception and the even more surprising response from the public. Producer Arnold Kopelson knew he was on to a good thing, but even he wasn't expecting particularly big things. 'People will see a new Brad Pitt,' he warned before the film was released. 'This movie is a risk because a lot of people are going to hate it, but it won't be ignored. It cost $20 million to make, not a lot by today's standards.'

The film certainly wasn't ignored upon its autumn 1995 release in the United States, and Kopelson need not have been preparing himself for a hostile reception. An opening weekend gross of $14.5 million in mid-September 1995 eclipsed the $8.5 million taken at the same time by Paul Verhoeven's hyped sleaze-fest *Showgirls*. By Christmas *Seven* had grossed over $84 million at the American box office alone, four times what the film had cost to make.

Although many critics felt some of the after-the-fact murder scenes were hard to take, they recognised an exceptional film when they saw one. 'Focus and film craft make *Seven* difficult to dismiss,' said Mike Clark in *USA Today*, while Michael Medved (author of the book *Hollywood versus America* that blames the movies for many of America's social problems) wrote in *The New York Post* that 'Both actors bring considerably more feeling to their characters than you might expect.' CNN's Carol Buckland commented: 'Brad Pitt comes on strong as the young cop. He goes a long, long way toward scuzzing up the glamour boy image. His hair is shorn, his face is stubbled and scratched. Pitt does bring a lot of interesting quirks to his character. He's almost always interesting to watch...even if he's half-obscured by murky shadows!'

The film was welcomed internationally too, seen as a throwback to a gritty, 1970s style of film making. *Sight and Sound* in Britain picked up on the literary references that run through the film, including Dante, Chaucer, Thomas Aquinas and Shakespeare. *Empire's* cover line declared it the 'scariest film every made'. '*Seven* isn't just a movie, it's a psychological trip through hell that leaves your head spinning. Not since *The Exorcist* has there been a mainstream Hollywood movie as extraordinarily dark, bleak, intense and monumentally scary as this. *Seven* goes for the gut...it never lets up. For the ending alone, this is simply unmissable,' wrote Mark Salisbury.

The continuing re-invention of Brad Pitt was noticed by many critics, who saw *Seven* as another step in the actors move towards becoming a leading man in mainstream cinema. 'It is the combination of Brad Pitt and Morgan Freeman that accounts for its success,' said Derek Malcolm in *The Guardian*, while Andrew Preston in *The Daily Express* felt that 'Brad Pitt is at his best ever...' Geoff Brown in *The Times* thought that 'Pitt bounces around, eager for the fray,' as if the actor was exorcising the imposed stillness he had to display in *Interview With the Vampire*.

The critical reaction afforded *Seven* was welcome enough, but it was the audience who made the film a success by parting with their dollars and pounds in huge amounts to see the film. While Pitt had shared the screen with Tom Cruise in *Interview With the Vampire* and with Anthony Hopkins in *Legends of the Fall*, it was he who was the prime attraction for many of the people who went to see the movie. As well as confirming his position in the Hollywood pecking order, *Seven* also allowed director David Fincher to overcome the stigma that had been attached to him since the debacle of *Alien3*.

Although appreciative of good reviews, Pitt is not fond of the press and journalists. He understands the Faustian pact between movie stars and the movie magazines, but that doesn't make him comfortable with it. He is happy enough to talk about his work, but does not enjoy seeing things in print on his private life. 'How do I feel about reading that kinda stuff? It really depends on the day. Sometimes I laugh, other days I just pull down the shades and ignore it. I don't know why it happens. I guess people just want to twist things and hear the negative version.'

'The truth is I don't want people to know me,' Pitt has admitted. 'I don't know a thing about my favourite actors. I don't think you should – they become personalities. It seems to me that it would be better if they didn't know who you were. Then your character would be more believable. I don't know shit about Robert Duvall or John Malkovich, and they're my favourites...'

He has never liked the whole teen idol thing that has dogged his career. 'The thing about these articles,' he said of the teen magazine profiles and features, 'I sit down and give my life views, and it sounds like I'm walking around like a prophet. That's not true, 'cause most of the time I'm out cutting up and laughing and speeding in my car and whatever, whatever, whatever. Yelling at the TV and cranking the tunes...It's like "What's your favourite colour?" I don't know. I like a bunch of 'em.'

The attention of the fans got to be too much when a Hollywood bus tour company began running coach loads past his LA home on Sunday mornings. 'I started lofting eggs at them,' said Pitt, 'I thought that was fair. I'm, like, as open as the next guy, but when freaky people turn up at your home, it's like, Whoah! Get off the train.' Pitt was even the subject of a 'Dear Brad' site on the Internet where fans would leave letters to the star to be read by the public and Pitt himself, should he care to browse the Web. Most of the notes seemed to be from teenage girls declaring their undying love and their hatred of Paltrow. One example was typical: 'I'm Stacy and I really love you. I even have your poster on my wall and you are always looking at me. I know you love me and we are meant to be. So look me up sometime, and please, please, please write back soon. I love you always and forever.' It's hardly surprising Pitt was minded to throw eggs at people.

It wasn't only female fans, either. Pitt discovered his attraction extended to the gay community too, placing him top of a 'Twenty Sexiest Men' readers' poll in British gay magazine *Attitude*, followed closely on the list by Keanu Reeves and

Johnny Depp. Questions were put about his sexuality, according to Juliette Lewis: 'The gay rumour goes wild – for everyone. Like with Leo [DiCaprio], he was like, "Is Brad gay?" And I said, "Leo, you're gay, don't you know? Haven't you heard?".'

Ironically, Pitt was offered the role of a baseball player haunted by a psychotic fan stalker in *The Fan*. Producer Wendy Finerman (*Forrest Gump*, 1994) gave Pitt the script, but he expressed more interest in playing the character of the fan than the star, the latter role being too close to real life for comfort. The film was made in 1995 with Wesley Snipes as the ball player and Robert DeNiro as the fanatic.

In April 1995 Brad Pitt's new relationship became public when he and Paltrow attended the British premiere of *Legends of the Fall* in London. The couple attended the charity premiere at a Leicester Square cinema, in the presence of Prince Charles, at a screening that raised over £100,000 for the Prince's Trust charity. The media, however, were far more interested in the relationship between Paltrow and the 'Sexiest Man Alive'. Pitt's comment to waiting reporters was pithy: 'I've never been happier.'

The pursuit, however, was on. Realising they had a new hot Hollywood couple to rival the on-again, off-again, on-screen, off-screen romances of Johnny Depp and Winona Ryder and Tom Cruise and Nicole Kidman, the media pulled out all the stops to scoop exclusive snapshots of the new star couple.

Following their trip to London, and before Pitt had to return to Los Angeles to take up his role in Terry Gilliam's *Twelve Monkeys*, the couple took the opportunity of a holiday break on the exclusive Caribbean island of St Barts. Thinking themselves to be in a secluded spot, they spent time around their pool naked. The problem was they weren't alone. An enterprising French photographer spotted them and saw a chance to make some money.

His colour full-length shots of Pitt and Paltrow naked were first published by a French magazine, before being reproduced by a British tabloid, and finally ending up on display internationally on the Internet.

Pitt and Paltrow were mortified to discover that their private moments were being splashed all over downmarket publications for public consumption. 'It's pathetic that anything we do is news,' said Paltrow. 'I hate my privacy being invaded, especially since most of it is happening because of who I go out with. It hasn't anything to do with me or my career.' Paltrow called the British tabloid journalists, 'the most hideous creatures on the face of the Earth. It made me recede,' she said of the incident, 'because there are few people I can hang out with. There are few people I feel I can trust.'

Pitt was equally stung by his unintentional public nude scene: 'It was horrendous. It bothers me that they take pictures of these private, special moments and flash semi-naked pictures of my girlfriend. I see how it hurts her.' Pitt started a legal action against the photographer, the photo agency that handled the sale and two French publications. 'I wonder about the rights of privacy,' he said after his actions had begun, trying to play down the impact of the publication of the photos. 'I mean, it all ends up in the litter box anyway.' Pitt avoided pursuing the British tabloids as, unlike France, Britain does not recognise any easily enforceable right of privacy, especially for high-profile celebrities.

Back in Los Angeles after the tabloid tiff, Pitt had business to attend to. He was due to report to the set in Philadelphia of Terry Gilliam's *Twelve Monkeys*, in which he

Pitt was again cast against type in Twelve Monkeys, foregoing a macho role for the motormouth
lunatic Jeffrey Goines against Bruce Willis's James Cole.

was co-starring alongside action star Bruce Willis. Gilliam, one-time animator and
actor in the *Monty Python* team, had carved out a distinctive visual style in a series
of feature films including *Jabberwocky* (1977), *Time Bandits* (1981), *Brazil*
(1985), *The Adventures of Baron Munchausen* (1989) and *The Fisher King*
(1991). Known as something of a maverick in the Hollywood community, Gilliam
had never made blockbusters and some of his movies – particularly *Brazil* and
Baron Munchausen – had fallen foul of studio interference.

The Fisher King, a fantasy starring Robin William and Jeff Bridges, had
restored his reputation somewhat, but it was still another four years before he got
underway with *Twelve Monkeys*. In the intermediate years he'd tried to float
several projects, including remakes of *A Tale of Two Cities* and *A Connecticut
Yankee in King Arthur's Court*, and a film written by Richard LaGravenese,
scripter of *The Fisher King*. A long-mooted adaptation of Alan Moore and Dave

Gibbon's graphic novel *Watchmen* had also fallen by the wayside. When offered the script for *Twelve Monkeys*, a feature-length version of a 1962 surreal short called *La Jetée* by Chris Marker, written by David Webb Peoples (*Blade Runner*, 1982, *Unforgiven*, 1992) and his wife Janet Peoples, Gilliam jumped at it.

'I love the idea of trying to alter perceptions and shake people up and make them look at the world in a way they're not used to looking at it,' said Gilliam. 'I found it to be an intriguing and intelligent script. The story is disconcerting. It deals with time, madness and various perceptions of what the world is or isn't. It's a study of madness and dreams, of death and rebirth, set in a world coming apart.'

Twelve Monkeys is set in a post-apocalyptic 21st-century world, but instead of a nuclear war having almost wiped out mankind, it's a killer virus that originated in 1996. Survivors live under the earth, where they are about to use a newly developed method of time travel to try and prevent the outbreak of the deadly virus.

The subject chosen for the trips back to 1990 and 1996 is James Cole (a bald headed Bruce Willis), a criminal haunted by a fragmented

Madeleine Stowe as the psychiatrist Kathryn Railly, whose credulity is stretched to the limit by Cole's story of time-travel, in *Twelve Monkeys*.

memory from his childhood. Both in 1990 and 1996, Cole meets fanatical animal rights activist Jeffrey Goines (Brad Pitt), leader of the Army of the Twelve Monkeys, who may have been responsible for the release of the virus. He also encounters a psychiatrist, Kathryn Railly (Madeleine Stowe), who finds Cole's tales of time travel and killer virus hard to believe, thinking that he's as mad as Goines. Despite this, they develop a relationship, and Cole discovers that Railly holds the key to his accomplishing his mission.

'It's a fairly complicated film,' admitted Gilliam. 'On one level it's about whether or not Cole is mad or telling the truth. The rational person is Railly, a reasonable person with a reasonable view of the world confronted by things that are inexplicable. I think what I liked most were the rantings of Jeffrey Goines. David and Janet [Peoples] were putting the kind of things that we all feel but are terrified to say into the mouth of a madman. Suddenly they became funny...'

Brad Pitt was convinced he was the right actor to play the part of crazy Jeffrey Goines. So intent was he on changing his image, he even insisted on wearing brown

Time traveller James Cole finds the past a less than restful place.

contact lenses to disguise his blue eyes, and his *Seven* buzz cut was made even scruffier.

Before he even arrived in Philadelphia for the shooting there were frenzied so-called sightings of Pitt in the city. A local Philly radio station staged 'Brad Watches' in which a host invited listeners to phone in to report any sightings of the star. Prizes were even offered for anyone who managed to break into the star's hotel room and filch something significant belonging to the actor. As far as Pitt is aware no one took up the challenge. He was only around for two weeks, but he seemed to manage to drive Philadelphia wild, with very little effort.

More work went into preparing to play his part in the film. 'He threw himself into the role,' said producer Charles Roven, ironically the husband of Dawn Steel who had headed up Columbia when Gilliam had a fracas with the studio over their botched release of *The Adventures of Baron Munchausen*. To play the manic-depressive character, Pitt spent an additional two weeks before coming to the set in group therapy sessions and he checked into a Philadelphia psychiatric ward for a day – an event that didn't get reported by the Pitt-obsessed radio station. 'He was fully in character,' said Roven of Pitt's ward visit where only the institution's director knew who the young actor was. 'He's a perfectionist.'

'Brad Pitt really wanted to do the film,' Gilliam said. 'In many ways we were lucky because he was running away from the "Sexiest Man in the world" image, so he went the other direction and he certainly won't win that award for this film. People are going to realise how funny he is. His comic timing is wonderful. It's just very, very funny stuff he's doing and he comes across as absolutely crazy.'

Continued Gilliam: 'I always like the idea of casting against type. What's interesting is that Brad has the fireworks part in the film. It's like in *The Fisher King* where Jeff Bridges is in every scene, yet Robin Williams is the one who got a lot of the credit. When Brad's on, fireworks happen. He gets all the good lines. Bruce is doing all the real hard work, and Brad gets to come in and just steal scenes. Brad is pretty laconic in some ways, then suddenly he's a blabbermouth, jabbering away at high speed. I love doing that, playing with the public's perception of that star, otherwise it wouldn't be fun.'

More fun was had by Gilliam in searching out locations. He used various places

Director Terry Gilliam (left) directs Brad Pitt and Bruce Willis in *Twelve Monkeys*.

in Philadelphia, with the Greek revival Ridgeway Library turned into the abandoned Wanamaker's Department Store, headquarters for the time-travel planning scientists in the future, and the Eastern State Penitentiary standing in for a 1990s mental hospital. Some of the film was shot in Baltimore. Much of the film has the look and feel of Gilliam's epic *Brazil*. 'I can't seem to avoid it,' admitted the director of his distinctive, steam-driven visual style.

Bruce Willis, often typecast as the action man star of the *Die Hard* movies, was as keen as Pitt to branch out into character roles. For Willis that had meant films like *Nobody's Fool* (1995) and *Four Rooms* (1995). He could understand the significance of Pitt's role in *Twelve Monkeys* to his career: 'For Brad, this is the best thing he has ever done, by far. He was just out of his mind...'

Opening at the very end of 1995 in America, *Twelve Monkeys* went straight to number one in the national box office. *Entertainment Weekly* called Pitt's Jeffrey Goines 'a jabbering psychotic who may just be more dangerous than he looks. Pitt does a hammy, bug-eyed turn, but his manic reaction time and rabid, get-a-load-of-me deviousness works for the character, and for the film's central mystery: looking at Jeffrey we can't tell where the fanatic leaves off and the put-on artist begins. Something similar might be said of Gilliam, who turns a world falling apart into a funky, dizzying spectacle.' Writer Owen Gleiberman scored the film B+.

Todd McCarthy, *Variety*'s film critic writing in *Premiere* magazine, was impressed by Pitt's off-the-wall turn in *Twelve Monkeys*: '[Cole] must endure the feverish ranting of an inmate played by Brad Pitt, whose mannered monologues and gesticulations can leave no doubt as to his sincere desire to become a serious actor.'

Becoming a serious actor was next on his career agenda, but he had more personal matters to deal with first over Christmas 1995.

Pitt was convinced from the outset that he was the right person to play the mad Jeffrey Goines.

11 On the Rocks

Just as *Twelve Monkeys* opened at American cinemas and Brad Pitt found himself at the top of the box office heap once again, the young actor had more personal concerns on his mind. He returned home to spend Christmas with his family in Missouri, as he did every year, but this time he brought Gwyneth Paltrow with him. A few days before the holidays, Pitt decided to pop the question. If Gwynnie (as he affectionately called her) said 'Yes' to marriage, he would have some serious news to announce to his parents during the visit home.

The decision had been a long-time coming for Pitt. It had been his fear of commitment that had caused him to break off his romance with Juliette Lewis. Now, at the age of 32, he decided he was ready. There was just one problem – 23-year-old Paltrow wasn't. She said 'no' to marrying the world's officially sexiest man.

An anonymous source gave details of the failed marriage proposal to *The National Enquirer*, which ran the story at the end of January 1996. 'He thought the time was right,' said the source, 'and he just went for it. But Gwyneth didn't want to walk down the aisle just yet.'

Recalling his romantic antics as a teenager in Springfield, Missouri, Pitt had laid elaborate plans for his proposal. 'He and Gwyneth drove to an old, romantic mansion in a secluded city park in the hills of Hollywood. They ate. Then they were just laughing and having a good time, drinking their wine, when Brad got serious. He looked at Gwyneth and quietly asked her to marry him on New Year's Eve.'

'Gwyneth was stunned,' related the source. 'She looked at him for a moment, then she said, "No, not yet. Look around us, nobody in Hollywood gets married at our age and stays married. It usually doesn't last more than two years." Brad was disappointed, but he told her he understood. He was pretty upset. She explained that she was scared of commitment at that level. She told him she wanted to work hard on her career first, before they get married. Brad is beginning to want kids and Gwyneth isn't ready . . .'

Paltrow had expressed her long-term plans rather differently in a September 1995 issue of *Interview* magazine. In ten years, she predicted, 'I'll be married, with three or four children.' That tallied with the ambition expressed by Pitt in that December's *USA Today*, when asked what he wanted out of his relationship: 'Married, with bambinos and at home . . .'

Paltrow, however, had strong views on marriage and no intention of getting hitched until she was sure Pitt had changed his ways with women. 'My parents have been married for 25 years and my grandparents for 55, so I take marriage and family very seriously. I wouldn't marry unless I thought it was forever. We'll have to see what happens.'

As for Pitt, he claimed the days of dating his co-stars were over now he had found Paltrow. In the past, movie sets had been venues for social and romantic opportunity: 'We're dealing with an industry full of fascinating people. They understand what you're trying to do. I hear actors saying "I'll never date another actor." Well, I think just the opposite – if you can find a stable one, but I'm properly in love for the first time.'

'This last year I've been as happy as I've ever been.'

147

Brad with Jason Patric, as lifelong friends who try to help their buddies beat a murder rap in Barry Levinson's *Sleepers*.

As 1996 began, it seemed that marriage and children were off the agenda for Hollywood's hottest new couple. But their relationship was going strong, and the duo were spotted house-hunting in the Hamptons, an exclusive area on the USA's East Coast populated by the rich and famous. Although people in the area were used to seeing stars and celebrities in their midst, so fearful of being spotted was Pitt, that he took to wearing a yellow turban to hide his instantly recognisable good looks. (It was a ploy he would continue to use, hiding his face under a thick scarf and Adidas baseball cap when passing through Los Angeles International Airport in mid-January.) While looking for a new property to buy together, Pitt and Paltrow were staying in her Greenwich Village apartment in New York, with Pitt having all but abandoned the Beachwood Canyon, Los Angeles home purchased in 1994.

Living in New York was handy for Pitt's next film commitment. By September 1994 he began work on a starring role in *Sleepers* (1996), a crime drama directed by Barry Levinson. Levinson had first enjoyed critical success with *Diner* (1982), a character-based ensemble drama set in his native Baltimore, before finding mainstream success with *Good Morning Vietnam* (1987), starring comedian Robin Williams, and *Rain Man* (1988), with Tom Cruise and Dustin Hoffman. However, a personal project, *Toys* (1992), which also starred Williams, was an unsuccessful piece of whimsy supposedly in the vein of cult kids' movie *Willy Wonka and the Chocolate Factory* (1971). When it bombed at the box office, Levinson had already returned to his gritty Baltimore roots by directing the pilot episode of *Homicide: Life on the Street*, the innovative ciné vérité TV series for which he was also credited as executive producer. With the glossier *Sleepers*, Levinson was hoping to return to the hardboiled credibility won by *Homicide*.

Based on a best-selling novel by author Lorenzo Carcaterra, *Sleepers* tells the harrowing story of four New York kids – Michael, John, Tommy and Lorenzo himself – who inadvertently kill a street vendor during a robbery, for which they are caught and convicted. While doing time in a juvenile reformatory (as 'sleepers' – vernacular for juveniles on a long sentence), they are sexually abused by four guards led by a sadist named Nokes (Kevin Bacon). 15 years later, in the early 1980s, two of the four, John and Tommy (Ron Eldard and Billy Crudup), now grown up and back on the streets of their native Hell's Kitchen, encounter the gone-to-seed Nokes in a bar, sit down and introduce themselves, then shoot him dead. The other half of the foursome are drawn into the case – Michael (Brad Pitt), now the assistant district attorney, and Lorenzo (Jason Patric), a news-hungry tabloid reporter. The pair conspire, along with their local priest Father Bobby (Robert DeNiro), to get their old pals off a murder charge, with Pitt's character effectively aiding his courtroom adversary, hard-drinking defence attorney Danny Snyder (Dustin Hoffman).

Carcaterra courted controversy by claiming that his novel was, in fact, not a novel at all but non-fiction, and that he only changed names and locations to protect

For a maturing Pitt, the role of Michael in *Sleepers* was straightforward, but important in pushing him toward the frontline of leading man roles.

the identities of some of those involved. With the controversial murder trial of one-time sports superstar and movie actor O. J. Simpson fresh in everyone's memories, any film dealing with the manipulation of justice was sure to be controversial.

Critic Janet Maslin, of the *New York Times*, was particularly cynical. Of the original source material, she agreed with the literary critics that 'it sounded more Hollywood than Hell's Kitchen and prompted instant scepticism about the author's conveniently cinematic vision'. Of the film adaptation, she was just as scathing: 'It's possible that this is a candid account of Carcaterra's boyhood adventures. It's also possible that Santa and the elves spend all year at the North Pole, making a list and checking it twice . . . As directed by Barry Levinson and acted by an incredible collection of male stars, *Sleepers* settles the authenticity question by not allowing a whiff of real life into its universe.' Further compounding her disbelief was the unlikelihood of Pitt's character being allowed to work on the prosecution case after serving time with the defendants as a co-perpetrator, the fact that Irish-American defence lawyer Danny O'Connor, in the book, had become the Jewish Danny Snyder in the film, and that, 'By a series of remarkable coincidences that are described in an epilogue, neither Michael nor anyone else involved in *Sleepers* was available to help Carcaterra or Levinson (who wrote the screenplay) tell the tale.'

Of Brad Pitt's participation, she was a little more positive: 'Pitt, with a heavy New York accent and more Method mannerisms than the film's businesslike style can really support (there's lots of pained, thoughtful cigarette smoking), makes an attention-getting prosecutor if not a persuasive one. He provides some welcome energy as the film moves suspenselessly toward its easy, fundamentally cynical ending.'

Perhaps it was the geographical distance from the subject matter, but Kevin McManus on the *Washington Post* gave the film a much easier time: 'To see the movie is to forget the whole fact-versus-fiction issue. Levinson, helped by a very good cast, manipulates us so skilfully that, by the time those toughs enter the bar, we're practically panting for an act of vengeance . . . If the movie's first act feels like a darker *Diner*, the second act feels like something out of the [John] Grisham oeuvre. It features a pleasing mix of good-guy gumshoeing, smart-alecky dialogue and courtoom surprises . . . for the most part, Levinson tells the story – fiction or non-fiction – quite well.'

Apparently placed under great stress, Carcaterra went so far as to claim, 'There are days when I'm sorry I wrote the book because of the physical and mental problems it activated.' But the degree of professional involvement on the film – from Levinson through to the principal players – still convinced Carcaterra he had done the right thing, especially when his family made connections with the star. 'My daughter has become friends with Brad Pitt,' said Carcaterra. 'Since she's only 13, this has placed her as close to heaven as she's going to get.'

For a maturing Pitt the role was straightforward, but important in pushing him further toward the frontline of leading male actors. 'You've never seen him so shrewd,' a source told *Entertainment Weekly* of his five months working on the film, which wrapped in January 1996. A spokeswoman for Pitt confirmed the actor was now choosing roles with an eye toward the future: 'He's interested in stretching. It's the roles, not the image, he's concerned with.'

The female lead on *Sleepers*, out of an otherwise all-male cast, was the British actress Minnie Driver. She had first come to prominence in the TV mini-series *The*

Politician's Wife (1995) before securing a small role in the James Bond movie *GoldenEye* (1995). 'It's kind of a weird dynamic,' she told *Premiere*, 'being the only girl.' Playing Pitt's ex-girlfriend allowed the actress a chance to get to know her co-star, but strictly on-set only. None of the *Sleepers* cast seemed particularly keen on pursuing a social life together. 'These are not people who fraternise after work. They're not the party-hearty kind of guys. If I tell any one of the boys of my female take on the situation [the production], they kind of laugh.'

As Pitt and Paltrow had learned to their cost, the couple's every move had become media fodder, and Driver found herself approached by tabloid journalists asking her for the lowdown on the newsworthy couple. 'Everything is prefaced by "Is it true that . . . ?", "Is he doing this . . . ?", and "Is she pregnant?". I'm, like, "I don't bloody know – it's a day job!".'

Despite the tabloids hovering around the film's Manhattan locations, Pitt and Paltrow managed to get through the shooting of *Sleepers* without another media mishap on the scale of the St. Barts incident.

With *Sleepers* under his belt, Brad Pitt had a chance to enjoy the approval of his peers. Nominated for a Golden Globe award for Best Supporting Actor in the recently released *Twelve Monkeys*, Pitt was stunned to discover, on 22nd January 1996, he had won. In his random acceptance speech, he reflected the euphoria of both his professional and his private lives, thanking Gwyneth Paltrow, 'my angel, the love of my life'.

Voted by the Hollywood Foreign Press Association, the Golden Globes are regarded as a strong indication of those stars and films most likely to be nominated for the Academy Awards in March. Having celebrated his 32nd Birthday in December (entertained by a troupe of lesbian strippers arranged by his pal, singer Melissa Etheridge), Pitt's near-perfect year was capped by a major Hollywood award.

'This last year I've been as happy as I've ever been,' he explained. '[I've] been miserable, been genius, been humiliated, been congratulated, been put down – I mean the whole gamut of emotions. That's a pretty amazing year. I value that. Extremes. And it comes from acting. The hardest thing is to make it look easy.'

The Golden Globe Award was followed, sure enough, by a February 1996 Oscar nomination for Best Supporting Actor in *Twelve Monkeys* – but Pitt was to lose out to his *Seven* co-star Kevin Spacey, who won for *The Usual Suspects* (1995). 'It's a crap shoot,' he said of the Academy Award process, dismissing its relevance in terms of choosing roles. 'It's got to be personal in each film. If it sinks, it sinks, and if it floats, good for you, because I just don't put a lot of emphasis on it. Sure it would be flattering [to win], but most of the time I disagree with their [the Academy's] choices.' Nonetheless, the nomination itself was a further sign that he was being taken seriously by the Hollywood establishment – no longer noted purely for his looks, he was now acclaimed for his acting skills.

People magazine's 'Sexiest Man Alive' accolade, however, was still a curse and a blessing. 'He has a great sense of humour about it,' claimed *Twelve Monkeys* director Terry Gilliam. 'This is just his cross to bear for a while. Everybody tries to inflate him, but he doesn't need to be inflated. He's good, solid stuff, our Brad.'

'It's time to kill the myth, y'know,' said Pitt himself, exasperated, two years after the fact, by a public appetite that had been fed by the nude St. Barts photos. 'It got out of hand. I prefer to look a little more realistic. It doesn't relate to longevity,

Brad receiving his Golden Globe Award for best supporting
actor in *Twelve Monkeys*, January 1996.

y'know. It only really leads to a quicker burn out. I have to admit I had about a month where it threw me for a loop. But I asked for it, and you have to make some adjustments. Really, what do I have to complain about? Nothing. I've got it pretty damn good.' Such happiness wasn't to last. On-set battles and controversies would arise during the making of his next film – *The Devil's Own* (1997) – and personal problems would soon be looming over him.

Brad Pitt travelled to Northern Ireland at the end of 1995 to research his role in *The Devil's Own*, a thriller in which he was to co-star with Harrison Ford. He hoped to 'soak up the atmosphere,' according to his publicist, and was spotted, by an eagle-eyed movie fan, researching Ulster's history in the Linen Hall Library in Belfast. The fan later spoke to the *Belfast Telegraph*: 'He was happy to sign autographs, but it was clear that he didn't want it generally known that he was in town. He didn't want to be diverted from his studies in the library by celebrity spotters.'

Staying in the Europa Hotel, Pitt booked in under the plain pseudonym of Mr Williams (after his Christian name of William). Despite his desire to stay low-key, he also gained a limited taste of 'the Troubles' at first hand – in the form of punches, kicks and bruises by two youths who caught him looking in the window of a Protestant bookshop. 'They yelled abuse at me and just knocked me over and kept on walking,' reported Pitt to *Rolling Stone* magazine. Despite playing a character in *The Devil's Own* who is obviously an Irish Republican, he was attacked by Catholic IRA sympathisers simply because, according to the Royal Ulster Constabulary, 'He was in the wrong place at the wrong time.'

Neither was it all sweetness and light during production, with trouble mounting even before shooting began in New York on 5th February 1996. The film was initally something of a pet project for Pitt, who was the first actor signed. The first draft of the screenplay by Kevin Jarre (who also scripted *Rambo: First Blood Part II*, 1985) was written in 1987, with Pitt attaching himself to the project as an unknown in 1991. Over the years, as he stuck with it, his own stature in Hollywood grew, until, in 1994, the film moved into pre-production. By this time, his agents had struck a deal with producer Lawrence Gordon whereby Pitt was to be paid a reported $8 to $10 million to play the lead role of a fugitive Irish Republican gunman.

The film is set during the short-lived IRA ceasefire that lasted from September 1994 to February 1996 – the month that the film began production, when the IRA launched a major bomb attack against London's Docklands. Pitt plays Frankie McGuire, who is first seen as an eight-year-old child when masked members of a (presumably Loyalist) paramilitary storm the family home and shoot his father dead at the dinner table. After a chronological jump of 20 years, we see the grown-up Frankie escape from a shoot-out with British forces and flee to New York, under the assumed identity of Rory Devane. He's taken in by Harrison Ford's hospitable police officer, Tom O'Meara, with whom he builds a strong rapport – not least because both men are at the mercy of the hotheads they associate with, whether O'Meara's trigger-happy partner (Ruben Blades), or the violently unpredictable arms dealer Billy Burke (Treat Williams). The cop eventually discovers his house guest's hidden past and uncovers his bloody purpose in coming to America – to purchase a consignment of Stinger missiles on the black market, for use in terrorist attacks. Conscientious to the last, he tries to eschew his partner's shoot-first tactics and bring the Irishman in alive – although, inevitably, it ends in tragedy.

'I did it because it spoke to something on the human side – the emotional side, which is really all I'm interested in,' claimed Pitt, who wanted to play down any controversy by pleading ignorance: 'I don't know much about politics.' Later, after the film had attracted the wrong kind of publicity, Pitt conceded, 'I can only understand the crisis from afar, from books and interviewing people. What I got from that was pain on both sides.' Belligerent after the film had been so lambasted by the press, however, he demanded, 'I want to know why the British Empire is promoting this pain. Why can't the Empire make right its wrong?' Recalling how his home state of Oklahoma was divided into 'Lutheran, Methodist, Baptist' communities, all forms of Protestantism, he tried to parallel the situation with Northern Ireland: 'Like it matters, like who gives a shit?' Unfortunately, with several hundred years of sectarian hatred burned into them – little to do with religion, much to do with tribalism and injustice, real and perceived – the Catholic and Protestant extremists of Ulster did, indeed, 'give a shit' – as a naïve Pitt was made aware when attacked by Republican youths.

It was Pitt who suggested Harrison Ford as his co-star, keen to work with the older actor whose early years of struggle had parallels with his own. It surprised the producers when Ford agreed to take what had previously been perceived as a 'Robert Duvall-like supporting role', and he was quickly signed up – despite his $20 million salary requirement pushing the film into would-be blockbuster territory.

Director Alan J. Pakula, acclaimed for paranoid conspiracy thrillers *Klute* (1971), *The Parallax View* (1974) and *All the President's Men* (1976), had his hands full with the two superstars. Ford was long used to being the main focus of his films, and Pitt was fresh from his Golden Globe win and Oscar nomination for *Twelve Monkeys*, as well as the box-office success of *Seven*. The result was, almost inevitably, conflict between the two men, both of whom regarded himself as the lead and the other actor as a support. According to the film's producer, the two stars had different versions of the movie in their heads, in which their own character took centre stage. Soon after shooting began, Ford began tampering with the script, attempting to beef up his role and turn his ambivalent character into a hero. As one of the executive producers told *Entertainment Weekly*, Ford 'wanted his character to be showier, like Pitt's'.

Other screenwriters were brought in to revise or 'doctor' Jarre's script: crime specialist David Aaron Cohen (the disappointing *V. I. Warshawski*, 1991, and the underrated *Blood and Wine*, 1996) and comic-tinged crime novelist Vincent Patrick (also screenwriter of *The Pope of Greenwich Village*, 1984, and *Family Business*, 1989) were brought in to inject a little street wisdom; Terry George – co-screenwriter of *In the Name of the Father* (1993), based on the case of the wrongly convicted Guildford Four, and writer/director of *Some Mother's Son* (1996), based on the 'H' block hunger strikes where ten IRA men starved to death – was brought in to lend his uncredited view of the Irish conflict; while *Lethal Weapon 3* (1992) co-writer Robert Kamen (again uncredited) brought it all back to the level of an action movie. If ever a film was a case of 'too many cooks', then *The Devil's Own* was it. (Pakula himself also contributed a revised draft.) Pitt's character gained love interest in the shape of newcomer Natasha McElhone, while Ford's character was made more heroic, in deference to the actor who had claimed, 'the character in the original script would have been very difficult to accept'.

As relaxed as they appear together, Brad and Harrison Ford were reputedly jokeying for the position of lead role in *The Devil's Own*.

Production of *The Devil's Own* slowed as all the additional rewrites took place, pushing the budget up from almost $70 million to nearer $100 million, and the shooting schedule ran over the proposed mid-June 1996 finish date. As the stars' egos continued to clash – wags on the set dubbed the film 'Star Wars' – the producers of Pitt's next movie, *Seven Years in Tibet* (1997), became so concerned that they delayed their production start by almost two months.

The new script, however, was not to Pitt's liking. According to Pakula, there had originally been 'a lot more stuff in Irish-American bars, a lot more stuff about the Irish-American world, which Brad loved, and which I felt was not necessarily that germane to the story'. In an echo of his displays of egotism on *Johnny Suede* and *Legends of the Fall*, Pitt fought his corner against both his director and his co-star – worried that, as Pakula and Ford had previously worked together on the thriller *Presumed Innocent* (1990), they were colluding to boost Ford's role. After a further revision of the script by Pakula, Pitt stormed off the set, claiming the script was no longer the film he had agreed to make. 'I think he panicked that we were trying to make this into a totally different film, a *Patriot Games* 2, where he'd be the heavy and Harrison would chase him and kill him,' admitted the director. Pitt returned to work the following day and his publicist rationalised the delay as due to inclement weather. The real reason for his rapid return, however, was the threat of a $64 million lawsuit, based on the studio's pre-sale of the film's overseas distributions rights on the strength of his name.

Pitt in the thankless role of an irish gunman in *The Devil's Own*.

Ford's PR people were equally keen to play down stories of battles on the set, dismissing 'all these ugly rumours'. However, an insider gleefully spilled the beans. 'Harrison wasn't about to play second fiddle to Brad Pitt, suddenly "the sexiest man alive",' claimed the source. 'They wouldn't even look each other in the eye, much less talk to each other. You could cut the tension with a knife.'

The shooting of one scene, in particular, attracted the attention of a scandal-hungry media. Attempts were made to block off several New York City streets for a sequence where the two main characters came to blows. However, news photographers knew this would be the picture which summed up the whole troubled production. When Pitt spotted one of them at a second-floor window, he waved his movie-prop pistol at the photographer as threateningly as if it were a real gun. The resulting picture ran in newspapers around the world.

As the stars jockeyed for position, the rest of the cast and crew began to get weary as the production ran on into August. Actress Margaret Colin, one of the stars of the smash hit *Independence Day* (1996), was playing Ford's wife, but had had enough by the time July rolled around. 'The feeling is we've got to deliver a hit,' she said, 'and we'll keep shooting until we have enough film to make a hit. I'd like to finish up now. It's too long.'

When *The Devil's Own* finally wrapped, Pitt was due to travel to India to star (for a fee of $8 million) in director Jean-Jacques Annaud's $50 million adventure film *Seven Years in Tibet* – one of two movies based on the life of the Dalai Lama, Tibet's Buddhist spiritual leader, then scheduled for production. Based on a true story, Pitt was to play Austrian climber, Heinrich Harrer, an Olympic gold medallist who escaped to Tibet from British troops during World War II, ultimately becoming the tutor to the Dalai Lama as a boy. The competing film was, ironically, directed by Martin Scorsese and scripted by Harrison Ford's screenwriter wife Melissa Mathison (*ET: The Extraterrestrial*,1982). Entitled *Kundun* (1997), it was also set to focus on the early life of the Dalai Lama, who was forced into exile in India when China invaded Tibet in 1950.

Bizarre rumours suggested Ford had 'kidnapped' Pitt by delaying completion on *The Devil's Own*, in order to give his wife's project a head start. John Jacobs, president of world-wide marketing at the production company Mandalay, was irked by the unavailability of his star. 'We desperately want to get going,' he said in July, as Pitt and Ford battled for the soul of *The Devil's Own*. 'Every time *Devil* pushes back, we have to push back. Maybe now the end is in sight for them, but no-one likes to have a movie with problems like *The Devil's Own* is having.'

Even when the production wrapped, Brad Pitt's troubles were not over. In an interview in *Newsweek*, he was unusually frank about his bad experience: 'It was the most irresponsible bit of film-making – if you can even call it that – that I've ever seen.' Pitt went on to claim the script was 'dogshit' and that he tried to back out of the movie until the producers threatened him with a lawsuit. It was not the kind of publicity the studio wanted. Having originally signed Pitt for the film in 1991, and worked with him up to its release six years later, producer Lawrence Gordon was upset by the actor's comments. 'I tell you what really hurts,' he said, 'I know he didn't feel good about it, but I know that what he said was interpreted in some way incorrectly. What he said was that the process was lousy, he didn't have a good time making the film, he wanted to get out of the film. He didn't say it was a bad film.'

Brad Pit and Paul Noonan in New York's Staten Island, the setting for part of *The Devil's Own*.

Just as rapidly as Pitt had left and returned to the production, however, he quickly claimed to have been quoted out of context. He issued a statement which read as a complete *volte-face*, as if the words had been drafted for him by the studio: 'What resulted from this challenge [making *The Devil's Own*] was hard work and dedication from people that I've grown to love and respect, and a film I am very proud of.' The damage limitation exercise was too late, however, and Pitt simply looked as if he was making a forced retraction. 'It was completely my fault,' he claimed later. 'I did not clarify what I meant and just ran a bunch of thoughts together. Every few years, when I think I've got it figured out, I get myself into some Charlie Brown mess.'

Making amends with Alan Pakula afterwards, Pitt spent $3,000 on a first edition of *Finnegan's Wake*, by Irish author James Joyce, to give to his director as a gift. 'It was one of the most generous and thoughtful gifts I've ever received – it's the 183rd copy, signed by Joyce himself,' said Pakula.

Harrison Ford, for his part, claimed that his and Pitt's battles had not been against each other but had been fought in aid of the film. 'I think we did well under trying circumstances to pull it all together,' he said. 'It was certainly a movie without a script at some very important junctures. It's regrettable it had to be done that way.' Both he and Pitt would be recalled a year after shooting had begun, in February 1997, to reshoot the ending. Again, Ford dismissed tabloid claims that the ending was re-done to massage the vanity of either of the stars. 'It's the same ending, just better. We have a better staging of it, and I get shot as well, but mostly it was to get a better photographic relationship between the two of us.'

The trouble with *The Devil's Own*, after all the fuss, is that it's not a very good film. Pitt does well in the thankless role of the Irish gunman, to whom the audience is supposed to be sympathetic, but the conflict between him and Ford's upright cop is too schematic, the inevitable ending signalled about halfway through the film with Pitt's line, 'Don't expect a happy ending, this is an Irish story.' One of the film's more surprising successes is Pitt's skill with the Irish accent. 'He spent months practising a Belfast accent,' said Pakula, referring to how dialogue coach Brendan Gunn, a native of Belfast, had worked hard with Pitt to erase his American inflections. It was the only part of the ill-fated movie which went well.

Essentially a thriller about an Irish gunman from an unnamed terrorist group on the run, *The Devil's Own* was politically neutral: neither pro- nor anti-IRA. As with British director Carol Reed's *Odd Man Out* (1947), an Irish fugitive (played, in the earlier film, by James Mason) is an outlaw at war with the establishment, though it's never explained how or why. Unlike *Odd Man Out* (retitled *Gang War in the US*, the Mason character, like Pitt's, never identified as an IRA man), *The Devil's Own* was made after 28 years of 'the Troubles' in Ireland and looked naïve and disingenuous in its failure to address the social situation it exploited.

Stateside opinion on the film was divided. Richard Schickel of *Time* was sympathetic: 'This is really quite a good movie – a character-driven (as opposed to whammy-driven) suspense drama – dark, fatalistic and, within its melodramatically stretched terms, emotionally plausible.' He did, however, express reservations about the younger lead's credibility in his role: 'Pitt and the script cheat a little with his character, not investing him with quite the fanatical glitter a political gunman ought to exhibit.' On balance, the 'nays' had it. Roger Ebert, in the *Chicago Sun-Times*, disagreed with Pitt's character's assertion that his story was an intrinsically Irish one: '*The Devil's Own* is an American story, to such a degree that audiences will be able to watch this movie in total ignorance of the history of Northern Ireland, and be none the wiser at the end . . . at no point in the movie, to the best of my recollection, are the words "Catholic" or "Protestant" ever uttered, even though sectarian conflict is at the heart of the Troubles.' Further, Ebert pointed out the contradictory nature of the title: *The Devil's Own* presumably applied to its terrorist main character, while his presentation in the film – as an anti-hero at worst, with the 'villain' tags reserved for the arms dealer and an amoral British intelligence agent – belied such demonisation. 'My best guess is,' conjectured Ebert, 'he's a villain given a moral touch-up because he's also a movie star.'

The Devil's Own met with the inevitable controversy when it was finally released in Britain in early summer 1997, after all other overseas territories. Apart from the supposed taboo of featuring a thinly-disguised IRA man as an anti-hero, outrage was fuelled when Diana, Princess of Wales took her two sons to see the film. Under the pretext that the film carried a '15' certificate and Diana had persuaded the cinema manager to admit her younger son, 12-year-old Prince Harry, the Princess was pressurised by the tabloids' reaction into issuing an apology. (She looked particularly naïve when she claimed to be unaware of the film's subject matter.) It was just one of many incidents dogging a movie that generated controversy but little applause.

1996 had more unpleasant surprises in store for Brad Pitt, when, late in the year, two forgotten aspects of his past resurfaced to embarrass him. The first was a film made in 1988, between *Cutting Class* and *Happy Together*, which he hoped had been lost forever. *The Dark Side of the Sun*, a low-budget weepie about medical illness, had been made in Yugoslavia and then lost during the Balkan war. Pitt played an American teenager whose skin melted if exposed to the sun – later described by sardonic reviewers as a leather-masked version of *The Boy in the Plastic Bubble*, the John Travolta TV movie.

As a 24-year-old unknown, Pitt had answered the $1000-per-week casting call for a 'good looking blond guy' to play Rick, who is searching Europe for a cure to his bizarre skin disorder. In the only role in his career to require extensive make-up, the young actor spent two hours every morning having chemicals applied to his face that could only be worn for a short time. The film's producer, Angelo Arandjelovic, later praised Pitt's professionalism. 'He was first on the set every morning. He gave 110 per cent. Even when he was still an unknown, women would throw themselves at him. They fell for his boyish looks. Someone actually broke into the production offices and stole all of Brad's publicity shots.' Pitt co-starred with actress Sheryl Pollack, playing a local woman with whom he falls in love. 'There were rumours about him and Sheryl, but I know Brad turned her down,' claimed Arandjelovic.

Shortly before editing was about to begin, the film was lost. The years of civil war that followed in the region ensured that it remained so, until Arandjelovic tracked it down late in 1996. 'The film was hidden by a colleague,' confirmed Arandjelovic. 'Then it was lost as we all fled the fighting. When the war calmed down I sent people to find it. It's a dream come true – Brad's star shines very bright today. There couldn't be a better time for the world to see his first movie.' Keen to cash in on Pitt's superstar status, Arandjelovic raised funding to finish the editing and distribute the film on video. Pitt simply ignored the rediscovery of *The Dark Side of the Sun* – but his silence didn't stop newspapers around the world publishing gruesome pictures of his young self in skin disease make-up. Released to the US home video market, the film met a mix of indifference and derision without doing harm to the career of Brad Pitt.

The next ghost from the past arrived via reports on tabloid TV show *Inside Edition* and in *The International Herald Tribune*, also from 1988. Both claimed Pitt had been arrested and charged with a breach of the peace for exposing himself. *Inside Edition* claimed Pitt and two friends, during a break from shooting *Cutting Class*, had decided to 'flash' at on-coming traffic, and that, according to a police report, the young actor pulled down his shorts and exposed himself. Pitt reportedly pleaded no contest, paid a $450 fine and was given two years probation. In 1996 his publicist, Cindy Guagenti, denied the story outright, but it only served to emphasise how Pitt's new superstar status was focusing the spotlight on him ever closer.

With the bitter experience of *The Devil's Own* behind him, it was a relief for Pitt to head off to make *Seven Years in Tibet* – in which he was the only star name. Producer Iain Smith, executive producer of British epics *The Killing Fields* (1984) and *The Mission* (1986), had secured the rights to Heinrich Harrer's autobiography in the mid-1980s. Hollywood Buddhist Richard Gere had once been pencilled in to play Harrer, but, as the film neared production, Pitt was considered to have better 1990s box-office potential. He had already expressed an interest in the role, as had many other Hollywood actors, but it was director Jean-Jacques Annaud (*The Name of the Rose*, 1986, and *Quest for Fire*, 1981) who sealed the deal, when he discovered Pitt shared his passion for photography.

Pitt played Harrer, a mountaineer who, in the autumn of 1939, set out to climb one of the highest peaks in the Himalayas. At the outbreak of the Second World War, he and fellow climber Peter Aufschnaiter (played by David Thewlis) were imprisoned by the Allies but managed to escape, finding refuge in Lhasa, the holy city of Buddhist Tibet, which was then a closed territory to foreigners. Though Harrer had abandoned his unborn son and his wife in pursuit of mountaineering glory, he became the tutor to the Dalai Lama – from whom he learned much. The young spiritual leader was also fascinated by his Austrian guest, from whom he learned the ways of the West, christening him 'Yellow Head'. (This being a reference to his blond hair.) Harrer also witnessed the cruelty of the Red Chinese Army toward the Tibetans, and how the materialist dogma of Marxism-Maoism tried to crush their spiritual values underfoot. Finally, at the age of 21, the Dalai Lama himself was forced to flee into exile on the Indian subcontinent.

The film was originally meant to shoot in India, but, as the Indian Government feared economic sanctions by the Chinese government, they refused permission. The rival Dalai Lama film, Kundun, also faced trouble when the parent production

Brad Pitt in *Seven Years in Tibet*, starring as Heinrich Harrer, the Austrian mountain climber who escapes allied imprisonment in India, at the outbreak of the Second World War, by fleeing to Tibet .

company, Walt Disney, was threatened with a Chinese economic and cultural boycott, forcing the producers to shoot in Morocco. Harrer, who was consulted as an adviser on *Seven Years in Tibet* and met with Pitt and Annaud, felt the Chinese action helped promote the movie. 'It's not only in America and Europe,' he told the *New York Times*. 'I am hearing from people in India, Bhutan, Nepal, all over that region, who say they are now very anxious to see the movie.'

Before shooting began, Pitt hooked up with co-star David Thewlis to begin a strenuous period of preparation. Pitt clearly enjoyed working with Thewlis, praising him as 'probably the best actor of our generation. What he did in *Naked* [1993, Mike Leigh's social-realist psychodrama, with Thewlis as charismatic street-scum] is as good as anything Brando or Pacino has done.' The pair endured a variety of training exercises together to prepare for the physical nature of their roles. They had to learn to ice skate, which involved secret midnight sessions practising at a specially rented rink in Los Angeles. Both had to overcome their fear of heights and learn to climb under the supervision of two veteran mountaineers, as many scenes would be shot in controlled mountainside conditions. Pitt, Thewlis and their instructors spent two weeks in the Austrian Alps and the Italian Dolomites getting to grips with the basics of climbing skills. 'It can be addicting,' said Pitt of his exhilarating learning experience. 'Never to be forgotten.' Nonetheless, he later admitted, 'some days I could not wait to get down. The truth is, I am shit scared of heights.'

Seven Years in Tibet was an epic shot in a variety of exotic and not-so-exotic locations around the world – mainly in Mendoza and Buenos Aires, Argentina, but Pitt also travelled to Vancouver in Canada, Santiago in Chile, Lienz-Kaerten in Austria, and even Leamington Spa in the United Kingdom.

Pitt was mobbed when he arrived at Buenos Aires International airport, despite the best efforts of security personnel from the Argentine Ministry of the Interior. He was flown to remote Uspallata in the President's private jet, but, even there, in a town with only two streets, Pitt was surrounded by local girls when eating at a restaurant. 'That was all fine,' he shrugged, under the protection of two bodyguards who kept the fans at a distance. 'The little girls are sweet, but then there were hundreds of paparazzi. They were just everywhere.'

'It was very interesting to see what Brad's life was like here,' noted Thewlis. 'He couldn't go out. I could go to a bar and hang out, but he couldn't even do that without causing a riot! His response was great – he kept a very level head about it. His way of handling it was to remain totally focused on his work.'

'Half of the Tibetan population is here and half of it is in Morocco making Kundun,' said actor B. D. Wong, who played the controversial Tibetan official who brokered the surrender to China. Also on set was Jetsun Pema, the real Dalai Lama's sister, playing her own mother in the film. To confuse matters, her real-life daughter was playing her mother's mother in *Kundun*. 'She called me last night,' said Pema, 'saying "The scene I just played, I was pregnant with you!"'

Production in Argentina, on a huge recreation of the city of Lhasa, was bedevilled by constant dust storms. The problems served only to enthuse Annaud even more about the project. 'Here's a guy who still gets thrilled and excited every day,' said Pitt of his director. 'The worse the weather gets, the happier he is, you know. The harder the elements, the more he loves it.' Annaud managed to pull off a remarkable coup towards the end of filming. Shooting in Tibet had seemed an absolute impossibility, due to the Chinese occupation, but the director managed to sneak a crew into the country along with acting doubles for Pitt and Thewlis. Directing from Argentina by fax and phone, Annaud was able to secure significant location footage to lend authenticity to his movie.

As with *The Devil's Own*, Pitt himself worked with an accent coach, aiming this time for the perfect Austrian accent. 'I'm hoping to become the Meryl Streep of my generation,' he joked of his perfectionism. 'It forces me to work really hard, because I never studied drama or acting techniques.' Despite his lack of drama training, Annaud was also impressed by how his leading man threw himself into the emotional vortex of method acting. Rehearsing a scene where Harrer receives divorce papers from his wife in Austria, Pitt decided the only way he could authentically represent pain was to feel it at its most intense. Moving the scene from understated sadness to full-on histrionics, Pitt insisted his character should hurl himself in despair onto a barbed wire fence. With his upper body wrapped in gauze, it took several takes before he achieved the desired effect – slumping slowly to the ground after hugging the barbed wire. 'I think this movie meant a lot to Brad,' Annaud would understatedly observe. 'People still think of him as a good-looking teenager. I think he's fighting for self-respect. It's about his professional honesty.'

Having had his fill of controversy with *The Devil's Own*, Pitt was disappointed to be caught up in more political fall-out over *Seven Years in Tibet*. German news magazine *Stern* discovered that Harrer, aged 84 in 1997, had been a member of Hitler's SS with a rank equivalent to sergeant, and that he may have joined the Austrian wing of the Nazi Party as early as 1933, when it was still illegal in that country. The piece was accompanied by a photograph of Harrer and Hitler together, with the Führer congratulating Harrer on a climbing expedition. 'I have a clean conscience,' Harrer insisted to a news agency, but the Simon Wiesenthal Centre in Los Angeles – who, after consulting their extensive Holocaust files, concluded there was no evidence Harrer had been involved in crimes against humanity, and that he had been a sports instructor in the SS – were concerned that he should omit such details from his autobiography. 'He hasn't even used this high-profile, very painful opportunity to say, "You know what? I'm 85 years old, but this is such a crucial issue to me, I'm gonna take a hard look at it,"' complained Rabbi Abraham Cooper, associate dean of the Wiesenthal Centre. 'A war criminal he is not. But he has failed because he's decided to take a public role in Tibet, one of the most sensitive and important human-rights issues, and arrogantly by saying, "Oh, no, no. That stuff's [his Nazi past is] not important."'

'I met Harrer, who is now in his eighties, and liked him,' an apparently stunned Pitt told an interviewer. 'I didn't ask him a thing about his past, because I felt inhibited about playing a person still living. Acting is about interpretation, not about knowing who he was more than 50 years ago, or what he had been through.' Touching on defensiveness, the actor dropped his guard just enough to admit: 'Would I have taken the part if I'd known the truth? Probably not, because I'd have looked at the story and the man in a whole different way.'

Annaud revealed at that point how he had previously known about Harrer's political involvement, revealed by an old photo of him wearing a backpack emblazoned with a swastika. In fact, after the *Stern* article, Annaud claimed to have phoned the old man and told him, 'Heinrich, I want you to know that Brad has been playing you as a Nazi,' claiming that his directions had somehow made this dark aspect implicit in the performance. 'Before the takes, I would say, "Give me your Nazi look here,"' claimed Annaud. But Pitt himself was bemused, finding the remark a little disingenous. 'Jean Jacques said, "I wonder . . .". I remember him saying it once. But "Play it like a Nazi?" No. I wouldn't know what that meant.' However, a last-minute voiceover by the actor acknowledged his character's Nazi Party activism very early on in the film – while a later part of the first-person narrative claimed he 'shuddered to recall' his affiliation with the men who subjugated the Jews, and other minority groups, even more ruthlessly than the Chinese crushed Tibet.

With *Seven Years in Tibet*, Brad Pitt had set out to prove he could handle serious roles in mainstream pictures. 'Brad understands Hollywood,' said director Annaud of his star. 'He understands that all those people who are rich and famous go from the glorious party straight to the analyst, because they don't respect themselves. They become rich and famous doing shit, and they know it. Brad doesn't want that.' *Seven Years in Tibet* was selected to close the Toronto International Film Festival in September 1997, with Pitt and Thewlis in attendance. Release in the United States was set for October 1997 – the vital pre-Christmas period for possible Oscar contenders.

Overall, however, the critics, whose reactions ranged from lukewarm to enthusiastic, gave it a far more positive reception than paying audiences. '*Seven Years in Tibet* is an ambitious and beautiful movie with much to interest the patient viewer,' praised Roger Ebert, with one major reservation, 'but it makes the common mistake of many films about travellers and explorers: It is more concerned with their adventures than with what they discover.' Ultimately summarising the film as 'about two characters [Harrer and the Dalai Lama] and . . . told from the point of view of the wrong one,' the veteran *Chicago Sun-Times* critic still had doubts about the credibility of Pitt as an actor rather than merely a movie star: 'the Harrer character is not forthcoming. Brad Pitt plays him at two speeds: Cold and forbidding at first, and then charming and boyish. He might have been more convincing if he'd been played by, for example, Thewlis. But *Seven Years in Tibet* is a star vehicle: Pitt is required to justify its $70 million budget . . .' The less sceptical viewpoint was represented by the *Austin Chronicle's* Russell Smith, who lauded the film for its 'perfect ratio of moving interpersonal drama and visual enchantment,' while praising Pitt for transcending his heart-throb status: 'even the straightest women and gayest men [may be] repelled by Pitt's willingness to play Harrer as every inch the arrogant, preening shitheel he seems to have been . . . his performance here – unmannered, wide-ranging, and effortlessly controlled – buries any remaining doubt that he's one of his generation's best actors.' However, the box office was not burdened by too many customers eager to see if Brad Pitt could cut it in a serious lead role.

Pitt had to overcome separation anxiety while working in Argentina on *Seven Years in Tibet*. He spent two hours a day calling Gwyneth Paltrow on his cellular phone, and, at $6 per minute, quickly ran up a bill in the region of $65,000. Paltrow was in London, starring alongside British actress Emma Thompson in a new adaptation of Jane Austen's *Emma* (1996). This same occupational hazard had been a recurring problem for Pitt and Juliette Lewis, but greater efforts were made to overcome it this time around. 'Constant separation is the worst thing for a relationship,' said Paltrow. 'It was a case of lots of letters to each other. Letters are so much better

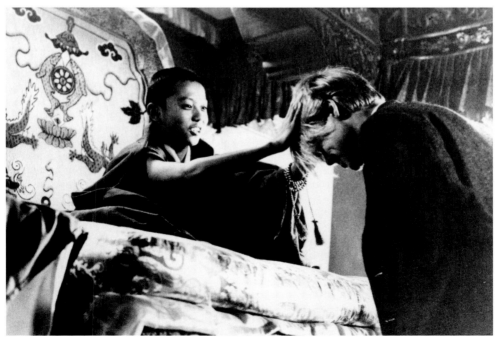

Above: Brad Pitt with English co-star David Thewlis in *Seven Years in Tibet*, and below with Jamyang Wang who starred as the young Dalai Lama, with whom Pitt's character developed a close friendship.

than the phone. You can always interpret things wrongly over the phone.' She even turned down a co-starring role as Emma Peel in the *Avengers* movie alongside Ralph Fiennes, her part taken by Uma Thurman in the badly-received 1998 production. 'I really wanted to do it, but in the end I had to say no,' she confirmed. 'It would have meant a long separation from Brad and I couldn't bear it.'

Pitt finally got Paltrow to agree to marriage, proposing for the fourth time when she visited him in Argentina, after serenading her. When he produced a $35,000 diamond ring he had specially designed himself, she finally gave in and said yes. An engagement party was held back in Los Angeles, attended by showbiz pals.

Pitt's engagement to Paltrow also saw the re-emergence of his ex-girlfriend, actress Juliette Lewis, to speak to the press about their former relationship. 'I still haven't got over him,' she admitted in an interview, 'and I probably never will.' Though it was three years since the end of their relationship, Lewis, now 23, claimed, 'I was truly in love. I'm resigned to the fact that I'll always be in love with him.' Since their split, her career had progressed: she had starring roles in *Natural Born Killers* (1994) and *Strange Days* (1996), and appeared alongside Leonardo DiCaprio in *The Basketball Diaries* (1997). Despite this, she had succumbed to the lure of drink and drugs, reaching the stage where her father checked her into a rehab centre in Clearwater, Florida – run by the controversial Church of Scientology, which she once tried to persuade Pitt to join.

She blamed the end of her relationship with Pitt for her later problems, such as cocaine addiction and a string of unfulfilling affairs: 'Brad and I were together from when I was 16 to 20. I was just so low and felt so bad about my life. My love for Brad was so enormous that when it went awry, nothing seemed to hold any excitement anymore.' Despite this, Lewis had the good grace to remark that Pitt and Paltrow made a good couple. 'Brad and me are old now. I think he and Gwyneth are cool. I know what Brad's tastes are, so it didn't surprise me at all when he and Gwyneth got together.'

Pitt was thinking purely of the future, buying two houses close to the one he already owned in Beachwood Canyon to create a secure 'compound' for he and Paltrow to live in. The simultaneous purchases cost the film star close to $1 million – only a fraction of his now-standard $12 million per film fee. A friend of the couple saw the house purchases as ideally complimenting their luxurious lifestyle. 'It means Brad can have one, Gwyneth another and a third for the staff,' she said, adding optimistically, 'maybe the third could be a nursery . . .' Pitt even reputedly considered staging the wedding ceremony in the grounds surrounding the houses. The couple also bought what the tabloids dubbed a 'love nest' in London, a $1 million mansion near Chelsea's famous King's Road. The ideal retreat while Gwyneth was shooting *Sliding Doors* (1998) at Shepperton Studios, the residence came with its own security staff primed to keep an eye out for tabloid snappers. 'They've fitted right in,' said a star-spotting neighbour, 'but then, they are the right kind of people.'

Everything seemed to be going perfectly for the perfect Hollywood couple. They even planned to work together, co-starring in a film about the adventures of a couple of karaoke singers to be called *Duets* and directed by Paltrow's father, Bruce. It all seemed too good to be true – and so it proved. Paltrow decided she couldn't face going through with it all when Pitt's doubts and fears of commitment began to surface again. Hollywood's golden couple suddenly and unexpectedly called off the wedding. The summer 1997 announcement actually made the 6 o'clock news across the USA, heralding one of the most public break-ups in modern Hollywood.

Its causes, however, remained a source of speculation. First in the firing line was Pitt, for whom breaking off longstanding relationships had become a personal habit. 'He's broken up with every girl who talks marriage to him,' a friend claimed to have warned Paltrow early in their relationship. ('That was before he met me,' Paltrow replied, over-confidently.) 'I am not anti-marriage,' said Pitt himself, forced to defend a track record of two highly visible broken relationships. 'My parents have been married for 35 years and I want it to be for life. I want to be a husband and a father. I will one day wear the ring, the suit, and kiss the bride. It was not meant to be,' he asserted, as if to put a full-stop to the episode.

James Cruise, a friend of Pitt's, claimed Paltrow had put great pressure on him to marry once she accepted his proposal – which she supposedly also pressurised him into making in the first place. According to this version of events, Paltrow had been secretly following the controversial relationships guide *The Rules*, subtitled *Time Tested Secrets for Capturing the Heart of Mr Right*. However, as marriage drew nearer, Pitt's fears and uncertainties grew. 'She did it out of a deep, deep love for him,' claimed Cruise. 'She got the damn ring, but she never truly got Brad because his heart wasn't in it. After the engagement party, Brad was more down than ever.'

'He spent months designing Gwyneth's engagement ring,' confirmed Robert Kamen, script doctor on *The Devil's Own*. 'He designed it, and he would sit there and draw it, draw it, draw it. He was in love, and I thought for sure it was going to go through, because he had this whole midwestern values thing.'

As Paltrow had begun making big plans for the wedding, however, the input of her parents seemed more important than that of her husband-to-be. In fact, her mother, actress Blythe Danner, was both a confidante and a role model. 'She could have had a bigger career,' claimed Paltrow of her mother, not with sadness but with admiration, 'but she chose to stay home with her children when they were young. I can't tell you how much I respect that.' Gwyneth was clearly a home-maker in the making.

Discovering sample wedding invitations the Paltrow family had printed, Pitt blew his top. 'They had a huge fight,' claimed Cruise, who watched the end of the fairy-tale Hollywood romance. 'The thing that ended it was when Gwyneth terrified Brad by telling him she planned to give up her career, have his kids and just be a housewife. He told me, "I'm ruining this poor girl's life. She's got a real future in films and she's ready to give it up for me." Brad was freaked out.'

Another source of resentment to Pitt was the feeling of being railroaded into the *Duets* project. He eventually told Paltrow to forget the joint venture. 'He felt used,' said another pal. 'Brad is no fool. He knows his value. I don't think he was happy to lend his name to a project he didn't control. Of course, Gwyneth would do the movie – she's Bruce's daughter – but what's in it for Brad?' When he pulled out, Columbia, the project's backers, temporarily pulled the plug on the film.

Paltrow, for her part, became suspicious of Brad's commitment when he announced his need for more time on his own. Rather than postpone their wedding, she decisively told him to 'forget it' altogether. When Pitt agreed, Paltrow stormed off in tears, leaving her ring behind her. According to James Cruise, Pitt blamed himself for letting the situation go so far. 'Brad told me, "I should never have agreed to marry her. It ruined everything for us. We were so happy."'

Other explanations for the unexpected break-up ranged from the whole thing as a publicity hoax, with a quiet secret wedding planned, to differences in the pair's backgrounds: Pitt, the Missouri boy, had rebelled against his early life expectations and kept his eye trained on the path less travelled; while the preppie-ish Paltrow, born to money and educated at New York's exclusive Spence School, had eased herself into a career that fitted her like a comfortable glove. 'I think she taught Brad a lot about existing in the klieg lights,' refelected their mutual friend, producer Paul Feldsher, 'and I think he taught her a lot about it being OK to live out of them – that it doesn't mean you don't exist . . . Brad is incredibly sophisticated in the truest sense of the word, but in terms of the language of sophistication, Gwynnie's got that down . . . She's very familiar with the topography of a sophisticated international life. And Pitt's not.'

Or, as Pitt himself would later explain of regional and social class differences (though not speaking directly of Paltrow): 'I don't have the East Coast vocabulary in which all I say is packaging. The upper East Coast schooling. It's very different from private schooling in Missouri, you know, but I work on it.'

Long periods spent working apart on films were also blamed – as, with echoes of Juliette Lewis, was a significant age gap, with Pitt then 33 and Paltrow only 24. 'People forget that she's really young,' a friend noted. 'The bottom line is, she's only had a few boyfriends in her lifetime.' Even more intriguing was the A Star is Born theory: both Lewis and Paltrow were relatively unknown when Pitt first took up with them. As their screen careers and public profile grew, so Pitt's insecurities came to dominate the relationships. A Hollywood writer who knows Pitt explained, 'Brad has always wanted to be a star. He has an inner drive and he won't allow anything or anyone to interfere with his aspirations. As his power increases, so do his suspicions. It's the star syndrome. You think people are taking advantage of you. You're fearful that people are trying to run your life, to tether you. Brad's relationship with Gwynnie and her family fed into all of that.'

Pitt's partygoing and Paltrow's homely nature were another source of conflict, although Paltrow emphatically denied they had split due to Pitt's flirtatiousness. Jean Black, Pitt's make-up artist and longtime friend, agreed with her: 'When Brad's in love, his loyalty and commitment are beyond reproach. Despite what the press says about him stepping out or whatever, in the eight years I've known him, I've never seen that side of him.'

'The desperation to uncover a reason "why" has produced information that is false, unfair and foolish,' Paltrow concurred in a press statement. 'Not only is Brad Pitt beyond reproach, but he is a man of extreme integrity and goodness.'

The press was also blamed, the excessive interest in the minutiae of their lives supposedly driving the couple apart. As Paltrow said, 'People have pushed too far, climbed over too many fences and scanned too many phone calls. You just get tired of it all.'

'I'd settle for truth,' echoed Pitt on the subject of constant press harrassment. 'Not too much to ask for, is it? But truth doesn't always sell, and on the gossip side, there are some petty people. They talk shit about everyone, and suddenly it's given credibility . . . a story about somebody's misery is more entertaining than a story about somebody's happiness.'

Brad Pitt portraying the living incarnation of the Grim Reaper in Martin Brest's *Meet Joe Black*.

But for now, he was left to deal with the detritus of his two-year relationship. The nude photographs taken two years previously at St. Barts – intrusive pictures that still spoke of happier times – had been reprinted in the August 1997 issue of *Playgirl*, the glossy magazine for women. Splashed across the front cover was the unambiguous tease: 'Brad Pitt Nude'. This time, Pitt leapt into action with his oft-threatened lawsuit, claiming 'invasion of privacy and infliction of emotional distress'. 'Enough's enough,' he fumed. 'I don't feel that when our forefathers made the laws they thought of 600-millimeter lenses. People say, "He's famous, he has no right to privacy." I didn't read that anywhere in the Bill of Rights.'

His suit was only partially successful at first, when Los Angeles Superior Court Judge Robert O'Brien ordered the publisher to cease distribution of that issue but did not order the recall of issues already on news stands. The defence mounted by Playgirl lawyer Kent Raygor emphasised how the photographs were over two years old and had already been published in Europe and on the Internet, without intervention from Pitt. The publicity surrounding the case only served to give the August issue of *Playgirl* immediate collector status, and increase the 'hit' rate on all the Internet sites that still featured the images. However, a second hearing resulted in the complete withdrawal of the magazine from distribution, and the publisher agreeing to pay an undisclosed amount of damages.

Joe Black (Brad Pitt) falling in love with Susan Parrish (Claire Forlani) in *Meet Joe Black*.

While his relationship with Gwyneth Paltrow was dying a sudden death, Brad Pitt had been rehearsing for the role of Death himself. In *Meet Joe Black* (1998), a film loosely based on the 1934 fantasy *Death Takes a Holiday*, Pitt played the title character – the living incarnation of death, who gives up being the Grim Reaper for a while and takes a holiday on earth.

After stealing the body of a handsome young man killed in a road accident at the beginning of the film, Death, rechristened Joe Black, visits a 65-year-old publishing tycoon by the name of William Parrish (*Legends of the Fall* co-star Anthony Hopkins – suggested for the part by Pitt after Gene Hackman backed out). Announcing he has come to deliver Parrish from this life via a fatal heart attack, Black is told that he's 'just some kid dressed in a suit'. 'The suit came with the body I took,' protests Black. But Death does indeed take a holiday when he grants the strangely ethical, unruthless multi-millionaire a stay of execution in order that he might teach him a few lessons on the value of life, and falls in love with Parrish's daughter – a doctor named Susan (Claire Forlani), bemused to find the attractive Joe Black she briefly met in a coffee shop (immediately before his death) has become aloof and introverted. As Susan teaches him of the joys of love and sex, Joe lends a hand to Bill Parrish as predatory businessmen move in on the sick tycoon. Enough leeway is granted for Bill to come to terms with making his final curtain call, giving a grand exit speech at his birthday party before Joe walks him off through a cascade of fireworks.

Pitt was initially sceptical about a plot which had the ageless spirit of mortality introduced to life's beauty by a saintly Rupert Murdoch figure: 'I thought, Marty [Brest]'s made some good movies, but there is no way I'm doin' this picture. And then I got the script. It's actually quite beautiful.' Similarly impressive was his fee. Pitt asked for $20 million and 15-20 per cent of the gross for the role, twice as much as the highest amount he had received for a film. He didn't get it, but did manage to increase his going rate by 75% to $17.5 million – Universal Studios felt it was worth the financial risk, after Pitt's performance in a series of high-grossing films without actually taking top billing. Director Martin Brest (who made *Scent of a Woman*, 1992 and *Beverly Hills Cop*, 1984) started shooting the movie on 10th August 1997, most of Pitt's scenes during the two-month shoot taking place in the Aldrich Mansion in Providence, Rhode Island, owned by the local Catholic Diocese. The original *Death Takes a Holiday* was a whimsical comedy featuring Fredric March as the suave Grim Reaper. Although Pitt had recently insisted he was 'certainly not avoiding romantic comedies', the sedate tone of *Meet Joe Black* was a little more sombre. On set, too, he was not having a good time. Location reports claimed he was depressed by his separation from Paltrow, barely eating or sleeping, and giving an increasingly detached performance. 'It's like he's on autopilot,' said one source. 'She practically left him at the altar, but he dreams they'll reunite.'

Unfortunately, the creative outcome of this melancholic period was no more positive. 'Exiting an advance screening of *Meet Joe Black*,' lamented *Rolling Stone*'s Peter Travers, 'I filed into an elevator with others who had just spent a punishing three hours watching Brad Pitt act like Death . . . One groggy observer raised his bleary eyes and said to no one in particular, "Fucking long."

'Fucking right. *Meet Joe Black* is a movie about death that stubbornly refuses to come to life . . . The movie saddles good actors with one-dimensional roles. And Pitt barely gets that . . . What the role needs is the sly whimsy of Johnny Depp in

Benny and Joon and the soulful longing of Nicolas Cage in *City of Angels*. What it gets is Pitt trapped as a passive bystander – allowed only a few cracks about death and taxes . . .' Richard Schickel agreed, his *Time* review stating that, as the audience watched Martin Brest's film 'disappear into the blond hole of Pitt's affectlessness, we have plenty of time to observe just how profoundly he has misconceived Death.' Pitt portrayed the Grim Reaper, Schickel said, as 'sort of a surfer dude to help us catch the curl of our last wave gracefully,' and pointed out the story's fundamental flaw: why does Death, an immortal figure in every sense, need a rich businessman to introduce him to the essence of existence? 'Who would know more about life than the figure who confronts us in our final moments, when all pride, all pomp, all defences are stripped away?'

Reviewing the film's video release, *TV Guide*'s Maitland McDonagh looked on the bright side of death: 'if you're in the right mood to let it wash over you it's very warm and fizzy indeed.' As for Pitt's performance, she was equivocal: 'he mostly stands around looking boyishly cute, which he does far better than anything else that's asked of him: The scene in which Death trades homespun metaphysical chitchat with a dying Caribbean woman (who sees straight through his toy-boy disguise) in a lilting Jamaican patois is positively painful.' In UK film magazine *Empire*, reviewer Adam Smith concurred: 'Pitt, saddled with an almost impossible role, reveals the profound darkness of his true nature by "walking funny".' He was also much less tolerant of the 'almost unbearably lengthy talking scenes leading to a running time of nearly three hours, leaving the movie like death itself these days, neither quick nor painless.' The crux of his criticism – 'in the end Brest drenches what could have been a pleasing if flimsy rom[antic]com[edy] with money and cheap sentiment, producing a sort of It's a Wonderful Death' – echoed many times around the world.

While Pitt's private life was on the rocks, the film offers continued to flood in. Choosing selectively, however, was not as easy a task as it seemed in the fickle and unpredictable world of Hollywood. He had already been stung by the process of making *The Devil's Own*, and his character's political affiliation in *Seven Years in Tibet*. 'You get caught up in the offers,' Pitt acknowledged. 'They don't always want you for the right reasons. I'm not talking about the money – it's the way they come at you. It's very flattering and they dangle a lot of carrots.'

Some considered Brad Pitt prime superhero material. Fans of Marvel Comics' *The X-Men* voted in an Internet poll for Pitt as the best likely screen personification of Archangel, an angst-ridden X-Man. However, Chris Columbus (*Home Alone*, 1990), then preparing his big-screen version of the Marvel comic, did not take the hint. While the actor was not offered the part, it's hard to gauge whether he would have had any enthusiasm for it after the ersatz comic-book flop of *Cool World*. (Ultimately, Columbus was taken off the project. The successful 2000 production of *X-Men* would be helmed by *Usual Suspects* director Bryan Singer.) One other comic book-style role that he turned down was the lead in the cyberpunk-science fiction film *The Matrix* (1999) – which, thanks to Pitt's first refusal, would revitalise the career of Keanu Reeves.

Ben Stiller – writer-director of teen love story *Reality Bites* (1994), who had previously hoped to make a film about Rolling Stones fans with his friend Pitt – offered him the lead in an adaptation of Scott Smith's novel *A Simple Plan*. The book is a tale of greed and disaster sparked by the main character's discovery of

$4.4 million in a suitcase on a crashed plane. It seemed promising material, but Pitt turned the offer down – though he also persuaded Stiller that neither of them should speak of his refusal, so that other actors would not think the role wasn't worth taking. (Without his star, Stiller would be replaced by director Sam Raimi, who featured Bill Paxsom in the lead of his 1998 production.)

He even refused to consider the part that many would consider a natural for him. 'There's a fantastic, beautiful script on the life of James Dean,' said Pitt of a proposed biopic, for which the producers had also considered Johnny Depp and Leonardo DiCaprio. 'No way would I touch it. I'd be a fool to do it. At best, you could copy him, but there was a magic, an internal magic, that I think you would be foolish even to attempt . . . I couldn't pull it off. And the other guys don't look like him, and that would disappoint the audience.' (Dennis Hopper, the actor who had worked with both Jimmy Dean on *Rebel Without a Cause*, 1955, and Brad Pitt on *True Romance*, begged to differ. 'Brad Pitt has got star quality written all over him,' he said of the actor who, though nine years older than Dean when he died, he considered the best man for the job. 'He's very versatile and has a kind of crazy compulsion.') Reputedly, however, Pitt had a fear of becoming like Donald Turnupseed, 'the guy who pulled out in front of James Dean and decapitated him' – known only by association, for the wrong reason.

Pitt needed a hit film to take his mind off of personal relationship problems, and *Meet Joe Black* was clearly not that film. He was philosophical enough, however, to reflect on his situation and count his blessings. 'Life is tough and it's crooked, but it's pretty fantastic,' he acknowledged. 'I'm starting to be, like, Disappointed Guy [in the eyes of the press], and that's not the case either. Moments like this go in cycles, and it's just when you get comfortable that something's going to mess you up.'

'I think what Brad's saying is "I'm not all fucked up and neurotic,"' explained Alan Pakula, who, despite the difficulties of *The Devil's Own*, had retained a great respect for the actor. 'Complexity to the press can sometimes mean that.'

'One of the scenes I love in Joe Black,' said Pitt, 'is when my character says, "You do the best you can, and if you're lucky, you can take some perfect pictures with you." And I wouldn't trade any of the rotten times. They're vital to defining who you are, what you want, how you want to live.' However, despite his musing on the life-enhancing message of the film, the morbid side of its theme seemed to have rubbed off as he opined, gloomily, of the end of his relationship, 'Loss is one step behind death.'

12 Punching His Weight

The element of Brad Pitt's personality that fights against what is expected of him was hinted at in a 1999 cameo role. 'Once you walk into money,' he had previously acknowledged, 'it separates you, and it separates the outside world's perception of you. That's what I'm afraid of.' *Being John Malkovich* (1999), directed by first-timer Spike Jonze, was a surreal comedy hinged on screenwriter Charlie Kaufman's wacky conceit of people being able to enter the head of intense character actor John Malkovich, one of Pitt's acting heroes, as if it were an apartment room. Recognisable in brief walk-on parts were actors Dustin Hoffman, Michelle Pfeiffer, Winona Ryder, Charlie Sheen, composer Philip Glass – and Brad Pitt, playing himself in a self-mocking send-up of superstar narcissism, smiling brainlessly for the press as he walks up the red carpet to a film premiere.

The end of the 1990s seemed to usher in a more positive cycle of his life. Getting over his relationship with Gwyneth Paltrow, the two remained friendly while Pitt entered into a relationship with Jennifer Aniston, best known as Rachel in the *Friends* sitcom, and Paltrow hooked up with actor-writer Ben Affleck.

Even so, there was a sense that Pitt had to choose his next roles carefully. *The Devil's Own*, *Seven Years in Tibet* and *Meet Joe Black* had all failed at the box office and, to a large degree, in critical terms. It was a crucial period if he wanted to punch his weight as an actor, rather than just coast on the reputation of being a pretty-boy movie star.

Of the savaging received by both *Meet Joe Black* (which Pitt admits to referring to on set as 'Meet Joe's Crack' – though he insists it was 'a term of endearment') and his performance, Pitt later insisted, 'I just figured it was my turn . . . Because, look, I represent the guy who's got everything. I deserve a beating, you know what I'm saying? . . . I'm not that guy. But I see that guy out there sometimes – what he's turned into – and, you know, I want to beat him up. I want to slap him. The me out there who's not me.'

As if out of a sense of synchronicity, his next major role would offer him the chance to both beat up and be beaten. It would also be his most audacious career choice to date, arriving from out of left field. 'Being able to choose is an even greater challenge,' Pitt confirmed. 'Back when I had to take any job I could get, it was easier. I want to do something new, every time out. Wouldn't it be great if I was in a movie and some people didn't even recognise it was me . . .'

'I think he suffers – or feels that he suffers – for his great good looks,' spoke Laura Ziskin, president of corporate production house Fox 2000, of the problem many people wish they had. 'Someone described him as ice cream on the screen. You can't resist him. But I think his good looks become a motivation for him to do something more daring.' At the same time, Pitt emphasised the freedom that wealth can bring, by insisting he would choose projects on the basis of how much they interested him, rather than out of desperation for another success: 'If you start making choices out of fear, you're fucked.'

As it transpired, Ziskin had a very specific project in mind for him. *Fight Club*

'I think his good looks become a motivation for him to do something more daring.' (Laura Ziskin, producer of *Fight Club*)

175

was the debut novel of Oregon service mechanic Chuck Palahniuk. When he wrote it in 1996, scrawling it on a clipboard as he worked under a truck, Palahniuk decided, 'this will never be published, so why censor myself?' Like the narrator of his novel, the author had a job in the motor industry that he regarded as unfulfilling and ultimately meaningless – fixing trucks not in need of repair to note the procedure for maintenance manuals. As inspiration for his malcontent characters, the author based them on friends who felt pretty much the same way as he did. 'It was more like dictation than writing,' Palahniuk said of the book that came fully formed. 'It sort of wrote itself.' One friend, a carpenter, spiced up his life by making salvage raids for materials on condemned buildings; at odds with modern civilisation, his friend Palahniuk noted, 'He's one of those neoromantic people who think if the Y2K bug happens, we'll all be better off.' While the millennial bug never did crash our computers and end our way of life, the carpenter's apocalyptic fantasies became the basis for Tyler Durden: *Fight Club*'s iconoclastic mouthpiece. Another friend, a young woman, became the basis for Marla Singer, an edgy emotional voyeur who gatecrashes illness support groups.

On the back of a buzz created by its publisher and Palahniuk's literary agent, however, the book was optioned by Fox 2000 while it was still in galley form. Its theme, so close to the end of the 20th century, has since been described as 'millennial'; its content is the fantasies and activities (often intertwined) of modern men who feel all meaning and passion has been sucked from their lives by the cold comfort of consumerism. Their response: to go to any extremes to bring the feeling back. Their starting point: one-on-one violence. As Pitt later explained of the film adaptation: 'The point is more to receive a punch [than to throw one]. It's for connection, for direction, for feeling – for some answer to impending numbness.' Or, as Tyler Durden spouts: 'We don't have a great war in our generation, or a great depression, but . . . we have a great war of the spirit. We have a great revolution against the culture. The great depression is our lives.'

As the first of a number of books where marginal characters find meaning in extreme, slyly subversive or terroristic activities, *Fight Club* bought the reclusive Palahniuk – who seems to dislike our sanitised modern culture as much as his character Durden did – a woodland farmhouse outside Portland where he could live, sans TV, cut off from the outside world. Criticised for its supposedly dubious politics, *Fight Club* (1999), the movie, and its creator owe much to the worldview of 19th century German philosopher Friedrich Nietzsche, and his concept of overcoming oneself. 'I volunteer at a homeless shelter because I am terrified of the homeless,' explained Palahniuk. 'I work at a hospice taking care of dying patients because they scare the crap out of me. And a friend took me to her med-school lab so I could dissect cadavers. Until I walked into that room with those three dead bodies and cut their heads off, I was just terrified at the idea. By doing these things, I'm afraid of so much less.' Or, in Nietzsche's words, 'That which does not kill us will make us stronger.' For her part, the friend who inspired the character of Marla was the same friend who arranged for Palahniuk to dissect dead bodies. Her only reciprocal request was that, should Palahniuk ever become famous, she wanted him to arrange for her to meet Brad Pitt.

'I read scripts weekly,' spoke Pitt of the typed bombshell he received. 'After a while you just start seeing the same thing, and you start hearing the same voice. And out of nowhere comes this voice, which is Chuck Palahniuk.' (The screenplay

Entering a more positive cycle of his life, Pitt embarked upon a new romance with *Friends* star Jennifer Aniston.

Brad in the role of Tyler Durden, the iconoclastic mouthpiece of David Fincher's *Fight Club*.

adaptation was in fact written by fellow newcomer Jim Uhls – though he was very faithful to the source material.) For Pitt, *Fight Club* was the answer to his fears of predictability and artistic stagnation. 'At this point you can go into the grocery store and know what aisle to go to to find me,' he reflected. 'I feel this out there. I'm perverting that expectation in this one. There's freedom in that.'

For Ziskin to move forward with what was basically a commercial and critical risk, she also needed a credible director. Enter David Fincher, who, since directing Pitt in the gothic-*noir* thriller *Seven*, had refined his vein of urban paranoia with *The Game* (1997), an extended *Twilight Zone*-like tale of a powerful businessman, played by Michael Douglas, whose life is turned inside out by unseen hands. Though *The Game* was not received as enthusiastically, *Fight Club* promised to fit the thematic territory Fincher had staked out: nightmare cities, where life owed more to his dark imagination than to any documentary-type observation.

As with many, Palahniuk's narrative delivered a shock to Fincher – but it was the shock of recognition: 'I knew who the [main] character was because he was me,' the director admitted. 'At some points in my life, I've said, "If I could just spend the extra money, I could get that sofa and then I'll have the sofa problem handled." As I was reading Chuck's book, I was blushing and feeling horrible. How did this guy know what everyone was thinking? And I also know, just from personal experience, that if I could choose to be someone else, it would be Brad Pitt [in the character of Tyler Durden].'

Second male lead Edward Norton, 29 at the time of the late 1998-early 1999 filming, was chosen to play the first-person narrator (given no name in the novel, referred to as Jack in the film). Already an Oscar nominee for his role as a violent racist skinhead in *American History X* (1998), he said of the director, 'I don't think there's anybody else in our generation who could have made this movie. Fincher is the only one who knows as much about narrative and intention as he does about gels and f-stops and the latest CGI stuff. I think he's – '

'Picking up where [the recently deceased Stanley] Kubrick left off,' interjected Pitt, the co-star who had formed a close rapport with Norton. 'I'm gonna leave that one up to the scholars, but that's what I think.' Praise indeed.

As to the unlikelihood of golden boy Pitt in the role of a leader of the alienated and disaffected, Fincher was having none of it. 'It's probably a character that's closer to Brad in real life than most people would be comfortable knowing,' he insisted. 'There is a childlike sense of anarchy to things that interest Brad. He is a kind of a shit stirrer and one of those people who is, "Huh? Is that the current thinking? I don't really buy that. I have to think about it, more, but that seems like bullshit to me." I think he understood the themes of emasculation and disenfranchisement, as odd as that may seem. I think there's a side of him that said, "OK, I relate."'

Norton agreed: 'I think that Tyler was a great outlet for Brad. He has this great irreverence. Brad's natural instincts are toward flatulent self-exposure, scatology. Tyler was such a creation of Brad's natural mischievous impulses, and I think all his best instincts were set loose by that part . . . there's a highly stylised, comic surrealism where you're breaking that fourth wall and sort of winking at the audience. Brad's great at that wink at the audience.'

Female lead Helena Bonham Carter used the part of Marla – the chain-smoking recovery groupie who gatecrashes Jack's voyeuristic private world – as a calculated departure from her public image as British costume-drama queen. 'She had to be powerful in her own right,' she said of the character who seems always, but not quite, on the edge of self-destruction, 'and not just used and abused. I think Marla is somebody who might use and abuse herself, but it's her choice . . . She's still just the girlfriend [of each of the main characters, though her dogging of Jack leads her to have sex with Durden]. But as girlfriend parts go, it's a pretty great one.' She was, nonetheless, initially cautious about the material: 'I thought it could be very dangerous – provocative for provocative's sake. About how men who feel emasculated need to prove themselves violently, physically, which I've always found faintly pathetic.'

It was a reservation that came to be shared by many critics, but Norton was evangelical in his enthusiasm: '*Fight Club* has a generational energy to it, a protest energy. So much of what's been represented about my generation has been done by the baby boomers. They dismiss us: the word slacker, the oversimplification of the Gen-X mentality as one of hesitancy or negativity. It isn't just aimlessness we feel; it's deep scepticism. It's not slackerdom, it's profound cynicism, even despair, even paralysis, in the face of an onslaught of information and technology.'

Dr. Jekyll and Mr.Hyde; Tyler Durden (Brad Pitt) with Jack (Edward Norton) in *Fight Club*.

Fight Club would ultimately mean many different things to its participants. To Pitt, by now in his mid-thirties, the participants' nihilism seemed part of a personal rather than social malaise: 'I grew up with a lot of structures – my high school, the church, whatever club was going on – and I certainly never felt like I belonged to any of 'em. I never felt a part of those who seemed so exuberant,' Pitt claimed, as if the self-professed 'insider' who made the high school sports teams and hung with the 'cool crowd' was desperate not to be left out of this alienation thing (which rather destroys the point of alienation).

'Every friend I gave it [a viewing copy] to went, "Mmm. Yeah! That's us,"' said Norton of *Fight Club*'s contemporary potency. 'I'm not saying nobody over 45 is going to understand it. But it won't surprise me if a great many people go, "Huh?"' Despite claiming he was no fighter, physically-fit Pitt – who bulked up for the role – and the wiry Norton – who slimmed down – came within a hair's breadth of the real thing. 'I clipped you once, didn't I?' Pitt reminded Norton during press chores for the film. 'In the face. Just enough to wake you up.' Norton concurred, recalling his contact with his co-star's slender six-pack: 'I cracked my thumb on Brad one time. On his stomach. And we both caught knees in the chest. Cracked ribs. Just had the wind knocked out . . . You obviously can't cut loose. But we shot some things wide enough that there was no way to fake it. That's when it got a bit . . .'

'Unchoreographed,' laughed Pitt, remembering the times they came close to a genuine fight club. 'We didn't train a whole lot,' he admitted, 'because these guys aren't supposed to be professional fighters. Again it's not about beating someone up. It's about the experience of a punch, the experience of pain and the wake up that could bring.'

Fight Club opens with a computer graphic sequence representing the main character's 'cave': his internal world, modelled on the anxiety centre of his brain. As the narrative begins, he has a gun held in his mouth by Tyler Durden (Pitt). The camera pans rapidly down 30 storeys as Durden speaks of a bomb that's primed to explode and parked, Oklahoma-bomber style, in a van outside in the street.

In flashback, Jack (Norton) is shown to be a college graduate working for a motor corporation, a cynical job in which he measures the cost of out-of-court settlements against that of recalling vehicle models after fatal accidents. He measures satisfaction in terms of money earned and products consumed, is addicted to buying furniture from IKEA ('I'd flip through catalogues and wonder what kind of dining set defined me as a person') – and is becoming a walking wreck, an insomniac with little sense of self-worth. His only release is to attend support groups for the terminally ill, where he can wallow in an emotional catharsis that allows him to sleep nights. As he puts it, 'When people think you're dying they really listen to you.'

At his first meeting for sufferers of testicular cancer, he encounters two people who will play major roles in the bizarre turn his life is about to take: Bob (rock star Meat Loaf) – a former weightlifter and steroid abuser who, since his gonads were amputated, has developed hermaphroditic breasts – and Marla (Bonham Carter), described in a cancerous metaphor as 'the little scratch on the roof of your mouth that would heal if only you could stop tonguing it'. Marla, tells Jack she has technically more right to attend the group than him. 'Her lie reflected my lie,' he says of the fellow 'tourist' he becomes obsessed with. Eventually, they agree to divide up the support groups between them (Marla gets ascending bowel cancer, Jack gets TB, as Marla's smoking doesn't go down too well).

Jack's life is so meaningless that he fantasises about his plane crashing on inter-state business trips. It is on one such trip that he meets Tyler Durden (Pitt), a louche dude with a goatee beard and 1970s-style clothes, and his life starts to take on new meaning. The (ostensibly accidental) destruction of his home when his apartment suffers a gas explosion ends Jack's yuppie lifestyle. When they meet at a bar, Durden lays the condition for Jack to take refuge in his home: 'I want you to hit me as hard as you can.'

Jack is introduced to the world of Tyler's nihilistic pranks: Tyler splices subliminal images of penises into an animated family film (as with malevolent prankster Guy Grand in Terry Southern's novel *The Magic Christian*, played by Peter Sellers in the 1970 film – an apparent influence on Palahniuk). He urinates in the soup at a posh restaurant where he works part-time. He prints safety information cards to replace those on airplanes, showing passengers about to crash in a state of blind terror. (Fincher made a *Fight Club* trailer which he hoped might be sent to theatres without explanation, where Pitt gives a safety information talk before breaking off to ask, 'Did you know urine is sterile? You can drink it.') He steals and recycles the liposuctioned body fat of the pampered rich, 'the richest cream fat in the world' – then sells it back to them as luxury soap at $20 a bar.

Jack enters the derelict gothic-wreck home of his liberator, where they live as a strange, almost homo-erotic 'odd couple'. Soon, the two men's form of violent catharsis wins adherents all over (and outside) their unnamed city, a silent brotherhood who acknowledge each other by their facial injuries. 'The first rule of Fight Club is,' says Durden, 'you don't talk about Fight Club . . . The third rule of Fight Club – someone yells stop, goes limp, taps out, the fight is over [this is a well-regulated school of brutalism] . . . And the eighth and final rule – if this is your first night at fight club, you have to fight.' The participants of Fight Club become addicted to experiencing pain, fear and anger simply to know that they're truly alive. ('That's what Tyler's saying,' emphasised Fincher. 'How can you exist if you've never had these experiences? You're not really existing, you're just buying all this stuff so that it looks like you have a life. So that when people come over to your house for a glass of Chardonnay, they can go, "Wow, this guy's got it all together."') Challenging Jack to name the historical figures he would like to have fought, Pitt gets the best lines when he states his desire to bash a notorious pugilist (Hemingway) and a revered pacifist (Gandhi).

Jack is soon attending work in a serene but badly battered state, his voiceover offering such useful pieces of information as 'you can swallow a pint of blood before getting sick'. But he is followed to his new home by Marla, after a suicide attempt, who becomes Tyler's (casual) lover rather than his, and causes friction between the two.

Burning Jack's hand with the lye manufactured as a by-product of his 'luxury soap', the ever-more extreme Durden tells him, 'It's only after we've lost everything that we're free to do anything.' His 'masculinist' philosophy encourages enthusiastic fight-clubbers – including big-breasted Bob – to begin a social disruption campaign by comically picking fights at random with strangers. Jack blackmails his boss into a pay-out by threatening to tell about their corporate practices and convincingly beating himself up, all the while screaming, 'please don't hit me again!'

As Durden's extremity escalates, Jack watches in horror as he makes a 'human sacrifice' by threatening to shoot a young Asian convenience store clerk at gunpoint – then releases him on the condition he returns to veterinary school to fulfil his ambitions, and stops wasting his life. Terror is a gift in this sense, reminding the youth, in Tyler's words, 'This is your life, and it's ending one minute at a time.' As the members of Fight Club shave their heads and dress in black shirts, Durden directs a campaign of sabotage he calls Project Mayhem, referring to them as 'Space Monkeys' – after the astronautic chimps sacrificed 'for the greater good' in the 1950s space program. Despite the accusations of 'fascism' levelled at the film, Durden instils his followers with self-loathing equality rather than a 'superman' ethic: 'We are all a part of the same compost heap. We are the all-singing, all-dancing crap of the world.' 'We're the middle children of history, raised by television to believe that someday we'll be millionaires and movie stars and rock stars, but we won't. And we're just learning that, so don't fuck with us.' 'Self-improvement is masturbation, self-destruction might be the answer.' 'Let's evolve – let the chips fall where they may.' As their campaign escalates to setting off explosions, Bob is shot dead and becomes the movement's martyr.

Jack is offended by how Tyler has made Fight Club a vehicle for his own madness – but, when he tracks Marla down, she insists she has been having sex with *him*, and recaps that show him fighting with himself and burning his own hand reveal that Durden is his dark 'doppelgänger'. When Jack tracks down his alter ego, we return to the opening scene of Durden holding Jack at gunpoint as a series of time bombs are about to detonate and blow up skyscrapers belonging to the main credit corporations – though, in a kind of 'terrorism lite', Tyler is considerate enough to ensure no one is left in the buildings. To the backing of grunge-rock band the Pixies' 'Where is My Brain?', Jack destroys Tyler, his Freudian *id*, by shooting *himself* through the face.

In the cartoon-apocalyptic ending, wounded Jack tells Marla, 'You met me at a very strange time in my life,' as massive corporate buildings start to collapse and an insert of a male sex organ appears – onscreen too long to be 'subliminal' this time. (In order to retain his US 'R' rating, Fincher had to insure the penis was not erect, and, most importantly, that it was adorned with black pubic hair, 'so no one would think it was Brad's'.)

Fight Club was essentially a big-budget Hollywood movie ($20 million of its $63 million budget reputedly spent on Pitt's fee alone) that went to great lengths to reach the cutting edge. 'You have to be careful not to say, "*Fight Club* is about the appeal of nihilism, or the cleansing effect of violence or pain,"' Norton insisted to *Premiere*. 'Because that's not what the movie's about. That's what Brad's character is suggesting to mine.'

'As an option,' reinforced Pitt. And this is where *Fight Club* backs off from espousing its main character's dangerously challenging philosophy and becomes much more conventional entertainment – with Tyler Durden revealed as the subconscious of the repressed, conventional Jack, a plot device that harks all the way back to the many versions of *Dr. Jekyll and Mr. Hyde*.

For Pitt, *Fight Club* was the answer to his fears of predictability and artistic stagnation.

'Tyler was such a creation of Brad's natural mischievous impulses,' claimed co-star Edward Norton.

'In *Fight Club*,' observed Ed Norton, 'there is a great subversive inversion of the expectations that are loaded onto Brad. There's this great perversion of the notion of the person who other people wish they were like.' Indeed, in the words of Tyler Durden to his host personality Jack, 'I look the way you want to look; I fuck the way you want to fuck.'

Despite the hard edge, Brad Pitt – face permanently bloodied and bruised once the fight club is up and running – still looks like a bloodied, bruised Adonis. As a testament to how, according to one acquaintance, he 'won the gene pool lottery', his features seem have been adorned with purple beauty marks rather than brutally altered. Ostensibly eschewing a glamour-boy image in favour of something more substantial, Pitt still took the time out to pose in 30 naked torso shots promoting the film. Even his feisty-looking haircut, with the shaven sides, was a love token from glamorous girlfriend Jennifer Aniston. 'Please don't make it a cute moment,' he implored of an interviewer, 'just say she shaved me,' insisting he wanted 'to be mean and ugly'.

'We wanted to shave his head even more,' revealed Fincher, 'but Laura Ziskin was averse to this idea. "Don't make him ugly!" she said. "You broke his teeth, you shave his head – oh my God, what are you doing?"'

At his own suggestion, Pitt had the caps on his front teeth filed down so that they appear slightly broken later in the film. 'It works for the part,' he acknowledged. 'I don't want to make it like Nicolas Cage-eating-the-cockroach-sensationalism kind of thing. I chipped my teeth as a kid, so I have the luxury of playing with the teeth as another bit of the arsenal to adapt to the character . . . It's just that little bit extra; it's the detail you find in a great painting, in a great song.'

With his professed lack of concern about dentistry, and his cigarette-smoking habit, Pitt is a minor dissident in California, with its 'health fascism' and belief in cosmetic perfection. 'You are not your haircut,' he insisted, deliberately copying Tyler Durden. 'You are not your shiny white teeth . . . I find this kind of focus on exterior beauty, things, clothes, cars, truly insidiously damaging.'

As an attack on consumerism and the yuppie ethic, however, *Fight Club* is only skin-deep. Durden preaches that, 'You are not your bank account. You are not the clothes you wear. You are not the contents of your wallet' – but this was ironic, to say the least, for the wealthy movie star renowned for the fine taste with which he furnished and decorated his Californian Craftsman-style house. 'Can I just tell you the most offensive thing about Pitt?' film producer Paul Feldsher, a personal friend, joked with a *Vanity Fair* journalist. 'He's got all this money, he's really well paid, and he's got really good taste. That's fucked. It's so much easier to take when someone with money spends it on really hideous things, but Pitt has an unbelieveable eye. We can walk into a store together and he'll see the tiniest thing that anyone might have missed, and he'll nail it right away.'

And this from the man whose onscreen rhetoric contained the line, 'Fuck Martha Stewart', an attack on the US media's queen of 'home and lifestyle'. In fact, when *Fight Club* itself became a commercial commodity – spawning posters, videos and DVDs – the ultimate irony was contained in the words of Tyler Durden, intoned by Pitt, over a soundtrack cut by techno-dance duo the Dust Brothers:

Tyler steals and recycles the liposuctioned body fat of the pampered rich then sells it back to them as luxury soap.

Helena Bonham-Carter in the role of neurotic, chain-smoking Marla in *Fight Club*.

'Deliver me from Swedish furniture. Deliver me from clever art.'

'The question has to be asked: "What track are we on?"' insisted Pitt of the 'message' that diverged from his own lifestyle. 'Tyler starts out in the movie saying, "Man, I know all these things are supposed to seem important to us – the car, the condo, our versions of success – but if that's the case, why is the general feeling out there reflecting more impotence and isolation and desperation and loneliness?" If you ask me, I say, "Toss all this, we gotta find something else." . . . I'm the guy who's got everything, I know. But I'm telling you, once you've got everything, then you're just left with yourself . . . it doesn't help you sleep any better, and you don't wake up any better because of it. Now, no one's going to want to hear that. I understand it. I'm sorry,' he apologised audaciously, 'I'm the guy who's got to say it.'

As to what was going to sell the film, however, he was more cynically realistic: 'It'll get caught in the morality net. We're gonna get hammered. The week that Seven came out, [talk show host] Kathie Lee Gifford said on her show, "It is your moral imperative to avoid this movie." If we don't get that on this one, then we've done something wrong.'

On that count, *Fight Club* did very well indeed – perhaps a little better than anticipated, when it was denounced for extolling neo-Nazism. After the preview screening at the Venice Film Festival in September 1999, 'We were just standing up out of our seats,' testified Norton, 'and Brad turned to me and said, "I can't imagine that I'll ever be in a better movie than that."' However, those critics who disapproved reacted with near-hysteria. (As with Quentin Tarantino's *Reservoir Dogs*, 1992, *Fight Club* was already gaining a much exaggerated reputation as 'the

Despite the hard-edged appearance of Tyler Durden, Brad still looks like a bloodied, bruised Adonis.

most violent film ever made'.)

Most extreme was Alexander Walker of the London *Evening Standard*, who, professing himself an opponent of censorship, tends to bewail any film that offends his sensibilities. Norton's point about the generational perception gap could not have been better illustrated. *Fight Club*, according to Walker, was 'an inadmissible assault on personal decency . . . The [fight club] members are predominantly blue-collar, working-class casual workers, the very people from whom the Nazis drew their most brutal bully boys . . . it uncritically enshrines principles that once underpinned the politics of fascism, and ultimately sent millions of Jews to the death camps . . . The comparisons with what the Nazis did to the Jews, whose bones and fat they rendered for bars of soap, was being openly recalled by Jewish critics in Venice . . . In any well-adjusted society, its stars would feel a backlash of public indignation well beyond the box-office. Edward Norton is one of America's most gifted actors; Brad Pitt one of its most personable. Both, curiously, played Nazis in two earlier films, *American History X* and *Seven Years in Tibet*. For their future good, they should explore the world beyond *Mein Kampf*.'

It should be stressed here that, despite the many horrors of the Nazi Holocaust, accusations that soap was made from human fat have never been scientifically confirmed. And, as Amy Taubin said in her article on *Fight Club* in *Sight and Sound*, 'if you've ever lived in LA, where women have fat suctioned out of their bodies as casually as they go to the hairdresser, your first association would not be with Nazi concentration camps. Misogyny, maybe; anti-Semitism, no.' The nearest thing to Nazism in the movie is the agents of Project Mayhem chanting, 'His name is Robert Paulsen!' of the deceased Bob – reminscent of the Nazi martyr Horst Wessel – but this is in the spirit of black comedy, as is Durden's claim that home-made napalm is easily manufactured from gasoline and orange-juice concentrate (which also made Mr Walker apoplectic).

Even Roger Ebert, often one of the USA's more perceptive critics, contended, '*Fight Club* is the most frankly and cheerfully fascist big-star movie since *Death Wish* . . . It's macho-porn – the sex movie Hollywood has been moving toward for years, in which eroticism between the sexes is replaced by all-guy locker room fights . . . The fact that it is very well made and has a great first act certainly clouds the issue.' Ebert complained, rather snobbishly, 'the movie stops being smart and savage and witty, and turns to some of the most brutal, unremitting, non-stop violence ever filmed . . . Although sophisticates will be able to rationalise the movie against the behaviour it shows, my guess is that audiences will like the behaviour but not the argument . . . they'll buy tickets because they can see Pitt and Norton pounding on each other; a lot more people will leave this movie and get in fights than will leave it discussing Tyler Durden's moral philosophy . . . the message in *Fight Club* is like bleeding scraps of Socially Redeeming Content thrown to the howling mob . . . *Fight Club* is a thrill ride masquerading as philosophy.' (This particular philosophy being heavily influenced by Nietzsche – the shadows of whose 'superman' ethos, adopted by the Far Right, worried Walker and Ebert, though the German philosopher rejected his countrymen's anti-Semitism.)

'What is heaven supposed to be?' responded Pitt, to the politically-correct idea that no one should ever give offence or instigate conflict. 'Where no one says anything bad about each other? Where everyone's helpful? You're basically talking about boredom . . . The point is, don't pacify yourself.'

In the UK, the British Film Board of Film Classification were concerned enough to cut two scenes of violence: 'in the first Brad Pitt is beaten up at length. The second is where Ed Norton beats up a blond boy to ruin his looks. We're quite stern . . . on promoting sadism as a source of pleasure . . . here the point was made and then followed by a long scene where a helpless victim has his face smashed up.'

In *The Guardian*, Peter Bradshaw praised 'a witty and seductive performance from Brad Pitt who has never been better' but attacked the film as 'a strident, shallow, pretentious bore with a "twist" ending that doesn't work' (and, it should be said, owes something to *Performance*, 1970 – the surreal drama that ends with gangster James Fox shooting decadent rock star Mick Jagger in the head, only for Jagger to take over the thug's mind and body in the final frames). 'Frankly, as Brad ponces about the place with his trousers hitched down to his hips, to show off as much pert musculature as possible,' mocked Bradshaw, 'he looks like he couldn't fight his way out of a pair of Calvin Klein boxer briefs. Has anyone connected with this film ever actually been in any fights?' Amy Taubin in *Sight and Sound*, on the other hand, was entranced: 'Pitt, who has never been as exquisite as he is with a broken nose and blood streaming down his cut body, emerges as an actor of economy and control who can rivet attention merely by turning his head.'

Ultimately, critical hand-wringing was insignificant in the face of approval from the target audience (though the film was not the commercial success Fox had hoped for). '*Fight Club* Kicks Yuppie Ass' ran the heading on the *Coffee Shop Times* website. '*Fight Club* is the gun to the head of consumerist America,' reviewer Robert Zimmer, Jr. announced with excitement. 'The pistol's cocked. Say what you will about the explicit nature of the fight scenes, or director Fincher's tendency to trip up his storytelling with his fixation on stylism – he wants us to stop reading the J. Crew catalogue, turn off Must See TV, and ask what the hell our lives really mean.' As the fan cult around *Fight Club* grew, so it was assumed that Chuck Palahniuk had based his concept on a real-life phenomenon. The author was amused to find that people (particularly women) would beg him to take them along to attend the secret fight clubs he had obviously gained access to. 'I'll be like, "No, it's made up; it's fake,"' he admitted. 'It just breaks people's hearts.' When informed that 'fight clubs', of a kind, did actually exist, the author expressed his approval: 'If there wasn't a need, people wouldn't do it. And I'd rather have them beating the crap out of each other than walking into McDonald's with a sawed-off shotgun.' But the genuine fight-club culture had more to do with traditional fisticuffs than philosophical masochism - particularly in Britain, where unlicensed and bareknuckle boxing would become familiar territory to a pugnacious Pitt.

Tabloid press speculation, meanwhile, was more concerned about the seriousness of Brad Pitt's relationship with Jennifer Aniston than with the meaning of *Fight Club*.

Pitt had first become involved with her on the rebound from Gwyneth Paltrow, back in summer 1998. In her mid-twenties, *Friends* star Ms. Aniston was already a veteran of showbusiness – daughter of a Greek actor named John Anastassakis, she was the god-daughter of Greek-American *Kojak* star Telly Savalas, and first appeared on television at the age of 15. If anyone was primed to survive the pressures of a Hollywood relationship, it was Jennifer Aniston – indeed, her first date with Pitt was reputedly brokered by agents working on behalf of them both.

The press asked the usual intrusive questions, speaking aloud to themselves: Was there any future in a relationship with a serial break-up artist? Was marriage even a remote possibility, given his track record? Pitt's response to the prying was sanguine. 'What's a bigger high?' he asked in return. 'Spending your life with another – I feel I'd be quite good at it. If I find it, I find it. If I don't, I don't. But I think that with another person in your life you have the opportunity to get further, to grow more.'

In August 1999, after *Fight Club* had wrapped, Bill and Jane Pitt had been flown by their son from Springfield, Missouri to Hollywood to get to know the woman the press pegged as a potential daughter-in-law. As part of their holiday itinerary, the aesthete Pitt took them to see original houses built by the legendary modernist architect Frank Lloyd Wright up in the Hollywood hills. Over the past year, he had taken Aniston on tours of Mediterranean Europe and the North African coast, and on a holiday to Acapulco, Mexico that the gossip columns referred to as a 'trial honeymoon'. In Portugal, they had sought an unlikely anonymity under the names of 'Mr. and Mrs. Vegas'; at the Alhambra Moorish palace in Granada, Spain, upon recognition they agreed to pose for photographers for five minutes. 'Then they'd fuck off,' Pitt casually related, 'and you'd find them in the bushes half an hour later, because they've got that pic with us picking our nose or scratching our sweaty crack.' (Photos of Pitt and Aniston's Spanish holiday would later be syndicated worldwide.)

In sequel to these romantic sojourns, Pitt also gave Aniston a three-carat diamond ring which – despite prompting from the press – the actress never referred to as an engagement ring. Making stories out of speculation, unconfirmed reports linked her recent visible loss of weight to the insecurity she supposedly felt about their relationship. 'They have a perception of Jen from the show [*Friends*] and they take her character as being man needy,' complained Pitt, 'and so they present her in that way, chasing, and they create this whole scenario, and then they say we're getting married, and because I did a movie about Tibet and because she's Greek, we're going to have a Tibetan-slash-Greek wedding, and we're going to ride yaks into the sunset.'

But all this speculation, according to Pitt, was simply on account of their not providing the press with the sideshow they wanted. 'We just didn't participate,' he asserted. 'We just wanted to see if something was going to grow on its own without any outside influence. We just wanted to keep it special. Keep it ours.'

Back home in Springfield, Missouri, with the mom and dad who were reputedly very enamoured of his new girlfriend, Pitt indulged his aesthetic interest in architecture by working with his father on a property development site. 'We're going to do something where everybody's got land and space,' he said of their 50-house development. 'I'm in a frenzy. I want to build cities! I'm quite mad with it.' Speaking of his immersion in architectural design, and how he would also like to open a 'chair museum', influenced by art-deco architect and chair designer Charles Rennie Mackintosh, Pitt made a telling observation: 'I've noticed that if I was ever in a chaotic relationship, I was always very into linear thinking, very proportion-divided off, very strict, almost like Frank Lloyd Wright, in a sense. In this relationship thing I'm in now, I find myself going more toward the whimsical, this free-flowing, free-form architecture. I respond more to cleanness and a modern perspective.'

Pitt had lived through enough public relationships to know not to look for some fairy-tale romance. 'It's not love itself that to me brings on happiness,' he reflected aloud. 'I'm just saying more perspective [makes for a sense of well-being] . . . As we're going into the 21st century, I think we're far enough along – we know enough now, that no one can save you. I go crazy when I read a script and one character says, "I can't live without you." It drives me crazy. Because we're teaching the wrong thing . . . it falls into the happily-ever-after bullshit that does not exist.'

While Pitt spoke of love in existential terms, he admitted it was largely due to his sensitivity about the press: 'The gauge comes up and I start monitoring when we start talking about the relationship, only because of the ways it's been perverted in the past, and I'm hypersensitive. But I will say this about Jen: she's fantastic, she's complicated, she's wise, she's fair, she has great empathy for others . . . and she's just so cool.'

With such equilibrium in his emotional life, only the smallest dark clouds blotted the domestic horizon. Court orders had to be taken out against an obsessive female stalker, 19-year-old Athena Rolando, who broke into one of Pitt's houses during his absence and reputedly spent ten hours in his underwear – briefly becoming a kind of mini-celebrity herself in the US media. 'But who wants to hear me complain?' acknowledged Pitt, keeping his sense of proportion. 'What's the point? I don't have a say. It doesn't surprise me. It doesn't alarm me, either. It's gross, and it's what I expect.'

Less predictable was his decision to appear on a summer 1999 cover of *Rolling Stone* wearing a dress. Purportedly a comment on his perceived 'male bimbo'

Brad claims of Jennifer, 'She's fantastic, she's complicated, she's wise, she's fair, she has great empathy for others . . . and she's just so cool.'

status, Pitt was obscure about his intent, claiming he 'just wanted to create some other world – some alternative to modern living'. The male sex symbol getting in touch with his female side had, it seemed, joined the wealthy anti-materialist and the non-violent pugilist as the latest in a line of rich contradictions.

The non-violent pugilist was soon to raise his bruised head again – resurrected by a casual meeting Pitt had a couple of years earlier. Guy Ritchie, then 31, director of frantic British gangland comedy *Lock, Stock and Two Smoking Barrels* (1997) and, later, amour of Madonna, received an unexpected call when he was on a promotional visit to Hollywood. Pitt had an admiration for the Brit gangster film – 'it's got this great energy, the way it weaves these characters together,' he observed, calling it 'pretty genius'. 'So I went knocking on his door,' said the Hollywood superstar, as if it was an everyday event. 'I called him up and said, "Loved it, got anything in the next one?" And he told me about this Irish fighter guy.'

'I never really expected him to say yes,' admitted Ritchie. 'But he came through.' Indeed, with a total working budget of £3 million, approximately one quarter of the actor's highest fee thus far, Ritchie's next compendium of criminal caricatures, *Snatch* (2000), could be said to benefit from Brad Pitt's charitable nature – and his fondness for playing against type. 'I think the original character was supposed to be about 300 pounds,' Pitt admitted, 'but somehow it still fit. He [Ritchie] just made it work.'

However, Pitt was not motivated by charity so much as admiration. 'He fulfils for me some kind of [Sam] Peckinpah fantasy,' he compared the brash former pop-video director and karate black-belt to the late American frontiersman director. 'Anyone who says he's arrogant is threatened by the fact that he knows what he wants. He has absolute faith in his decisions – not that he's going to make the right decision, but that, if it is not right, he has capabilities to figure it out.'

Shooting in December 1999, Pitt, with Jennifer Aniston in tow, drifted amiably into the London pub culture. Renting a flat, he also turned up everywhere from a go-kart track in Battersea to quaint countryside pubs. 'He won us all over,' confirmed co-star and ex-footballer Vinnie Jones, as well known in his soccer days for his violent temper as for his playing skills. 'My attitude is that I don't care whether you're Brad Pitt or Billy the builder, this is me and either we have a crack together and enjoy each other's company or we don't.' Thankfully, Pitt was 'up for the crack', as they say. 'I've read some rubbish printed about Brad,' confirmed Jones, 'but I kept my opinions to myself until I met the geezer . . . He's as straightforward as they come. There's nothing else to look for other than what you see. He liked a game of cards in his trailer – well, you couldn't call it much of a trailer – and his was always the busiest place on set.'

As fellow *Lock, Stock* veteran Jason Statham confirmed, Pitt 'lost plenty at poker', but was happy to be a part of such an unpretentious ensemble. 'He's one of the only Hollywood people I've ever met who isn't constantly looking over your shoulder,' said co-star and near-namesake Jason Flemyng. 'I was worried,' admitted Ritchie's producer, Matthew Vaughan, 'because on *Lock, Stock* . . . everyone got on with each other and there was a brilliant team spirit. I thought that Brad's presence would throw all that away. But, to my surprise, he contributed towards it.'

'The cast of *Snatch* blew me away,' enthused Pitt, taken with the quaint British vernacular. 'These guys, you would think that the movie was secondary to them.

From Hollywood heartthrob to pure 'pikey' as 'One Punch Mickey' O'Neil in Guy Ritchie's Brit-flick *Snatch*.

Guy Ritchie, director of *Snatch*, on location with Brad Pitt.

They're having chess battles in between set-ups for the shot, shouting, "Fuck you, you cunt!" As a loner, I was really taken with the camaraderie these guys have together.'

'Brad's a film star in the Paul Newman-y sense. I can understand what the kids go bonkers about,' said Ritchie, paying back the compliments. Having confessed to early reservations about employing a pretty-boy Hollywood actor on a Brit flick full of rough-house character actors, the director came clean with his opinion: 'I don't mean to blow smoke up his ass, but he was experimental, interesting, and intelligent.'

For his role of Irish bare-knuckle fighter 'One Punch Mickey' O'Neil, Pitt went through a change of visual image that took him from Hollywood golden boy to pure 'pikey' in leather trilby and stubble. The first step was to emblazon his body with temporary (though authentic-looking) tattoos, provided by specialists Images in Ink: the Madonna (the Virgin Mary, not Ritchie's fiancé) and red roses on his chest and abdomen, with a snake appearing out of his pants; the Last Supper of Christ and a dove of peace on his back; and, as described by make-up artist Fae Hammond, 'At Brad's own request we added a dog and a running man on his wrist. It was all in an ink that lasts three days, during which time he couldn't have a shower.' Apologising for his lived-in odour, he also had to be given a lived-in face. 'We had to get rid of the golden boy look,' confirmed Hammond. 'He also had a false bridge added to his nose to give it a thicker edge because he has a perfectly shaped nose of his own which looked wrong.'

To complement the boxer's nose, he had to train in basic boxing skills that had not been required for *Fight Club*. Pitt's trainer was a Romany gypsy named Bobby

Frankham – tipped as a possible British light-heavyweight champion, until an unfortunate 1987 incident when he punched a referee – who Pitt visited on a traveller's site in Watford, a satellite town on the M1 motorway outside London, with a British bodyguard known as 'Safety Dave' in tow. Since his expulsion from mainstream boxing, Frankham had fought a long string of bare-knuckle fights on gypsy encampments across the UK, all of which he claimed were undefeated. 'My mum cooked him a typical gypsy meal [of wild rabbit stew], and he loved it,' said a clearly impressed Frankham. 'He . . . just sat outside the mobile home, laughing and joking with everyone.' (Despite Pitt's easy-going affability, he later conceded in a US interview: '*Snatch* was definitely scuzzy, but they lived in trailer parks, so there was no way around that.')

Pitt was praised by Frankham for his physical fitness and for 'studying my mannerisms'. 'He is all muscle and looks the part,' acknowledged Ricky English, a professional boxing coach on hand to teach Pitt the Marquess of Queensbury rules. Pitt would tell the audience on Jay Leno's chat show how this new image, created by *Fight Club*, and subsequently *Snatch*, was pure play-acting: 'I'm not a fighter. I don't like hitting people, I don't like getting hit . . . It hurts! . . . I want no part of it,' he protested, joking that his last real-life fight was 'back in 1982,' when he 'ended up squeezing the guy's satchel'. As he joked of his need for prosthetic make-

For the role of Mickey in *Snatch*, Brad needed prosthetic make-up to mis-shape the otherwise perfect bridge of his nose.

up, 'I got this kinda cute pixie nose. That says: this guy doesn't fight.'

Despite this, English claimed of Pitt, 'Like Ray Winstone [a considerably chubbier hard-man – veteran of Brit crime dramas from *Scum*, 1979, to *Sexy Beast*, 2000], he could have been a fighter if he had not gone into acting. He has all the right attributes.'

Finding an authentic voice for One Punch Mickey was, Pitt admitted, 'the 40-foot free-throw with 3 seconds left on the clock . . . 3 days before I was supposed to start this thing, I was in a panic, I couldn't figure what I was supposed to do . . . I had a head start,' he admitted, 'I've done an Irish accent before, a Northern accent . . . first you start with a melody, everything kind of goes up, it's all very lyrical.' In terms of professional chemistry, however, Pitt took his lead from a stateside contemporary: Benicio Del Torro, appearing in the film as 'Frank Four Fingers'. 'In trying to find my character for *Snatch*, I looked to what Benicio did in *The Usual Suspects*,' he confirmed of the near-unintelligible Puerto Rican character Fenster, replicating the effect with an Irish accent. 'He was kinda the first guy that made it OK to be incomprehensible, and so, borrowing from him, we went with this and it really worked out for us.'

To stress the distinctive accent of the Irish 'tinkers', as opposed to the Romany 'pikeys' (descended from the original Middle-Eastern gypsies) who had taught him to box bare-knuckle, Vinnie Jones also 'hooked him up with some gypsy friends just south of London. Brad visited them for a day and just nailed it, like he'd been speaking that way all his life.' Indeed, Ritchie claimed one of the most delicious aspects of making *Snatch* was obtaining the services of a superstar who normally commands a multi-million dollar fee, then having him speak unintelligibly throughout. At one point, he claimed, he was thinking of having him subtitled.

Though on an equal billing with several other characters, Pitt's One Punch Mickey is central to the frenetic plot of *Snatch*, for which – with so many characters whose fragments of story cut across each other – Ritchie felt obliged to make freeze-frame introductions: Jewish-American thief Franky Four Fingers (Benicio Del Toro) is acting as courier for an 86-carat diamond stolen from a jeweller's in Belgium; on his way back to meet with gangland fence Avi (Dennis Farina) in New York, he stops off to place a bet on an unlicensed boxing tournament in London; it's here that he has a nasty run-in with gun runner and ex-KGB agent Boris the Blade (Rade Sherbedgia), and is himself snatched by two black pawnshop owners, Sol and Vinnie (Lennie James and Robbie Gee), and their massively corpulent driver Tyrone (Ade), out to rip off the diamond.

While Bullet-Tooth Tony (Vinnie Jones) is hired by Avi to get the diamond back, One-Punch Mickey O'Neil (Pitt) is recruited as a replacement in the bare-knuckle boxing tournament by new promoters Turkish (Jason Statham) and Tommy (Stephen Graham), and told to go down in the fourth round. However, Mickey has his own ideas, as he wants to win the bout and buy his old mother a mobile home. But the ominous shadow of grey-haired local villain Brick Top (Alan Ford) falls over the event, and Turkish, Mickey and his family all run the risk of being disposed of at Brick Top's country smallholding – chopped up and mixed with pig swill, as is his habit. Add to this a further 'snatch' from the Anglo-Jewish jewellery market of Hatton Garden, and the film becomes a bloody farce in the most enjoyable sense.

In many ways, the film is an extended remake of *Lock, Stock and Two Smoking Barrels* – though Jews, Americans, Irish tinkers (or gypsies) and West Indians are

Brad was accepted as 'one of the lads' by the predominantly British male cast of *Snatch*.

added to the range of coarse Anglo-Saxon characters. Vinnie Jones' Bullet-Tooth Tony is the same basic menacing enforcer/collector as Big Chris in the previous film, at one point repeating his schtick of slamming people's heads in doors (accompanied on the soundtrack by Ritchie's fiancé Madonna singing 'Evening Star'), and the violence is both more cartoonish and more excessive: an unfortunate dog gets opened up when he's believed to have swallowed the diamond; more gruesome and yet more comical, the black gang from the pawnbrokers' shop are fed to Black Top's pigs.

Pitt was accepted both as an ensemble player and as 'one of the lads': to the extent where a return trip to attend the film's August 2000 premier entailed a night's drinking at Walthamstow Greyhound Stadium in east London, courtesy of dog-racer Vinnie Jones (with Jones' advice on 'form', Pitt even managed to back some winners), then back to where the other half live – a £2,000-a-night penthouse suite in central London's Metropolitan Hotel, where Pitt, Ritchie and their mates ordered up 48 cans of Guinness and four packs of cards, so that they could drink and play poker till dawn. (Adopting Irish inflexions had helped Pitt develop Irish tastes – he subsequently installed an Irish-style pub, complete with Guinness pump, at his Hollywood home.)

The following evening, Pitt was met by the sight of 4,000 fans, mostly teenage girls, pushing against the barriers outside the premiere of *Snatch* at London's Leicester Square Odeon. Stepping out for a while to shake hands and talk to them, he told the police inspector charged with controlling the crowd, 'I owe it to them [the fans]. I want to say hello.' Informed that some young fans were being crushed at the front of the barriers, and threatened with arrest if he didn't help defuse the hysteria, Pitt reluctantly withdrew.

In its homeland, the press made no bones about the derivative (if enjoyable) nature of the film. Unfairly attacking him for sparking off the 1990s Brit-gangster genre, old-school Brit film-maker Sir Richard Attenborough accused Ritchie of propagating 'the pornography of violence'. *Empire* magazine's critic, Andrew Collins, was more realistic about his appeal: 'Guy Ritchie is Quentin Tarantino. Young, visionary writer-director makes big splash with debut feature: a cheap, stylised crime caper that meshes snappy dialogue with excessive gunplay and a hip soundtrack. But . . . for the all-important follow-up, did he [Tarantino] remake *Reservoir Dogs*? No. But that, in effect, is what Ritchie has done with *Snatch*. This should have been – but isn't – his *Pulp Fiction* . . . as a director he's unsurprisingly prone to every pop-video camera trick in the box, and as a writer he's almost pantomime. In terms of his heavily-stamped trademark style, *Snatch* is identical to *Lock, Stock* . . . Why bother?' The review did concede, however, 'if you liked *Lock, Stock*, you'll like this . . . even though *Snatch* is almost actionably similar . . . for many that will be its selling point.' As for the film's US import, praise was unequivocal: 'Pitt pitches his indecipherable "pikey" just right, drawing on the physicality of *Fight Club*, the insanity of *Twelve Monkeys* and the dodgy accent of *The Devil's Own*.'

Back on the golden boy's home ground, the *San Francisco Examiner*'s Joe Leydon agreed with the general assessment of his director: 'Once again, Ritchie has greedily ransacked assorted pop-culture sources – everything from Quentin Tarantino to Damon Runyon, from '30s gangster melodramas to '70s blaxploitation flicks – to concoct a crafty crazy quilt of farcical comedy, ferocious mayhem and fast-break exuberence. [In fairness to Ritchie, the idea of stealing inspiration from Tarantino – who gleaned inspiration for his own crime movies from many sources, including blaxploitation – is on the level of one thief robbing another.] . . . There is a great deal less artistry than artifice in this frenetic pastiche. But Ritchie is ingeniously clever in constructing his knotty plot, and earns extra points for tying the various threads together with such a satisfying flourish in the final scenes.'

As for the cast, 'There are no real heroes to speak of, but the actors are everything they need to be for this shaggy-dog story to have appropriate bite. And a few notables – especially Statham, Jones, Farina and Pitt – actually manage to generate a rooting interest in their disreputable characters.' In *Rolling Stone*, Peter Travers was more specific in his praise: 'Brad Pitt has more fun than anybody as Mickey O'Neil, an Irish gypsy, mama's boy and lethal bare-knuckle boxer . . . Pitt's indecipherable accent is a one-joke hoot on which the actor plays hilarious variations.'

In the interim, while the world was Brad Pitt's oyster he was more tightly focused on his private universe. In the 1910-built house in East Hollywood where he was experimenting with his own ideas of interior design ('I'm interested in ways to make minimalism seem warm,' he claimed, influenced by the modernist and 'organic' styles of Lloyd Wright and his contemporaries), his mooted 'chair museum' seemed to be getting underway. As described by *Esquire* magazine, the interior contained, 'A retro bubble chair lined with fake fur. Tan leather sofas. A metal chair that slides in and out of the wall. A love seat at the foot of the stairs, for when you are so in love, you can't make it to the next floor without stopping to smooch.' Pitt's creativity was impressive, but these were the kind of items that, if they went on sale at an upmarket furniture store, would make Tyler Durden declare war on society.

As ever with Pitt, some short-term working acquaintances had become long-term friends. Jason Flemyng, from *Snatch*, went out to dinner with Brad and Jennifer while he was working in LA: 'this will sound strange,' he almost apologised, 'but it was so nice to be around normal people. We just ate Mexican food and talked nonsense.' As for Pitt's companion, Flemyng could not have been more taken – Aniston was 'a female Brad. Couldn't be more gorgeous, yet utterly without vanity.' It seemed as if they were finally fulfilling the role of the perfect Hollywood couple that Pitt and Gwyneth Paltrow had once given up. 'They finish each other's sentences,' remarked a personal friend, film director James Gray, 'they're two peas in a pod. Gray recalled dining with them in April 2000, two months after Pitt ended his stint on *Snatch* and was trying, unsuccessfully, to give up smoking: 'Jennifer was telling him to wear his patch. She's trying to get him not to smoke, but she smokes. He says, "Don't smoke either, honey!" and she says, "Well you quit first!" They're perfect together.'

As to his own relationship, Pitt claimed, almost clinically, 'I've done my homework. I want to know why things go wrong, when I'm culpable and when I'm not. I want to know why some relationships work and some don't. I want to know how I can not make the same mistakes.'

On 27th July, 2000, it seemed that Brad Pitt had finally put the mistakes in his emotional life behind him. His press spokeswoman, Cindy Guagenti, announced that the much speculated-upon wedding of Pitt and Jennifer Aniston would take place in two days time. The official announcement was, however, pre-empted by a more personal communication. 'Brad didn't want Gwyneth to find out from the media that he was getting married,' revealed a friend to the tabloids, 'and knew on Tuesday [the 25th] that he wouldn't be able to avoid a public confirmation for much longer. So he called her up to tell her it was happening and to say that he hoped she'd be happy for him.'

'Gwyneth very graciously gave her blessing,' confirmed a Paltrow family friend on their behalf, 'but obviously out of respect for Jennifer she will not be attending the wedding.' (All other guests had been invited, and sworn to secrecy, several weeks previously.) Pitt, who had invited Paltrow to attend, attributed his current calmness and happiness to his bride-to-be, claiming, 'Jen's taught me to meditate and communicate in a more Zen-like fashion.' To a contented Brad Pitt, there was every reason to reconcile his emotional past and future, and keep everybody as one big happy circle of friends.

13 A Poster Boy for Manhood

The venue for the wedding of Brad Pitt and Jennifer Aniston, on Saturday 29th July, 2000, was kept a secret until the very last moment. It was eventually revealed as the massive beachfront mansion of millionaire TV executive, Marcy Carsey – producer of *Roseanne* and *The Cosby Show* – in the exclusive Californian neighbourhood of Malibu. Jennifer Aniston had happily told friends that she wanted the wedding 'all of Hollywood never forgets'. She was not to be disappointed.

The cost was budgeted at a cool $1 million – which included minor extravagances such as $25,000 for floral arrangements from La Premiere of Beverly Hills (including lotus flowers floating in a specially built fountain – 'Brad wanted the Zen garden look', explained one of the florists, enhanced by brown sugar candles imported from Thailand to decorate the reception marquee), and $7,000 for a firework display ('they wanted it big, grandiose, the greatest effects that we had,' the pyrotechnic company said of their 13-minute display). The 200 guests included all but one of Aniston's *Friends* co-stars – Courtney Cox, Matthew Perry, Lisa Kudrow and David Schwimmer, with Matt LeBlanc sending his apologies from Hungary, where he was filming – Pitt's former co-stars Sir Anthony Hopkins (*Legends of the Fall* and *Meet Joe Black*), Morgan Freeman (*Seven*), Bruce Willis (*Twelve Monkeys*), Edward Norton (*Fight Club*), actresses Cameron Diaz and Salma Hayek, Guy Ritchie and Madonna, rock star Sting and his actress wife Trudie Styler. (In the weeks running up to the big event, Brad and Jennifer had joined the former Police vocalist on stage at the Beacon Theatre in New York City, where he serenaded them with his new single 'Fill 'Er Up': 'We're going to get wed / So fill 'er up, son / Don't be staring / That's real diamonds she'll be wearing.')

Security was tight, but then the bride and groom were concerned about one particular prospective gatecrasher: the besotted Athena Rolando, who had failed to attend psychiatric counselling sessions in the wake of her conviction for stalking Brad. Pitt made provision by hiring security consultant Moshe Alon – a former agent of Mossad, the Israeli secret service, who, since coming to Hollywood, had worked for ageing glamour queen Elizabeth Taylor – to keep out both unwanted guests and, most crucially, uninvited members of the press. Reputedly, there were almost as many security guards as guests, with Alon's team backed up by a complement from the local sheriff's department. To supplement these precautions, all guests had to sign confidentiality agreements – with the incredible penalty of a fine of up to $100,000, if they released photographs or gave accounts to the press – and Pitt's lawyers had sent legal-warning letters to every helicopter charter company in southern California, informing them that action would be taken against anyone who colluded with the paparazzi to take aerial photographs. (This did not stop fans of the couple taking to sea on everything from inflatable waterbeds to chartered yachts, to try to witness the wedding from afar.)

The couple even contacted the Federal Aviation Authority to try to clear airspace around the house for the day, on the pretext that helicopters, combined with the noise from the wedding, would violate local decibel limits. The authority refused, but Aniston tried to keep it in perspective. 'Jen finally said, "Look, if they [the paparazzi] get the picture, they get it,"' Pitt later admitted. '"Don't forget what the day is about." She was right.' The city authorities were co-operative enough, however, to impose a three-day closure of the local section of the Pacific Coast Highway, and a temporary total parking ban, with guests – who had been flown into the locale at a total cost of $35,000 – driven to the wedding from Malibu High School, five miles away, in buses with blacked-out windows. As one of Carsey's wealthy neighbours said: 'This is more like a military-style operation than a wedding. You'd think we were at war.'

At 6.30 pm, the event proper began with a six-piece band and 40-member gospel choir singing the classic song by 1930s crooner Al Bowlly, 'Love is the Greatest Thing'. Cue Jennifer Aniston, preceded by flower girls trailing petals and blowing soap bubbles, a ring-bearer and two bridesmaids, carrying a bouquet of Dutch roses.

'The paparazzi and I, we have a big game going on,' Pitt later admitted on The *Jay Leno Show*. 'And I started getting carried away with that, and Jen smacked me around, remembered why we were there.' Confounding the actor's most paranoid expectations, however, 'At the very last minute, when the ceremony started, the press backed off. And I really have to thank them because they were just so cool. They let us have our moment, they let us have what turned out to be the highlight of my life.'

Indeed, the press allowed Pitt and his bride to largely control the reporting of the event, issuing one single official black and white photograph ('Just a quick little photo, as we were walking out,' described Pitt. 'It's one of those deals where it was click, click, click and, "OK, we're done",): showing him in traditional black tuxedo by Parisian designer Hedi Slimane, with his best-man brother, Doug, 33, and father, Bill, in dark Prada suits, and Aniston in elegant, highly-expensive designer wear – white satin silk gown by Lawrence Steele; suede high-heeled sandals by Manolo Blahnik – with both in white gold wedding rings by jewellery designer Silvia Damiani, for whom Pitt apears in Italian TV and magazine ads. The actor and the designer had been conferring on the rings for the last seven months – indicating how long the planning of the wedding had actually taken. Inevitably, a bidding war soon took place over the rights to publish both the photo and a firsthand account of the wedding, with *Paris Match* magazine paying a reputed $3 million that was donated to charity by the Pitts.

The wedding vows that united Brad with his new wife, Jennifer Aniston-Pitt – as she is now officially known, though she remains Jennifer Aniston onscreen – were highly personalised. Pitt, quipping lightheartedly to defuse the seriousness of the moment, promised to 'split the difference on the thermostat'; Aniston, emotional, on the verge of tears, promised she would always make Brad's 'favourite banana milkshake'.

'It was an emotional service,' commented one moved guest. 'It was not like a business thing. It was friends and family and celebration.' This was complemented by extravagances like a retrospective slide show that depicted Brad and Jennifer growing up over the years, projected onto an outdoor screen – pure showbusiness. Even Lieutenant Thom Bradstock, of the LA County Sheriff's Department, felt moved to report that the guests 'were all laughing. Other times, people were clapping,' and that 'there was a big smile on Brad's face' throughout. Dakota

Horvath – a 12-year-old answer to Frank Sinatra spotted by Pitt as a night-club act – described how, as they cut through their six-tier wedding cake, 'They were looking into each other's eyes when they fed it to each other, and they were laughing with the cake in their mouths.'

After the ceremony, the broad selection of music featured a Latin jazz band, Gypsy Magic, and child crooner Horvath singing 'The Way You Look Tonight' as Brad and Jennifer took the floor, followed by Ed Norton and Salma Hayek. At 10 pm, the outdoor pyrotechnic display was accompanied by Pitt's choice of modern, independent-label rock music, including Jeff Buckley, Garbage and the melancholic Radiohead – personal favourites of Pitt, who regards them as nothing less than 'the Kafka and the Beckett of our generation'. The wedding party was also entertained by Pitt's friend, singer Melissa Etheridge, performing an unlikely acoustic version of Led Zeppelin's hard-rock sex anthem 'Whole Lotta Love', with actor Dermot Mulroney on the mandolin. Apart from Brad's rock 'n' roll favourites, however, the Aniston family made sure the celebrations echoed the style of an old-fashioned Greek wedding, with live bazouki music, traditional dancing, and plenty of enthusiastic plate smashing.

Sadly, there was one family member missing from the event: Jennifer's mother, estranged since making disparaging comments about her daughter on a TV chat show to promote a tabloid book on their relationship in 1996. Nancy Aniston was not even on the guest list.

Finally hitched, Pitt and Aniston were still leading the peripatetic lives of actors, often working many miles apart. With a gradually evolving film career, Ms. Aniston too was much in demand – earning $750,000 per episode for *Friends*. 'Distance is a beast,' conceded Pitt – though he had a method of communing with his loved one unavailable to everyday mortals. As he described to Jay Leno's audience, 'Fortunately, you can find *Friends* in pretty much any country . . . I get to see *Friends* in Spanish or in German.' (The audience was amused at this point by Pitt singing the *Friends* theme song in German.) Otherwise, long-distance love was conducted with state-of-the-art technology: 'We have web cams, with the little video file . . . you can't see movement really, it's like every 6 seconds it takes a picture and it's frozen. You'll be talking, then you'll say something else, then you'll laugh . . .'

As to agonising over his professional thespian as opposed to 'movie star' status, Pitt claimed that was all over: 'I've disconnected from it . . . I spent so much energy in the first portion of the fame game trying to fight that. It just became daunting and I missed the enjoyment of what was going on. I vowed not to do that any more.'

On the basis of doing it all just for fun (and, perhaps occasionally, for money), his first film since he finished *Snatch* at the beginning of 2000 was a joint effort with Julia Roberts. Although the pair had never appeared onscreen together, Pitt and Hollywood's favourite pretty woman were old friends. Roberts estimated, in a February 2001 *Entertainment Tonight* interview, that they had first met when they were both struggling actors, 17 years ago (although Pitt never arrived in LA until 1986, indicating she must have been two years out). As to why Hollywood's golden boy and girl had not worked together before, Pitt opined, 'I would guess we were a little obvious.'

'The fact that two working actors can both like a script mutually, and find time to do it, and find a director that's brave enough to go there . . . It's no small miracle,' Roberts chimed in during the same interview.

'This one came out of nowhere,' said Pitt, 'and the idea of us jumping into this kind of low-budget, gonzo, hit-and-run film just kind of appealed to us both.' The shoot saw him down Mexico way – on location in the remote village of Real De Catorce, and away from the cameras of the paparazzi – working on a film with a 'low budget' of a mere $35 million: hardly chickenfeed, but less than the usual combined fees of its two stars. ('It stayed within a pretty small budget despite us,' Pitt claimed, by now used to working on the overblown Hollywood scale.)

'It was several things,' Pitt said of the hybrid screenplay. 'The story is several genres within one movie. It's a romantic comedy, it's a road trip movie, it's kind of a heist film, there are Tarantino elements to it. The idea of plugging us into this thing with several characters, a movie that's about several relationships, sounded interesting to me.'

The privations of shooting in Mexico were minor, when offset against the benefit of working out of the public eye: 'It was paradise,' Roberts asserted, without equivocation. 'It was . . . a lost time, a lost space. The city that time forgot . . . Lots of rubble. Cock fights on Sunday.'

'It's the belly button of Mexico . . . You take one tunnel in, and a mile-and-a-half tunnel out,' confirmed Pitt. 'They only had one phone line in the whole town and

Brad in Gore Verbinski's violent-road-movie-cum-romantic-comedy *The Mexican*.

Hollywood's golden couple, Brad (Jerry) with on-screen girlfriend Julia Roberts (Samantha) in *The Mexican*.

you're sequestered up at the top of this mountain . . . there are things you have to get used to, like the burros [donkeys, the town's main mode of transport] outside your window at 3 in the morning. And, you know, there were always the scorpion checks. You check your shoes every morning. Check your clothes in the house . . . You check your sheets before you get into bed.' (Pitt joked that, by the time they left their isolated Mexican locale, 'We pretty much wiped out their culture, as a true American will. I think that they're all online because we brought in computers and fax lines and modems. They're all on eBay now.')

Director Gore Verbinski was formerly known for the Budweiser beer ad with the talking frogs, and his debut feature, the part-animated/part live action *Mouse Hunt* (1997). *The Mexican* (2001), too, had the quality of a brutal cartoon. Pitt's character, a buffoonish underworld gofer named Jerry, was perhaps the least menacing gangster in recent movie history. 'I call him the anti-[Steve]McQueen,' said Pitt, 'because there is nothing cool about him. But he's earnest and he tries and he's got a good heart. But very defensive . . . he's a chump.'

'I think Brad is entering new territory with this part,' praised Roberts, aware of her friend's desire not to be pigeonholed. 'He's not handsome, he has no stand-out quality. And he's so earnest doing it.' Of course, as many thousands of Brad Pitt fans would shout, by 'not handsome' Ms. Roberts meant that the cinematographer had downplayed Pitt's good looks rather than emphasised them.

'I find it very funny,' Pitt said of the film's basic plot premise, 'couples always fight a lot and it's always about nothing, about the silliest things. Well, we catch this couple at that moment in their life when they're just not getting along, nothing is working. And she's been hanging out for him, he's required to do one last job, as many movies go, and she's saying, "I'm not having it, I'm going on with my life" – and from there the hijinks ensue.'

'There is a familiarity that comes with the two of us,' said Roberts of hers and Pitt's *Mexican* double-act. 'I think in the instance of playing these characters we had a very limited amount of time to try to convey a lot of years. I think that challenge was really daunting at first, and then became appealing. In the first read through, we read through all the scenes and then said, "Okay, that was 7-and-a-half minutes. Is that it?" But we kind of made the most of it, and said, "Okay, this is a challenge. This isn't a flaw, it's a challenge." How can you really convey their relationship, their dynamic, their feelings, in this much time?'

As to whether the two main characters' uneasy relationship had any relevance to modern love in general, Pitt seemed to reach back into personal experience when he reflected, 'There are a lot of outs. If you want to find an out, you can find an out. You know, no one said that it's going to be easy, but if you can get past egos and your issues with being right and get back to what's there, you should never leave.'

The film opens with Samantha (Roberts) and Jerry (Pitt) waking up in bed together, then clashing in an hysterical argument which ends with her throwing his belongings from a balcony. From thereon, the film takes each of its main characters down a different narrative track for the next 75 minutes: Jerry is sent by his criminal employers (the reason for their screaming match) to Mexico to retrieve a handcrafted antique pistol (the 'Mexican' of the title) that could be evidential in a murder case – its past history recounted in sepia flashbacks. Jerry and his associates prove just as comically incompetent as they are corrupt, and he gets involved in inevitable gunplay and violence along the way.

The buffoonish underworld gofer Jerry, Brad's character in *The Mexican*.

Meanwhile, Samantha high-tails it from LA to Las Vegas, where she encounters some criminal characters linked to Jerry and narrowly avoids being shot when a hitman carries out a contract in a casino toilet. She is abducted by the same hitman, Leroy, played by James Gandolfini – better known as the mighty Tony Soprano, in *The Sopranos* mafia soap-opera. (*The Sopranos* is a particular favourite of Pitt, who claimed, post-production: 'I love Gandolfini. Me and Julia are going to start the Church of Gandofini.') Samantha is forced along on a ride where she and her abductor start to analyse her relationship with Jerry. (Leroy, though a killer, is played against type by Gandolfini as a sensitive gay man.) Ultimately, the violent climax which returns to Jerry's activities is a western pastiche, a literal 'Mexican stand-off' set in Mexico.

Perhaps not quite audacious enough to really carry off its hybrid concept, *The Mexican* met with the customary mixed reviews. *Village Voice* critic J. Hoberman noted how the symmetrical break in the storyline made it 'actually two different movies – or rather, two parallel star vehicles . . . the movie means to be edgy but cute. However, it negotiates its switchback mood changes with increasing difficulty. The breezy, convoluted scenario – with gangsters whining about their retirement packages and downsizing – start to resemble second-rate Elmore Leonard.' Ultimately, rather than a marriage of contrasting tones the critic saw it as a film with an identity crisis: 'Seeking to be that elusive thing, an old-fashioned screwball comedy with a modern body count, *The Mexican* is still squabbling with itself as it departs into the sunset.'

USA Today critic Mike Clark was more scathing, his review headed 'Mexican

Jerry may be a chump in *The Mexican*, but he will ultimately have to be a killer.

Brad and Julia both enjoyed the privations of filmings in Mexico, away from the intrusion of the paparazzi.

Goes South of Boredom'. 'Superstars usually avoid movies this spiritless,' he lamented, 'and it's tough to believe anyone could read this script and fail to realise the movie wouldn't end up going anywhere.' In the *Seattle Post-Intelligencer*, William Arnold was kinder, but chiefly on account of the lead actors. If the movie's central plot device seemed 'more laboured and irrelevant than most McGuffins – and the movie too long and convoluted – the good news is the star power shines through it all . . . Pitt is boyishly endearing, and holds the screen nicely – though, as he begins to show wrinkles and other distinct signs of physical ageing, one wonders if his appeal is going to make the transition to more mature parts.

'Roberts, also de-glamed and showing the signs of age, is even more striking. She makes us believe this character – her animosity towards Pitt is very funny, and her smile lights up the world. Together, the two of them are cute as a bug.'

The next movie was, almost as a further reversal of expectations, not part of a search for more idiosyncratic roles, but a big-budget ($90 million) action picture directed by Tony Scott – for whom Pitt, as young rising star, had contributed a cameo to *True Romance*. For the first time in nearly a decade, *The Spy Game*

209

(2001) offered the opportunity to work alongside Robert Redford – Pitt's one-time mentor, to whom he continues to be compared, at least in terms of the younger Redford's looks – though this time Redford was a fellow cast member. 'With this one, I figured, "Well, this is cool, I'll be able to sit down, swap stories, ideas, eye to eye." And as soon as I got there,' he admitted, 'I turned into a little kid again.'

'There', in this case, was the city of Casablanca and the village of Ouarzazate, both in Morocco – part of a frantic itinerary for location shooting that also took in Berlin, Budapest, London, Oxford and Washington DC. (After the extended period of recreation around the time of his wedding, Pitt was suddenly back into the actor's work ethic – 'I get a break for Christmas,' he said during location shooting in late 2000. 'I'll be with Jen in LA.') Morocco was also a (perhaps unlikely) location stand-in for Vietnam, as the original location, Haifa in Israel, was abandoned due to escalating tensions between the Israelis and the Palestinians. 'I would have liked to have gone to Israel,' said Pitt in Morocco. 'And as I stand here in my military fatigues, I must say, war is the dumbest thing I've ever heard of.' As with Pitt's comments on Northern Ireland, his opinion was heartfelt commonsense – but dismissive of how quickly people without shining careers, and without the freedom that wealth brings, can go for their neighbours' throats when centuries-old enmities arise in times of tension.

'Now, Mexico is romantic,' Pitt reflected on his previous film's location jaunt, 'but Morocco has got this romantic image and I don't know how they got away with that one.' Hardly untravelled, there were still aspects of north African life that were totally alien to the Hollywood star. 'Not anything scary,' he confirmed, 'but just little things. Like pooping in the street and this kind of thing that, as a Westerner, I didn't adhere to.'

The international storyline of *The Spy Game* centres on veteran CIA agent Nathan Muir (Redford), standing on the verge of retirement. When word comes that his former protégé, Tom Bishop (Pitt), has been arrested as a spy in China, Muir is stirred into action, while also sinking into his memories. The action is played out across two time-zones: the 'present-time' storyline focuses on Muir using every professional spook trick in the book to free Bishop from his captors; the flashback sequences begin in Vietnam, where Bishop, as a young Marine sergeant, is recruited by Muir to the agency. Their close professional association and friendship, however, is threatened by human rights activist Elizabeth Hadley (Catherine McCormack), and her romantic association with Bishop.

'This movie takes place over three decades,' Pitt explained to a reporter from *Details* magazine. 'Right now we're in the seventies,' he stated, demonstrating by removing a headscarf to reveal a very full head of blond hair. 'For the eighties, I think I'll go for the full Don Johnson mullet,' he joked. ' I like playing a soldier. It's like being 7 years old again. But listen to these lines: "Target in sight. Do we still have the go? Repeat, do we still have the go?" Being a grown man, I feel silly.'

When the interviewer responded with a 'What the hell, it's just a job'-type sentiment, Pitt gave a flash of the passion he obviously still feels for his profession: 'But I don't want it to be a job! I want it to be my life. Look, I'm in my thirties. I'm halfway done. I don't want to waste time.'

Reminded he was currently making a multi-million dollar action film, and that his next picture – a big-budget remake, in which he was just one of a number of Hollywood A-list faces (including Julia Roberts) – was hardly the mould-breaking material this questing actor was supposedly looking for, Pitt just reversed his stance and shrugged it off: 'That's career maintenance.' If ever an actor could afford to have it both ways, it was Brad Pitt.

With scarcely time to draw breath, the next film was a project with director Steven Soderbergh – who, since his debut with *Sex, Lies and Videotape* (1989), had slipped in and out of critical favour until his 2001 double triumph with *Erin Brockovich* and *Traffic*, both produced in 2000 and both nominated for a string of Academy Awards. (*Erin Brockovich*, with Pitt's pal Julia Roberts in the title role, won Soderbergh the Oscar for Best Director, while *Traffic* won Pitt's *Snatch* co-star Benicio Del Toro the Best Actor award.) 'He drives me crazy!' enthused Pitt. 'I gotta get next to him! I gotta rub up against him!' Pitt would indeed 'rub up against him', but on the unlikeliest of projects: a 2001 remake of *Ocean's Eleven*, the 1960 'Rat Pack' film starring Frank Sinatra, Dean Martin, Sammy Davis, Jr. and Angie Dickinson. 'Remember when everyone said they shouldn't remake *Lolita*?' responded Pitt to raised critical eyebrows. 'Well, I've seen the movie and it has its merit and there were things in the movie that I was affected by . . . Then I realised: it's Shakespeare. It's why you redo Shakespeare. To find your own personal version.'

But *Ocean's Eleven* wasn't Shakespeare (nor, indeed, was it *Lolita*). It was an unlikely 'heist' caper about an eleven-strong gang of World War II veterans, led by Sinatra as Danny Ocean, who stage a raid on a number of Las Vegas casinos on the same day. Leisurely paced, less a thriller than a vehicle for the big personalities and even bigger egos on display, *Ocean's Eleven* was too much a product of its era and of the show-business hierarchy of its time to be faithfully re-made. (Its chief influence on modern pop-culture was how Danny Ocean's suited-and-booted amateur thieves part-inspired the look of Tarantino's professional thugs in *Reservoir Dogs*.)

But Pitt clearly sees the remake as emblematic of its own time, not trying to recreate the pop-culture of 40 years ago – despite the fact that it's been claimed he takes 'the Dean Martin part' in the film, all the supporting characters have a different name and only the basic premise remains. '*Ocean's Eleven* is cool,' he insists. 'My guy is Dusty Ryan, that's his name. Or, at least I think so,' he admitted, not having yet seen the script. According to the film's pre-publicity, Ryan is the 'rich boy that's always up for a high risks game of chance. He's the sort of guy that wears $500 shoes and has effortless cool hair. He's just plain cool.' Pitt noted, with approval, 'I get to be Anti-Jerry in this one' – referring to his uncool character in *The Mexican*, 'the anti-McQueen'.

'This is an idea that Soderbergh and [George] Clooney had,' explained Pitt. 'They asked, "Why aren't there films like *The Great Escape* and *Bridge on the River Kwai*, where all these guys showed up and did a film? It's almost logistically impossible with people's schedules, people's deals. On this one, they assembled this great cast and people made their [salary] cuts and everything to go and do this thing.' While Pitt expressed disappointment at 'the people who wouldn't do it or couldn't do it' (including Bruce Willis and Mark Wahlberg), his excitement at making a parallel to 'the *Great Escape* cast . . . Chuckie Bronson and Ernest Borgnine and all these guys jumping on and doing a film' was fulfilled by a number of veteran actors in smaller roles, such as Eliott Gould and comedian Bill Murray, the latter reprising his role as a lounge crooner from TV's *Saturday Night Live.*

In the central role of Danny Ocean, the only character retaining his name from the original version ('The unshakeable constant always on the beat . . . can't lose if he tries leader of the Rat Pack' – the gang retaining the collective name of Sinatra and his cronies), George Clooney was ringmaster in a celebrity circus working on reduced fees that included Pitt, Casey Affleck (rising young star and brother of Ben Affleck), Scott Caan (son of James Caan, and star of teen TV), Matt Damon and Andy Garcia. Out of this ensemble cast, Pitt was also reunited with Julia Roberts in the revised Angie Dickinson role. ('Danny's ex-wife and the only crack in his perfect armour. She's the glimmer in his eye and she's another's doll for the time being and it's the only loss he's ever had. And he's looking at turning the long odds and taking her back.')

Not having worked together throughout their careers, in 2000-2001 Brad Pitt and Julia Roberts made two films together in a single year, through accident rather than design – 'It was a fatalistic fluke,' said Roberts of the happy coincidence, obviously far from displeased at the prospect. 'Brad never complains,' she noted of his behaviour during filming. 'If I had to describe him in two words, I'd say sunny disposition. He radiates it to everyone around him,' she almost gushed, adding that he was 'a very low-key, groovy guy'.

Of the plot itself, the essential details remain essentially the same – *Ocean's* eleven rob three big Las Vegas casinos (Bellagio, the Mirage and Treasure Island), but this time the distraction used by the robbers is not New Year's Eve, as in the original, but a major boxing event, featuring real-life fighters Lennox Lewis, still World Boxing Organisation heavyweight champion at the time of filming, and Wladimir Klitschko.

Ocean's Eleven caused unforeseen controversy on set: Lewis and Klitschko were performing appropriately in the roles of champion and contender, with Lewis offering the Ukranian (or his boxer brother Vitali, who also appears in the film) the chance to challenge him in real-life at a match mooted for the month of the film's release. This was in early April, when Lewis was still with the film crew in Las Vegas. He was also about fly to Johannesburg, South Africa, to fight little-rated contender Hasim Rahman in Johannesburg, South Africa on the 21st of that month – with much comment passed upon his late start for training in a region 6,000 feet above sea level.

Lewis brushed off the criticism, but when he began breathing heavily in the fifth round of the fight, Rahman saw his chance and went for a one-punch knockout – defeating Lewis and relieving him of his world championship title. With much animosity between the two fighters and a rematch set for the month before the release of *Ocean's Eleven,* the most vocal criticism came from those who accused Lennox Lewis of cutting his training time in half to play movie stars with George Clooney, Julia Roberts and pretend pugilist Brad Pitt.

Early reports of *Ocean's Eleven,* based on a rough cut screened in July 2001 and previewed on a George Clooney fansite, suggest the film may be undemanding entertainment for fans of the main stars: 'Clooney and Pitt, as the doctor says, have perfect chemistry across the whole film . . . Julia Roberts, with limited screen time and a very late introduction, does wonderfully with her scenes . . . this is no big statement piece or Oscar heavy nor is it intended to be . . . it's a very good, fun ensemble work that is smart and very, very cool.'

Brad on married life to Jennifer: 'The thing that surprised me is this pride that I now have when I look across at this woman . . . that we're embarking on this journey together.'

For his next role, Brad Pitt may revert to kicking against expectations. He has recently stated the criteria that he often (except in cases of 'career maintenance') seeks to rebel against: 'the leading man role [has] already been defined: the guy who can handle any situation. I understand why people want to see that. But there's no game in it for me.' However, the central character in *To the White Sea* is just about the most resourceful character that Pitt is ever likely to play.

To the White Sea, adapted from the novel by earthy American poet James Dickey, is a longstanding project of British producer Jeremy Thomas. (Dickey died, aged 74, in 1997, one year after Thomas acquired the rights.) Mooted to star Pitt as a World War II pilot shot down over Japan, director-producer team Joel and Ethan Coen took the helm on the basis that they discard the already existing screenplay (by David Webb Peoples and his wife Janet – screenwriters of *Twelve Monkeys*, for which Pitt was nominated for a Best Actor Oscar) and prepare their own. However, as is usual in the evolutionary development of a script, the Coens are said to have taken elements from the Peoples' version as well as the source novel.

Closely based on Dickey's second survivalist novel (after Southern man-against-nature epic *Deliverance*, filmed in 1970), the story follows B-29 gunner and former Alaskan hunter Muldrow as he undertakes an odyssey of a distinctly violent kind, to the desolate island of Hokkaido off the northern coast of Japan. The novel is an interior first-person monologue, with Muldrow commentating on how his early life prepared him for such an extreme test of his survival skills, and how he steels himself to commit increasingly violent acts in defence of his life. Audaciously, however, the screenplay is said to contain no dialogue after the first five minutes of the film, and no voiceover narration – challenging the Coen brothers and Pitt to perform a similar balancing act to director John Boorman and Lee Marvin in the uneven wartime survival drama *Hell in the Pacific* (1968) – albeit on a much more visceral level – by streamlining their style into a purely visual cinematic narrative.

The original novel and early drafts of the screenplay earmark *To the White Sea* as one of the most controversially dark and violent projects Pitt has been involved in. To ensure his own survival, the resourceful Muldrow, as well as withstanding torture, is seen to shoot, stab or impale any potential enemy who crosses his path – in a flashback sequence, he kills one of his own husky dogs back home in Alaska to prevent himself from freezing, and is later seen to cut a Japanese man's throat for the chance to steal his clothes. The film is a long-standing project, and its much-delayed production is due to begin in January 2002, shooting in Japan and Canada on a budget of $50 million.

Meanwhile, the star has been drawn into some other pet projects. One rumour, printed in *Spin* magazine in April 2001, claimed Pitt had been speaking with Mary Guibert, mother of singer-songwriter Jeff Buckley, who tragically drowned, aged 30, in 1997, about the prospect of playing her son on film. (Buckley is a personal favourite of Pitt, who featured his music during the firework display at his wedding to Jennifer Aniston.) Initial suggestions were that this would be the film of music journalist David Browne's joint biography *Dream Brother*: the story of Jeff and his similarly ill-fated father, folk and blues-rock singer Tim Buckley, who died from a drug overdose at 28. However, contradictory reports claimed the project would not be the Buckley story per se, but a rock 'n' roll saga where the Buckley figure is obliquely referred to as 'the Musician', and is one of a number of main characters. (Almost apologetic for his profession, Pitt had recently expressed his continuing obsession with rock music: 'I've had this frustration with film because we can't replicate feelings . . . it can't quite do what music does. Music has its own language.')

Another mooted project is the film of Jack Kerouac's seemingly unfilmable 1957 'beat' novel *On the Road*. With the film rights owned by Francis Ford Coppola, Pitt is said to be interested in taking the role of narrator Sal Paradise (a thinly disguised version of proto-beatnik/alcoholic/amphetamine addict Kerouac), with Billy Crudup (who co-starred with Pitt in *Sleepers*) as travelling companion, Dean Moriarty, closely based on the author's friend/inspirational muse/gay crush, Neal Cassady. The only incongruous factor seems to be the choice of director: Joel Schumacher, the journeyman who jumped from the urban paranoia drama *Falling Down* (1993) to *Batman Forever* (1995).

Whatever his next career moves, Pitt's passions remain his private life, and his sense of aesthetics, as expressed in his love of architecture. Asked what he might be doing if he didn't have a career as an actor, Pitt didn't hesitate: 'I would be building . . . I'm going to revamp LA architecture. I am, I'm serious,' he insisted. 'This is an amazing city with amazing architecture . . . after [1930s modernist architect Richard] Neutra, it just dropped off . . . You see what they're doing on Hollywood Boulevard, it's all built around commercialism. That's all right, but you can put some great design in there and you can evolve the architecture of the place, instead of building strip malls everywhere.' Strongly influenced by Lloyd Wright and modernist pioneers such as Henry and Charles Greene, who developed the customised cabin-style Hollywood bungalow, Pitt admits of his passion, 'I get angry, I get emotional.'

'I took a year off,' he describes the period after *Fight Club* wrapped, broken only by the British sojourn to make *Snatch*, 'and I did some experiments on redoing two places . . . I was just playing with an evolution of modernism with old-world materials, which keep it warm . . . But that's what I would be doing. And that's probably what I will be doing.'

Despite the snide remarks and insinuations cast his way over the years, Pitt as an individual seems to have too much depth to fall into the one-dimensional trappings of celebrity. 'I want to do something hands-on,' he insists, 'rather than just play golf, which is the sport of the religious right.'

After years of high-profile relationships and break-ups, he seems to have arrived at the emotional peak most people hope to attain during their lives. The reasons for the break-up of his former relationship remain obscure – although Pitt is said to refer coolly to his former amour as 'Paltrow', the minutiate of the affair remains guarded by privacy.

What is clear is that, on the personal front, things have changed. 'The thing that surprised me is this pride that I now have when I look across at this woman,' he says of Jennifer Aniston, 'that we're embarking on this journey together . . . I've never done anything like it and have never experienced anything like it . . . I believe in big romance,' he confirms, as if to dispel the perception of the flighty film star. 'It's just that these misconceptions of what it should be, it's dangerous. It's like prom night misconceptions of it supposedly being the greatest night of your life. It's putting too much on the things when you should let it be what it is and [be] finding the beauty in that.'

As for the immediate future of the seemingly perfect marriage, his wife has hinted time and again that she longs for children, and may even consider at some point – echoing Gwyneth Paltrow – giving up her career in favour of full-time motherhood. Being one half of the quintessentially modern Hollywood couple, she has also come to value, and to guard, her privacy, suing one celebrity tabloid whose photographer took blurred shots of her sunbathing topless: as she deadpans, 'We are actors but I don't know where we signed up for "You can climb over our walls and take photographs of us."'

While Aniston takes gradual steps in the direction of a serious career as a film actress, Pitt denies the story of an upcoming guest appearance on *Friends* as a 'vicious rumour that started in the commissary'. While stating that he's 'open to it', there is clearly no prospect now that the cast and crew have filmed the final season. In fact, the final scene of the final episode of *Friends* reveals that Aniston's character, Rachel, is pregnant. 'We were like, "Well, jeez, we've got it written in here,"' said Aniston of herself and her on screen character, '"it could come in nicely." But, you know, we'll see. All in good time.'

While stressing that she's not pregnant, however, the prospect is clearly on her mind: 'All of our friends have kids. Your priorities change, and it's about your home and enjoying the passage of time. Going to New York or Europe for five months isn't so appealing. And if it works out where we have kids, we'll sort of switch off and the family will go wherever we need to go.'

George Clooney, Pitt's *Ocean's Eleven* co-star who quipped, 'Well, there's a homely couple' when he saw Aniston visit the set, jokes that the progeny of the 'Sexiest Man in the World' and one of the most attractive women in Hollywood might 'just explode – [be] too much for Earth'. As for Pitt, the Hollywood golden boy hesitates at such responsibility, but is, at least, refreshingly honest about it: 'I'm still a little selfish. I'm sure I'll fuck them up somehow,' he jokes disarmingly.

John Stockwell, director of Aniston's upcoming movie *Rock Star* (2001, which also features Pitt's *Snatch* co-star Jason Flemyng), recalls driving home at 3 am after seeing a concert by the band Korn with Pitt, at a time when he was also considering taking a role in the film: 'He wakes her up [with a phonecall], but she's not mad, and he's just reporting in, not out of a sense of duty but out of love . . . It is sweet. So sweet it will give you diabetes.'

The Pitts' domestic life appears to be the golden pinnacle of the Hollywood dream, combining glamour, affluence and a sense of aesthetics. The couple recently spent $13.5 million on a palatial home in Beverly Hills – with tennis courts and a 35-seater cinema among its features – plus a further $11 million on a 400-acre holiday home on the California coastline. Originally built in the 1930s for actor Fredric March (who played the prototype of Pitt's character in *Meet Joe Black*), Ms Aniston had 'fallen in love' with the Beverley Hills house's design by architect Wallace Neff.

Pitt himself, while seemingly too embarrassed to discuss winning *People* magazine's 'Sexiest Man Alive' award for the second time, in November 2000, was lauded by the celebrity mag as 'a poster boy for manhood in the new millennium'. As unwanted accolades go, it could have been a lot worse. Those dual aspects of boyishness and manhood are combined in Brad Pitt, in the same way that his good looks, talent and knack for being in the right place at the right time came together so fortuitously.

Insinuations that his acting should not be taken seriously on account of his 'pretty-boy' status have proven hard to live down, even as he moves into his late thirties. 'Brad is one of the most attractive and talented men in the world today,' said the gay record producer David Geffen, and such honest appreciation of his sex appeal causes some critics to sneer. As Jim Harrison, author of the original novella *Legends of the Fall*, observes, 'The truth is, men resent good-looking men, more so than women resent good-looking women. It's sexual jealousy, what the French call the injustice of "the given".'

But if Pitt believes his attractiveness is, in some ways, a curse, then it's also a blessing. He is in the near-unique position of being able to pick and choose in his Hollywood career, to switch over at will from being a pretty face in a multi-million dollar blockbuster to stretching himself in a character role, on a more controversial or low-budget production. Such unpredictability may continue to ensure that Brad Pitt lives an even more charmed existence than he already appears to. As Alan J. Pakula, Pitt's director on an ill-fated film who, nonetheless, came to join his large coterie of friends, says of him: 'There's something about Brad that still seems like it's being formed.'

Filmography

Early Work

Extra in **Less Than Zero** and **No Man's Land**

Television Series

Dallas (five episodes)

Another World

Growing Pains
'Who's Zoomin' Who?'
USA, 1987, 30 minutes
Directed by: John Tracy
Script by: Tom Walla
Production Company: Warner Brothers
Cast: Alan Thicke, Joanna Kerns, Kirk Cameron, Tracey Gold, Jeremy Miller, Lisa Capps, Rachel Jacobs, Kevin Wixted, Brad Pitt

Head of the Class
USA, 1988, 30 minutes

21 Jump Street
'Best Years of Your Life'
USA, 1988, 60 minutes
Directed by: Bill Corcoran
Script by: Jonathan Lemkin
Production Company: Patrick Hasburgh Productions in association with Stephen J. Cannell Productions
Cast: Johnny Depp, Peter DeLuise, Cheryl Pollak, H. Richard Greene, Brad Pitt, Gina Nemo, Tiffany Helm, Laura Austin

thirtysomething
'Love and Sex'
USA, 1989, 60 minutes
Directed by: Marshal Herkovitz
Script by: Liberty Hodshall
Production Companies: The Bedford Falls Co / MGM/UA
Cast: Timothy Busfield; Polly Draper; Mel Harris; Peter Horton; Melanie Mayron; Ken Olin; Patricia Wettig; David Clennon; Richard Murphy; Cheryl Pollak; Brad Pitt

Tales from the Crypt
'King of the Road'
USA, 1988, 30 minutes
Directed by: Tom Holland
Script by: J. Johnson
Based on Tales from the Crypt / Two Fisted Tales, originally published by William M. Gaines
Music by Warren Zevon
Production Company: HBO
Cast: Raymond J. Barry (Iceman); Brad Pitt (Billy); Michelle Bronson (Iceman's daughter); Jack Keller (Car dealer)

Advert: **Levi Jeans** (1988)

Films

A Stoning in Fulham County (TVM)
USA, 1988, 100 minutes
Directed by Larry Elikman
Screenplay by Jud Kinberg and Jackson Gillis
Story by Jackson Gillis
Production Company: The Landsburg Company
Cast: Ken Olin; Jill Eikenberyy; Nicholas Pryor; Ron Perlman; Theodore Bikel; Olivia Burnette; Brad Pitt; Bill Allen

Cutting Class
USA, 1989, 91 minutes
Directed by Rospo Pallenberg
Screenplay by Steve Slavkin
Production Company: April Films
Cast: Donovan Leitch; Brad Pitt; Jill Schoelen; Roddy McDowall; Martin Mull; Brenda Lynn Klemme; Mark Barnett

Happy Together
USA, 1989, 92 minutes
Directed by Mel Damski
Screenplay by Craig J. Nevius
Production Company: Metropolis Motion Pictures
Cast: Patrick Dempsey (Christopher Wooden); Helen Slater (Alexandra Page); Kevin Hardesty (Slash); Marius Weyers (Denny Dollenbacher); Barbara Babcock (Ruth Carpenter); Gloria Hayes (Luisa Dellacova); Brad Pitt (Brian); Aaron Harnick (Wally); Ron Sterling (Trevor); Eric Lumbard (Gary); Michael D. Clarke (Steve); Wendy Lee Marconi (Dory)

The Image
USA, 1989, 110 minutes
Directed by Peter Werner
Screenplay by Brian Rehak
Production Companies: HBO Pictures / Citadel Entertainment
Cast: Albert Finney (Jason Cromwell); John Mahoney (Irv Mickleson); Kathy Baker (Marcie Crawford); Swoosie Kurtz (Joanne Winslow-Darvish); Marsha Mason (Jean Cromwell); Spalding Gray (Frank Goodrich); Brad Pitt (Steve Black)

Glory Days (TV series)
Six Episodes, 50 minutes each, Fox Network, 1990
Directed by Marc Laub
Created by Patick Hapsburgh
Cast: Brad Pitt (Walker Lovejoy); Spike Alexander (Dave Rotecki); Evan Mirand (Fopiano); Nicholas Kallsen (Dominic); Beth Broderick (Sheila Jackson); Robert Costanzo (Lieutenant V.T. Krantz)

Across the Tracks (AKA Nowhere to Run)
USA, 1991, 100 minutes
Directed by Sandy Tung
Screenplay by Sandy Tung

Cast: David Belafonte (Stanford Scout); Marisa DeSimone (Salesgirl); Bebe Drake-Massey (Mrs Fischer); Annie Dylan (Linda); Thomas Mikal Ford (Coach Walsh); William Garson (Salesman); Jaime Gomez (Bobby, Teammate #1); Garon Grigsby (Thompson); John Linton (Brad); Kent Lipham (Big Ed); Chuck Lyons (Officer); Mike Marikian (Andy, Manager); Ron Marquette (Paulie, Brad's Friend #1); David Anthony Marshall (Louie); Jack McGee (Frank); Cyril O'Reilly (Coach Ryder); Brad Peterson (Stolen Car Driver); Brad Pitt (Joe Maloney); Jami Richards (Melani); Rick Schroder (Billy Maloney); Carrie Snodgress (Rosemary Maloney)

Too Young to Die?

USA, 1990, 92 minutes
Directed by Robert Markowitz
Screenplay by David Hill and George Rubino
Production Companies: Spelling / Republic Pictures / Von Zerneck-Sertner Films
Cast: Michael Tucker (Buddy Thornton); Juliette Lewis (Amanda Sue Bradley); Brad Pitt (Billy Canton); Alan Fudge (Mark Calhoun); Emily Longstreth (Jean); Laurie O'Brien (Wanda Sledge); Michael O'Keefe (Mike Medwicki)

Thelma & Louise

USA, 1991, 124 minutes
Directed by Ridley Scott
Screenplay by Callie Khouri
Production Companies: MGM/UA / Pathe Entertainment / United International Pictures
Cast: Susan Sarandon (Louise Sawyer); Geena Davis (Thelma Dickinson); Harvey Keitel (Hal Slocumb); Michael Madsen (Jimmy); Christopher McDonald (Darryl); Stephen Tobolowsky (Max); Brad Pitt (J.D.); Timothy Carhart (Harlan Puckett); Lucinda Jenney (Lena, the Waitress); Jason Beghe (State Trooper); Sonny Carl Davis (Albert); Ken Swofford (Major); Shelly Desai (East Indian Motel Clerk); Carol Mansell (Waitress); Stephen Polk (Surveillance Man)

The Favor

USA, 1991, 95 minutes
Directed by Donald Petrie
Screenplay by Josann McGibbon and Sara Parriot
Production Company: Nelson Entertainment / Shuler-Donner Productions
Cast: Harley Jane Kozak (Kathy); Elizabeth McGovern (Emily); Bill Pullman (Peter); Brad Pitt (Elliott); Larry Miller (Joe Dubin); Ken Wahl (Tom Andrews)

Johnny Suede

USA, 1992, 95 minutes
Directed by Tom DiCillo
Screenplay by Tom DiCillo
Production Companies: Miramax Films (distributor) / Vega Film Productions
Cast: Brad Pitt (Johnny Suede); Richard Boes (Man in Tuxedo); Cheryl Costa (Woman in Alley); Michael Luciano (Mr. Clepp); Calvin Levels (Deke); Nick Cave (Freak Storm); Ralph Marrero (Bartender); Wilfredo

Giovanni Clark (Slick); Alison Moir (Darlette); Peter McRobbie (Flip Doubt); Ron Vawter (Winston); Dennis Parlato (Dalton); Tina Louise (Mrs. Fontaine); Michael Mulheren (Fred Business); Wayne Maugans (Ned Business); Catherine Keener (Yvonne); Joseph Barry (The Cowboy); John David Barone (Bernard); Tom Jarmusch (Conan); Samuel L. Jackson (B-Bop)

Cool World

USA, 1992, 101 minutes
Directed by Ralph Bakshi
Screenplay by Michael Grais and Mark Victor
Production Company: Morgan Creek Productions
Cast: Janni Brenn-Lowen (Mom Harris); Brad Pitt (Frank Harris); William Frankfather (Cop); Greg Collins (Cop); Gabriel Byrne (Jack Deebs); Kim Basinger (Holli Would); Michael David Lally (voice, Sparks); Michele Abrams (Jennifer Malley): Carrie Hamilton (Comic Bookstore Cashier); Stephen Worth (Comic Store Patron)

A River Runs Through It

USA, 1992, 123 minutes
Directed by Robert Redford
Screenplay by Richard Friedenberg
From the story by Norman MacLean
Production Companies: Allied Filmmakers / Columbia
Cast: Craig Sheffer (Norman Maclean); Brad Pitt (Paul Maclean); Tom Skerritt (Rev. Maclean); Brenda Blethyn (Mrs. Maclean); Emily Lloyd (Jessie Burns); Edie McClurg (Mrs. Burns); Stephen Shellen (Neal Burns); Vann Gravage (Young Paul); Nicole Burdette (Mabel); Rob Cox (Conroy); Robert Redford (narrator)

Kalifornia

USA, 1993, 118 minutes
Directed by Dominic Sena
Screenplay by Tim Metcalfe
Story by Stephen Levy
Production Company: Polygram Filmed Entertainment, in association with Viacom Pictures / Propaganda Films
Cast: Brad Pitt (Early Grayce); Catherine Larson (Teenage Girl); David Milford (Driver); David Duchovny (Brian Kessler); John Zarchen (Peter); David Rose (Eric); Michelle Forbes (Carrie Laughlin); Tommy Chappelle (Old Man); Juliette Lewis (Adele Corners); Judson Vaughn (Parole Officer)

True Romance

USA, 1993, 120 minutes
Directed by Tony Scott
Screenplay by Quentin Tarantino
Production Company: Morgan Creek Productions
Cast: Christian Slater (Clarence Worley); Patricia Arquette (Alabama Whitman); Dennis Hopper (Clifford Worley); Val Kilmer (Elvis); Gary Oldman (Drexl Spivey); Brad Pitt (Floyd); Christopher Walken (Vincenzo Coccotti); Bronson Pinchot (Elliot Blitzer); Samuel L. Jackson (Big Don); Michael Rapaport (Dick Ritchie); Saul Rubinek (Lee Donowitz); Conchata Ferrell (Mary Louise Ravencroft); James Gandolfini (Virgil); Anna Thomson (Lucy); Victor

Argo (Lenny); Paul Bates (Marty); Chris Penn (Nicky Dimes); Tom Sizemore (Cody Nicholson)

Legends of the Fall

USA, 1994, 132 minutes
Directed by Edward Zwick
Screenplay by Susan Shilliday and Bill Wittliff
From the novella by Jim Harrison
Production Company: Columbia TriStar
Cast: Brad Pitt (Tristan Ludlow); Anthony Hopkins (Col. Ludlow); Aidan Quinn (Alfred); Julia Ormond (Susannah); Henry Thomas (Samuel); Karina Lombard (Isabel Two); Tantoo Cardinal (Pet); Gordon Tootoosis (One Stab); Paul Desmond (Decker); Christina Pickles (Isabel); Robert Wisden (John T. O'Banion); John Novak (James O'Banion); Kenneth Welsh (Sheriff Tynert)

Interview With the Vampire

USA, 1994, 122 minutes
Directed by Neil Jordan
Screenplay by Anne Rice (& Neil Jordan, uncredited)
From the novel by Anne Rice
Production Company: Geffen Pictures
Cast: Brad Pitt (Louis); Christian Slater (The Interviewer); Tom Cruise (Lestat); Stephen Rea (Santiago); Antonio Banderas (Armand); Kirsten Dunst (Claudia); Virginia McCollam (Whore on Waterfront); John McConnell (Gambler); Mike Seelig (Pimp); Bellina Logan (Tavern Girl); Thandie Newton (Yvette)

Seven

USA, 1995, 123 minutes
Directed by David Fincher
Screenplay by Andrew Kevin Walker
Production Company: New Line Cinema
Cast: Brad Pitt (David Mills); Morgan Freeman (William Somerset); Gwyneth Paltrow (Tracy Mills); Kevin Spacey (John Doe)

Twelve Monkeys

USA, 1995, 124 minutes
Directed by Terry Gilliam
Screenplay by David Webb Peoples and Janet Peoples
Production Companies: Atlas Entertainment / MCA / Universal Pictures
Cast: Brad Pitt (Jeffrey Goines); Madeleine Stowe (Kathryn); Bruce Willis (Cole); Christopher Plummer; David Morse

Sleepers

USA, 1996, 105 minutes
Directed by Barry Levinson
Screenplay by Lorenzo Carcaterra and Barry Levinson
From the novel by Lorenzo Carcaterra
Production Company: Baltimore Pictures/Polygram Filmed Entertainment/Propoganda Films
Cast: Brad Pitt (Michael); Kevin Bacon (Sean Nokes); Robert De Niro (Father Bobby); Minnie Driver (Carol); Dustin Hoffman (Danny Snyder); Jason Patric (Lorenzo); Ron Eldard (Jon); Billy Crudup (Tommy); Brad Renfro

(Young Michael).

Devil's Own

USA, 1996, 107 minutes
Directed by Alan J. Pakula
Screenplay by Kevin Jarre/David Aaron Cohen/Vincent Patrick/Terry George/Robert Kamen
Production Company: Columbia Pictures
Cast: Brad Pitt (Rory Devaney); Harrison Ford (Tom O'Meara); Margaret Colin (Sheila O'Meara); Ruben Blades (Officer Edwin Diaz); Treat Williams (Billy Burke)

The Dark Side of the Sun

Canada/USA, 1997 (filmed in Yugoslavia, 1988) 101 minutes
Directed by Bozida 'Bota' Nikolic
Screenplay by Andy Horton and Zeljko Mijanovic
Cast: Guy Boyd (Father); Brad Pitt (Rick); Cheryl Pollack (Frances)

Seven Years in Tibet

USA, 1997, 131 minutes
Directed by Jean Jacques-Annaud
Screenplay by Becky Johnston
Cast: Brad Pitt (Heinrich Harrer); David Thewlis (Peter Aufschnaiter); B.D. Wong (Ngawang Jigme); Lhakpa Tsamchoe (Pema Lhaki); Mako (Kungo Tsarong); Danny Dengzongpa (Regent); Victor Wong (Chinese 'Amban')

Meet Joe Black

USA, 1998, 174 minutes
Directed by Martin Brest
Screenplay by Bo Goldman and Ron Osborne
Suggested by the play *Death Takes a Holiday* by Alberto Casella, adapted by Walter Ferris, and the screenplay by Maxwell Anderson and Gladys Lehman
Production Company: Universal Pictures
Cast: Brad Pitt (Joe Black); Anthony Hopkins (William Parrish); Claire Forlani (Susan Parrish); Jake Weber (Drew); Marcia Gay Harden (Allison); Jeffrey Tambor (Quince); David S. Howard (Eddie Sloane); Lois Kelly-Miller (Jamaican Woman)

Being John Malkovich

USA, 1999, 122 minutes
Directed by Spike Jonze
Screenplay by Charlie Kaufman
Prodcution Company: USA Films/Gramercy Pictures
Cast: John Cusack (Craig Schwartz); Cameron Diaz (Lotte Schwartz); Catherine Keener (Maxine); Orson Bean (Dr Lester); Mary Kay Place (Floris); John Malkovich (John Horatio Malkovich); plus cameo appearances by Charlie Sheen, Brad Pitt, Dustin Hoffman, Michelle Pfeiffer, Winona Ryder, Charlie Sheen, Philip Glass

Fight Club

USA, 1999, 135 minutes
Directed by David Fincher
Screenplay by Jim Uhls

From the novel by Chuck Palahniuk
Production Company: Fox 2000
Cast: Brad Pitt (Tyler Durden); Edward Norton (narrator); Helena Bonham-Carter (Marla Singer); Meat Loaf Aday (Robert); Jared Leto (Angel Face)

Snatch

UK, 2000, 102 minutes
Directed by Guy Ritchie
Screenplay by Guy Ritchie
Production Company: Ska Productions/Columbia Pictures
Cast: Benicio Del Toro (Franky Four Fingers); Dennis Farina (Avi); Jason Flemyng (Darren); Vinnie Jones (Bullet Tooth Tony); Brad Pitt (Micky O'Neil); Rade Sherbedgia (Boris the Blade); Jason Statham (Turkish); Mike Reid (Doug the Head); Robbie Gee (Vinny); Lennie James (Sol); Ade (Tyrone); Stephen Graham (Tommy); Alan Ford (Brick Top); William Beck (Neil); Andy Beckwith (Errol); Ewen Bremner (Mullet)

The Mexican

USA, 2001, 120 minutes
Directed by Gore Verbinski
Screenplay by J.H. Wyman
Production Company: Dreamworks
Cast: Brad Pitt (Jerry); Julia Roberts (Samantha); James Gandolfini (Leroy); J.K. Simmons (Ted); Bob Balaban (Nayman)

The Spy Game

USA, 2001
Directed by Tony Scott
Screenplay by Michael Beckner/David Arata/John Lee Hancock
Production Company: Beacon Communications/Universal Pictures
Cast: Brad Pitt (Tom Bishop); Robert Redford (Nathan Muir); Catherine McCormack (Elizabeth Hadley)

WORKS IN PROGRESS

Ocean's Eleven

USA, 2001, minutes
Directed by Steven Soderburgh
Screenplay by Stephen W. Carpenter and Ted Griffin
From the original screenplay by Harry Brown, Charles Lederer and Ted Griffin, Story by George Clayton Johnson and Jack Golden Russell
Production Company: Village Roadshow Pictures/Warner Brothers
Cast: George Clooney (Danny Ocean); Brad Pitt (Dusty Ryan); Julia Roberts (Tess Ocean); Don Cheadle (Roscoe Means); Matt Damon (Linus Zerga); Andy Garcia (Harry Benedict); Elliott Gould (Ruben Tischkoff); Casey Affleck; Scott Caan; Vitali Klitschko, Vladimir Klitschko, Lennox Lewis (boxers)

To the White Sea

USA, 2002
Directed by Joel Coen
Screenplay by Ethan Coen and Joel Coen
From the novel by James Dickey
Production Company: 20th Century Fox
Cast: Brad Pitt (Muldrow)